D1570469

IN STALIN'S SHADOW

Angelo Tasca

IN STALIN'S SHADOW

ANGELO TASCA AND THE CRISIS OF THE LEFT IN ITALY AND FRANCE, 1910–1945

Alexander J. De Grand

NORTHERN ILLINOIS UNIVERSITY PRESS

DEKALB, ILLINOIS 1986

Copyright © 1986 by Northern Illinois University Press
Published by the Northern Illinois University Press,
DeKalb, Illinois, 60115
Manufactured in the United States of America

Design by Jo Aerne

Library of Congress Cataloging-in-Publication Data

De Grand, Alexander J., 1938–
In Stalin's shadow.

Bibliography: p.
Includes index.
1. Tasca, Angelo, 1892–1960.
2. Communists—Italy—Biography.
3. Communism—Italy—History—20th century.
I. Title.
HX289.7.T37D4   1986
335.43′092′4 [B]   86-5121
ISBN 0-87580-116-1

Contents

Acknowledgments

Many people have helped in the preparation of this book and my debt of gratitude to them is enormous. Without the encouragement and kindness of the late Professor Giuseppe Del Bo, who placed the Tasca Archive at my disposition, this work would not have been possible. I owe a special debt to Dott. Elio Sellino, whose friendship and advice were essential to the completion of my work, and to the staff of the library of the Fondazione Giangiacomo Feltrinelli, who did everything in their power to make the research easier. I would also like to thank the directors and staff of the Istituto Gramsci in Rome, which allowed me to consult the Archives of the Italian Communist party, of the Istituto Storico della Resistenza in Toscana, of the Archivio Centrale dello Stato in Rome, and of the Centro Studi Piero Gobetti in Turin. The research was carried out in part under a Senior Research Fellowship from the National Endowment for the Humanities. Roosevelt University released me from some of my teaching obligations to finish the writing of the manuscript.

Angelo Tasca's children, Elena Dogliani, Valeria Tasca, and Carlo Tasca, generously shared their memories of their father, as did many others who knew him: Alfonso Leonetti, the late Giuseppe Berti, Andrea Viglongo, Gilles Martinet, Charles André Julien, and Daniel Mayer. Along the way many friends in Italy and the United States were of great assistance. Professor Leonardo Rapone shared his bibliographical knowledge and allowed me to see an advance copy of his study of the Italian Socialist party in the 1930s. I would also like to thank Professors Franco Della Peruta, Renzo De Felice, and Alceo Riosa. Professors Marion Miller, William Logue, Roland Sarti, and Jon Kofas read all of the manuscript and Anthony Cardoza and Linda De Grand read substantial parts of it. Their suggestions greatly improved the final work. Professor Charles Delzell, whose kindness to other scholars is legendary, spared me a quantity of errors. In addition, others helped in major ways: Elena Comolli, Amelia and Laura Francini, Antonio and Terri Sarcina, Luciana Capaccioli, Luigi and Caterina Lazzareschi, Umberto and Dana Giovine, and Antonio and Enrica Di Muccio. Finally, I would like to thank Mary Lincoln and the editors of the Northern Illinois University Press for making the preparation of this book for publication a pleasure. I dedicate the work to the memory of Ralph Helstein, one of America's great labor leaders, and of Alfonso Leonetti, who represented the best traditions of the Italian Left.

IN STALIN'S SHADOW

Introduction:
A Generation of Exiles

No generation of young Italians was so tormented as that born between 1890 and 1900. They came of age just as Italy embarked on the nightmare of World War I. The war caught them in their late teens and early twenties and, for many, became the omnipresent reality of the rest of their lives. The future Fascist leader Giuseppe Bottai once remarked that his generation knew nothing but war. But Bottai spoke more for those young Italians—Italo Balbo, Dino Grandi, Curzio Malaparte—who identified their aspirations with fascism and followed Mussolini from battle to battle until the ultimate catastrophe of World War II. For others, revolution, rather than war, provided the focal point of their lives. The Bolshevik Revolution and the abortive Italian revolution of 1919 and 1920 represented a personal rupture with the past and set them on a course that would lead to defeat and exile before the terrible Fascist years came to an end. Members of that generation were dispersed to Russia, to America, to France or England before they found their way home again. Some never returned. Like Antonio Gramsci, they died as internal exiles at the hands of the Fascist regime, or like Carlo Rosselli, the great democratic antifascist, they would be murdered in exile by Fascist thugs.[1]

Those who joined the revolutionary movement in the heady days after World War I had little idea where it would carry them. Italian and European socialism would be challenged and transformed beyond recognition by the events of the next fifty years: the rupture of the movement into Socialist and Communist parties, the rise of fascism and nazism, and the cold war. External events shaped individual destinies in strange ways. The ideals of one's youth often offered little guidance in the maze of twentieth-century political upheaval.

Angelo Tasca lived for thirty years at the eye of the hurricane. His career spanned the period of profound crisis for the European socialist movement; like that of a modern Ulysses, his fate seemed a plaything of a particularly vengeful god. Tasca was born in 1892 and, unlike many who were slightly younger, had practically completed his education and formed his political views before the war. He identified with the revolutionary, or Maximalist, wing of the Italian Socialist party. In 1919, disgusted by the senseless slaughter of the Great War and certain that the Bolshevik Revolution marked the dawn of a new era, Tasca joined Antonio Gramsci and Palmiro Togliatti in launching *L'Ordine nuovo*, which was to become the most famous of the revolutionary journals and a rallying point for the future leaders of the Italian Communist party.

During these first postwar years, Tasca and the other young revolutionaries sought a way to apply the lessons of the Bolshevik Revolution to Italian conditions. In the passionate debates over the factory councils, Tasca became the leading exponent of the values of the traditional unions and cooperatives and the chief protagonist in a bitter debate with Antonio Gramsci, who advanced the cause of the new forms of proletarian organization.

Tasca became a member of the new Communist Party of Italy (Partito Comunista d'Italia [PCI]) when it was formed at the Congress of Livorno in January 1921. After the split with the Socialist party, he worked actively, but with limited success, to draw into the new Communist movement the majority of revolutionary socialists who remained loyal to the old party. The effort to minimize the rupture with the past again brought Tasca into conflict with Amadeo Bordiga, Antonio Gramsci, and Palmiro Togliatti, now the major leaders of the PCI.

Tasca was also one of the first leaders of the Italian Left to understand the nature of the Fascist challenge in its double dimension: the problem of immediate tactics and the search for a long-term solution to the political-economic crisis that gripped Europe in the interwar period. While in the Communist party, he advocated a broad alliance of working class parties, even extending to the democratic middle class, to oppose fascism.

Despite differences over policy, Tasca remained in the leadership group of the Italian Communist party throughout the 1920s and in 1928 was sent to Moscow as its representative to the Executive of the Communist International. His arrival in Moscow just as Stalin triumphed over Nikolai Bukharin could not have been more ill-timed. Tasca, who admired Bukharin and supported his defense of the New Economic Program and his opposition to "social fascism," openly defied Stalin and attempted to rally the Italian party against the Soviet leader. Tasca's defiance earned him an expulsion on Stalin's direct orders from the Italian Communist party and from the International.

The decade of the 1930s represented for Tasca a progressive alienation from the past. It began when he worked on Henri Barbusse's *Monde* from 1930 to 1933. *Monde* was a political and literary biweekly that was close to, but not an official organ of, the French Communist party (Parti Communiste Français [PCF]). Tasca, because of his difficult relationship with the Communist International, occupied an anomalous position on *Monde* and toward Barbusse, who was a noted member of the PCF. Tasca's search for a revolutionary solution outside, but not necessarily hostile to the Communist party, ended in failure when he was driven from *Monde* by the Stalinists of the PCF.

Once out of the orbit of the Third International, Tasca was drawn to a dangerous revision of Marxism that paralleled that of the Belgian socialist theorist Henri De Man or of the French neosocialist Marcel Déat. Like De Man, who was the most influential theoretician in the Belgian Workers party during the 1930s but whose disillusionment with democracy led him to collaborate with the Germans during World War II, Tasca was convinced that the proletariat as such would never comprise a majority of the working population and that the key struggle between the Left and the Fascists was for the loyalty of the lower middle class. Tasca began to search for a new socialist "humanism" that would have an appeal beyond the working class. He was also attracted to theories of socialist planning formulated by De Man as another way of bringing the lower middle class and the proletariat together on a program that would be anticapitalist but also non-Marxist.

After several years in the political wilderness, Tasca rejoined the Italian Socialist party and began to contribute a column on foreign affairs for the French Socialist newspaper *Le Populaire* in 1934. Faced with the old problem of developing a strategy against fascism, but by now deeply suspicious of the Communist movement, Tasca joined with others on the right wing of social democracy who fought against a "united front" alliance between the Communist and Socialist parties. Anticommunism became his dominant passion during the 1930s. Within the Italian Socialist party he became the rival of Pietro Nenni, the party secretary and supporter of Unity of Action with the Communists. The debate between Tasca and Nenni that began in the 1930s would continue in other forms to paralyze Italian socialism as a political force in the years after 1945.

During the 1930s Tasca became increasingly interested in foreign policy, which he tended to view from a French rather than an Italian perspective. He joined the staff of *Le Populaire* in 1934, became a French citizen in 1936, and was deeply involved in the internal struggles within the French Socialist party (Section Française de l'Internationale Ouvrière

[SFIO]). His strong antifascism led him first to ally with the opponents of Munich and of appeasement; later, he seemed to become caught up in events beyond his control. The pact between Hitler and Stalin in August 1939 and the outbreak of the war suspended normal political activity.

In 1940 the defeat of France brought Tasca to a serious crisis of faith. He joined those French Socialists whose virulent anticommunism led them to collaborate with the Vichy regime. Convinced that the conflict between Socialists and Communists had played a large part in the disintegration of France during the 1930s, Tasca looked to Pétain's New Order for a sign of renewal. Tasca, who had directed the Italian language broadcasts for French radio before the war, rejected an offer of passage to London and continued to work as a civil servant and anticommunist propagandist under the Vichy government. Although Tasca eventually realized that Vichy was a failure and joined a Belgian resistance network that passed information to the Allies, his collaboration with Vichy from 1940 to 1944 cost him a postwar political career in both Italy and France.

After 1939 Tasca threw himself entirely into the struggle against the USSR and against the French Communist party. Hatred for the Soviet system became the moving force in his life. Even his writing, with the exception of the great *Rise of Italian Fascism*, became part of his crusade against the Soviet Union. Nothing remained of his early Marxism and revolutionary idealism. Faced with the impossibility of resuming a direct political role, Tasca turned to history to wage his battle. Drawing on his vast archive of documents and over one hundred volumes of diaries, Tasca attacked the Communist movement in a number of studies of the French Communist party and of Soviet foreign policy during the period of Stalin's pact with Hitler. His life ended in 1960 in bitter opposition to the movement that he helped to found and to which he had given his best years.

The political itinerary of Angelo Tasca was that of an entire generation of European intellectuals, not in the sense that they all arrived at Tasca's conclusions, but rather because they faced common problems and struggled against the same limitations. Tasca was not a wholly sympathetic figure. He lacked that touch of greatness that marked Antonio Gramsci. He was not always correct in the alternatives that he proposed, and, even when he was correct, events often conspired to render his options unworkable. Yet he possessed courage and intellectual honesty. His *Rise of Italian Fascism* still stands as one of the remarkable achievements of Italian historiography.

What follows is not a biography of Angelo Tasca in the strict sense. Details of Tasca's life are examined only to the extent that they were relevant to his political career. Moreover, the analysis terminates for all practical purposes in 1945, although the outline of Tasca's life from 1945 to 1960 is traced in an epilogue. The true subject of this book is the Italian

Left (and to a lesser extent, the French Left) from 1918 to 1945, studied through Tasca's activities. It centers on the troubled relationship between the Socialist and Communist movements from the origins of the split in the Bolshevik Revolution to the crises leading up to World War II. Once the proletarian movement broke into two distinct parties, there were only three options: continued civil war on the Left, absorption of one party by the other, or cooperation and alliance. Each of these strategies was attempted along the way. Tasca's career is an ideal medium for viewing the problems created by the split on the Left because he was involved in both parties and took clear positions on each of the three options. But Tasca's life is important in a larger perspective; it revolved around the essential issues that confronted the European Left during the first fifty years of this century: the integration of the Bolshevik legacy into socialist practice, the challenge of fascism, and the polarization caused by the cold war. In analyzing Tasca's political career, we can see the failure of the European Left to produce any universally accepted answers to these problems. More particularly, we can understand the difficulty that social democracy experienced in coming to grips with either the challenge of communism or that of fascism. The debilitating civil war on the Left would weaken and eventually neutralize the forces that worked for social change during the first half of the century. On a more personal level, this study provides to the author one more piece in deciphering the riddle of that generation of the 1890s that seemed to be born under the twin stars of war and revolution.

PART 1
THE COMMUNIST,
1892–1929

1

The Making of a Revolutionary Socialist

Italy, from the turn of the century to the outbreak of the Great War, experienced an era of great hope and equally great frustration. The period was one of rapid economic growth for both industry and agriculture. Cities such as Turin and Milan formed the factory complexes that marked the industrial revolution elsewhere; with this growth came the formation of a modern proletariat.

Politically, the years from 1900 to 1914 were a relatively optimistic time. After the unstable economic and social conditions of the 1890s almost led Italy on a course of authoritarian rule, the new century opened on a different note. Under the leadership of the liberal prime minister Giovanni Giolitti, who dominated Italian politics during the period before the war, there was an attempt to broaden the base of the political system to take into account the emerging labor force in the north and the new willingness of Catholics to work within the national state.

Giolitti sought chiefly to preserve the traditional position of the liberal political class that had ruled Italy since unification in 1860. He was not interested in profound reforms of the political system, although in 1912 he did introduce universal manhood suffrage that would make the continuation of traditional politics impossible.

As might be expected in a period of rapid change, critics appeared, on both the Right and Left, who rejected the course that Giolitti had chosen. Within the socialist movement there were increasingly bitter debates between the reformists, who felt that progress might be made by working with Giolitti within parliament for specific political and economic changes (recognition of the right to strike and the suffrage reform of

1912), and the revolutionaries, or Maximalists, who argued that the labor movement would be co-opted by Giolitti without effecting any real improvement in the lot of the mass of workers. At issue was the control of the Socialist party and of the General Confederation of Labor. The former was founded in 1892, struggled against political repression in the period from 1894 to 1899, and emerged under moderate leadership to enjoy a period of modest growth under Giolitti. The Labor Confederation, which was launched in 1906 and led by the moderate socialist Renato Rigola, remained the most important bastion of reformist strength.

But Italy was a deeply divided country. Class conflict simmered just beneath the surface. A decreased rate of economic growth after 1907 brought many of the social conflicts to the fore. Giolitti's gradualist methods were unable to keep pace with the polarization of the Italian political Left after the Libyan war of 1911–1912. A new generation of socialists arrived on the scene; like the young Benito Mussolini, they thought that the moment was right to break decisively with the old order. The Giolittian system unraveled when the imperialist conquest of Libya provoked a bitter and violent reaction against war and militarism among the politicized workers and peasants. Paradoxically, the great growth that had made reformism possible seemed now to undermine it. On the eve of World War I the young on both Right and Left pushed ahead with their call for a new Italy. The fragile and antiquated political structure of nineteenth-century Italy was about to enter the storm of war and revolution that would mark a definitive end of the Italian belle epoque.

PREWAR SOCIALISM AND THE YOUTH MOVEMENT IN TURIN

Pre-1914 socialism cannot be judged by standards of the modern political party. Steady gains in both arousing worker consciousness and improving organization were being made, but these were from a very low base. In 1908 there were still fewer than seven thousand members of the Socialist party in Piedmont, and membership in the entire country stabilized at around forty-five thousand between 1904 and 1908. In 1911 probably fifteen thousand workers were organized in Turin's industrial unions. The most notable of these, the Metal Workers Federation (Federazione Impiegati Operai Metallurgici [FIOM]), was able to enroll but 2,527 members, or 7.5 percent of the work force in the sector.

Apart from the small Socialist party, two other organizations, which would play an important role in Tasca's life, encompassed the bulk of organized workers, the Camera del Lavoro (Labor Chamber) and the Turinese Cooperative Alliance (Alleanza Cooperativa Torinese [ACT]), both dominated by reformist socialists. The relative stagnation of membership for both the national and the provincial movement up to 1911 led to growing discontent with reformism in the party and the unions. This discontent was especially acute in the young generation that rallied to socialism around 1910.[1]

The young perceived two problems as threats to the growth of the worker movement. The first was the absence of adequate leadership. Reformists were considered to be compromised by their dealings with Giovanni Giolitti and mired in petty negotiations for partial reforms that, however efficacious, failed to inspire militancy and sacrifice. The second problem derived from the first. Pragmatism without ideals, reform without an overall revolutionary strategy accounted for the loss of dynamism in the years before 1911. Many young intellectuals who came to socialism in the years leading up to World War I believed that the movement suffered from a profound ideological crisis that grew out of neglect of spiritual and cultural values. The situation seemed quite different from that of the late 1890s, when an earlier generation rallied to socialism as a fledgling movement struggling to survive against a repressive government. Somehow the old militancy had to be rediscovered. The old faith in gradual, but continuous, progress that inspired the reformist movement of the turn of the century had been undermined by a number of new sociological and political theories that used rationalist and positivist analysis for very different ends. Vilfredo Pareto and Gaetano Mosca exposed the limitations of democracy and the persistence of oligarchies. They were joined by Gustave Le Bon in questioning the progressive role that the masses might play on the political scene. Modern politics was shown to be open to emotional and irrational appeals. More than anyone else, Georges Sorel exercised a profound influence between 1898 and 1908, as young intellectuals used his ideas to turn the new theories of elites and of the role of the irrational in politics to the service of the revolutionary movement. Sorel's call for a new militancy struck a responsive chord in the young who wanted to break with the old order. They sought a proletarian vision that could be juxtaposed to that of the bourgeoisie. Antireformism and antimilitarism seemed to offer a start toward a new intransigence. An ideologically rejuvenated socialist movement might then reach out to the worker and peasant masses who had been unmoved by reformist appeals. War in Libya and the crisis of the Giolittian system offered the opportunity. The organizational decline of the PSI, which saw the Turin section drop to six hundred members in 1910, seemed to cry out for a few determined adherents who could make a difference.[2]

EARLY LIFE AND FAMILY BACKGROUND

Angelo Tasca was born into this Italy in transition on 19 November 1892 at Moretta in the province of Cuneo. His family was of Piedmontese origin from the valleys that sent poor peasants on seasonal migrations into

France in search of work. Tasca's parents separated when he was quite young. His father, a mechanic for the state railways, was a socialist, but of an instinctive sort, who responded more to his economic situation than to any formal ideology. Tasca's mother moved to southern France when she left the family. Although she kept occasional contact with her son and even helped him financially when he was at the university, Tasca clearly felt the impact of his parents' separation and the loneliness of an only child in a poor, single-parent family. The relationship between Tasca and his father was not without affection, but it was not close.[3]

When Tasca was still quite young, his father moved to Turin, where Angelo completed his secondary education at the Liceo Gioberti in 1911 and then enrolled as a scholarship student in the law faculty at the University of Turin. Subsequently, Tasca switched to the Faculty of Letters, in which he completed his university work. The first indication of his socialist activity was at the Liceo Gioberti, where he helped organize the local branch of the Federazione Giovanile Socialista Italiano (FGSI), which was the youth wing of the Partito Socialista Italiano (PSI). Tasca made his debut as a socialist orator in July 1909 by speaking against the visit of the czar to Italy.[4]

FIRST SOCIALIST EXPERIENCES

Angelo Tasca's socialism, like that of other young radical intellectuals of the pre—World War I period, was shaped by three factors. First was the domination of Italian intellectual life by Benedetto Croce. For intellectuals of the Left and of the Right, Crocean philosophy offered a vehicle for a critique of Italy's cultural development during the post-Risorgimento period. Thus, young Italians often arrived at Marx by way of Croce and Sorel rather than directly. Second, Tasca was caught up in the reaction against the Giolittian system, which seemed to embody the worst features of Italian life since unification: corruption, mundane administration, and compromise of ideals. Publications like *La voce* of Florence that sought to apply the lessons of militant idealism to the world of politics and economics argued that cultural reform was a prerequisite for any revival of the Italian nation. Large numbers of discontented young intellectuals rallied to *La voce* and then shifted their loyalties to *L'unità*, edited by the historian and dissident socialist Gaetano Salvemini. Salvemini's strict moralism and concern for the poorest and most disadvantaged regions of Italy motivated his hostility to Giolitti and made his brand of politics particularly appealing to the young. Finally, Tasca was shaped by antimilitarism. Hostility to the army reflected a deeper rejection of the kind of state produced by the Risorgimento.

DEFINING THE NEW MILITANCY: THE CONGRESS OF THE YOUTH FEDERATION IN 1912

The Socialist Youth Federation and its newspaper, *L'Avanguardia*, became the platform of those young socialists who sought a more revolutionary policy. The FGSI was founded and dominated for many years by the Maximalist Arturo Vella, but in 1912 its soul belonged to Benito Mussolini, the rising star of the PSI. In practice, however, the federation split over the best way to form revolutionary cadres. In September 1912 the congress of the FGSI brought the two factions into open conflict. Two future leaders of the Communist party, Angelo Tasca and Amadeo Bordiga, represented the contrasting positions. Bordiga believed that the socialist movement would stagnate if it concentrated only on education and culture: One did not become a socialist by reading scholarly journals, but rather by instinctive class feeling and concrete political action. Militant action would form leaders capable of making the revolution, and those leaders would be none the worse for not having studied Croce or Gentile.[5] Bordiga distrusted bourgeois intellectuals who came to socialism with all their cultural baggage in tow. He did not condemn culture per se, but he believed that until the schools were changed in the new proletarian society, there could be little hope for liberation through education.[6]

Tasca, representing the minority at the congress, approached the question of culture and the formation of a new revolutionary cadre quite differently. Although the socialism of his father and his own direct experience of proletarian life drew Tasca to the movement, his struggle for an education and his interest in literature, philosophy, and pedagogy defined the content of his socialism in terms of a cultural awakening that would precede a direct assault on existing institutions. Tasca called for a new relationship between politics and culture that would force a sharper ideological consciousness on the socialist movement and would bring an end to the politics of reformism.[7] He insisted that the cultural battlefield not be abandoned to the bourgeoisie. Nor was it necessary to create a wholly new system of education before the cultural battle could be won.[8]

THE UNIVERSITY OF TURIN AND THE *CORRIERE UNIVERSITARIO*

Although Tasca lost the debate with Bordiga at the FGSI congress, his ideas carried the day within the provincial section of the FGSI and among his friends at the University of Turin. It was at the university that Tasca met the young radicals who were to be the core of the *Ordine nuovo* group and of the future Communist party: Umberto Terracini, Antonio Gramsci, and Palmiro Togliatti. Their world was not that of Marx and Engels but of Croce, the liberal economist Luigi Einaudi, the radical historian Gaetano

Salvemini, and the economist and sociologist Vilfredo Pareto. It would have been impossible to escape from or to reject this legacy. Instead, the young Turinese took up the ideas of the day—free trade, a call for new rigor and honesty in political life, and philosophical idealism—and turned them to the cause of proletarian liberation. Tasca was the leader of the younger group of socialists, and his stand on the importance of culture met no opposition from his friends.

Culture in its broadest sense, as defined by the nineteenth-century liberal Francesco De Sanctis and by Benedetto Croce, gave meaning to politics by providing the object of political activity. Already in the first years after unification, De Sanctis had called for a new political culture for united Italy. Following closely in the footsteps of their masters, the young believed that only by setting ideal ends could politics rise above *giolittismo*, political bargains based on self-interest. The political role of the intellectual was to define these ethical ends. Gramsci, Tasca, and Togliatti were all "culturalists" before World War I in reaction to the dominant outlook in the party and in the unions. Not only did the reformists tend to avoid a discussion of ends to concentrate on short-term objectives, but they were generally drawn to the empirical social sciences and less interested in pure philosophy. Against this mentality Croce and his younger followers directed many of their critical salvos. But the mixture of Croce and Sorel, syndicalism and voluntarism, that the young opposed to the positivism and moderation of the reformists did not augment the intellectual clarity of their alternative. Out of this ferment, however, emerged a starting point not only for a revision of reformism but also of the Crocean idealism that had served as a weapon in the initial struggle.[9]

The Turinese expressed their ideas in the *Corriere universitario*, a university periodical; in the FGSI's *L'avanguardia*; and in the provincial socialist paper, *Il grido del popolo*. Of the three, the *Corriere universitario* was most suited to the development of the culturalist theme. It was not a socialist paper but was open to all currents and reflected the common ground shared by rebels on the Left and Right. There Tasca argued that culture was the process by which specialized knowledge was integrated into an operative world vision. Political activity took on meaning only in so far as it was supported by an adequate ethical framework. He rejected the positivism of an earlier generation, which seemed to reduce socialism to mere economic calculation. His socialism, Tasca insisted, developed from the theories of Marx, Engels, Antonio Labriola, and Georges Sorel.[10] Far from being a mechanistic explanation of historical evolution, socialism was the result of struggle and will. There was simply no iron law that made socialism the automatic outcome of the process of history. From Marx by way of Croce, Tasca came to believe that human consciousness was the agent of history. The process of revolution could never be separated from that of achieving a new consciousness.[11]

TASCA AND GRAMSCI

Tasca almost certainly had some influence on Gramsci's evolution toward socialism. During the 1912–1913 academic year they were in regular contact. In May 1912 Tasca presented Gramsci with a copy of *War and Peace*, dedicated "To the school comrade—today; to the comrade in battle, I hope, tomorrow." According to Renzo Martinelli, who has examined Gramsci's writings from these years, Tasca appreciated the qualities that Gramsci could contribute to the socialist movement and encouraged him to collaborate on the *Corriere universitario*. Both men shared a common belief that the major task of the socialist youth movement was cultural preparation.[12]

Yet Tasca's influence on Gramsci should not be overstated. The latter became a socialist in his own time and for motives that transcended personal friendships. Contacts and shared interests within a small university world did not translate into equal degrees of militancy or even common positions on important issues. Moreover, there was a real incompatibility of character between Tasca and Gramsci. Gramsci had a more original mind, which groped for solutions outside the traditional structures of Italian socialism while remaining within the Marxist tradition. But, quite often, Gramsci's political positions were too abstract and artificial for Italian reality. Tasca, who never entirely succeeded in integrating his various interests within a coherent framework, had a shrewder awareness of political realities than did Gramsci. Tasca's obvious love of knowledge for its own sake often communicated itself to comrades as pedantry. Toward a few close friends he could be extraordinarily sacrificing and generous, yet he carefully compartmentalized his life, and few people seemed to know him well.[13]

SALVEMINI, *LA VOCE*, AND THE STRUGGLE
AGAINST GIOLITTI

One of the characteristics that bound Tasca with Gramsci and the other young socialists at the university was an avid enthusiasm for *La Voce* and then for Salvemini's *L'unità*. Salvemini's hostility to the Libyan war, his defense of free trade, his intransigence on the southern question, and his strong sense of morality in public life made him an irresistible figure to the young. Tasca was among those who tried to persuade Salvemini to run for the vacant parliamentary seat in the fourth college of Turin in the special election of 1914. When Salvemini refused, the same offer was made to Mussolini, who was in 1914 still a new voice in socialist politics. These offers, both rejected, reflected the impatience of the young socialists with the established figures of the socialist movement.[14]

In a letter to Salvemini, written sometime after the election of 1914, Tasca reaffirmed his admiration for Salvemini's work and described the activities of the Fascio Giovanile Socialista in terms certain to appeal to Salvemini:

> We are all, or almost all, members of the party, because in these three or four initial years of study and of modest work, lived in continuous contact with the workers of the city and with the peasants, we understood that the Party still has an enormous hold on the spirit of the people and that it is not really a question of creating a new faith, but only of revitalizing and redirecting that original faith, which for better or worse *encompasses all the best aspirations of the humble.* It is true that renewal of faith is, in essence, *creation*; for which, alongside cultural preparation (which has its *ideal* value because it establishes the seriousness and the fecundity of the faith), an active participation of the young in the task of renewal is also necessary. . . . Ours is a rational mysticism, or better, the appreciation of the great mystical value of the ideal, as Sorel would put it.[15]

This letter clearly reveals Tasca's state of mind in 1914 (and perhaps that of his friends as well). Nowhere does Marx's name appear. Sorel's emphasis on militant idealism and on the force of will in history was far more attractive, yet the transition from culture to practical politics was still missing. There was no concrete program of action with a specifically socialist content. The issues that Tasca raised—anti-Giolittian politics, free trade, and antimilitarism—were shared by many dissidents of the Left and Right.

ANTIMILITARISM AND THE CRISIS OF INTERVENTIONISM

Antimilitarism was a fixed point in Tasca's political credo. In 1912 it drew him to Salvemini and to Mussolini, but at the same time it represented a limit to Tasca's admiration for both men. Tasca rebelled both against the military system's brutalization of worker and peasant conscripts and against any socialist support for a bourgeois war.[16] Thus, the crisis over Italian intervention in World War I, which lasted from August 1914 until May 1915 and drastically changed the face of Italian politics, caused Tasca to break with both Salvemini and Mussolini and led to a serious difference with Gramsci over the value of the "revolutionary" war. Although Gramsci never became an interventionist, he did waver when Mussolini shocked and scandalized the Socialist party by proclaiming the idea of "active and operative neutrality" in October 1914. Mussolini must have realized that there was some sympathy for his position among the young Turinese. In his search for support after his break with the Socialist party, Mussolini unsuccessfully invited Tasca to collaborate on the new *Popolo d'Italia*.

Tasca recalled that Gramsci even submitted an article to Mussolini; fortunately, it was never published.[17] Gramsci did, however, write a compromising article for *Il grido del popolo* entitled "Neutralità attiva ed operante" in which he argued in Mussolinian terms against the socialist policy of total opposition to the war and in favor of a flexible policy that would reveal to the proletariat the blind alley down which the bourgeoisie had led Italy. Gramsci attacked Tasca's condemnation of Mussolini and rejected the thesis that the war would work to the exclusive benefit of the bourgeoisie: The proletariat could use the war to become conscious of its revolutionary potential even if the moment for revolution had not arrived.[18]

Tasca, who was passionately opposed to the war, had plunged immediately into the campaign for neutrality. At the end of July he presented an antiwar motion from the provincial congress of the FGSI to the Turinese section of the PSI. In September he joined Bruno Buozzi and other prominent socialists in calling for absolute neutrality. In *L'avanguardia* he dismissed the fears about an Austro-German victory as no excuse for the PSI to abdicate its responsibility to the international proletariat.[19]

After Mussolini's defection to the interventionist cause, Tasca appealed to him to reconsider and recalled his past contributions to the party. On the issue of the war, "the purest antiproletarian expression," Tasca would not compromise. Typically, however, he turned, not to Marx, but to Sorel for inspiration. War was a negative myth, the symbol of all that worked against the proletariat, whereas revolution was a positive ideal. The revolutionary impact of the war presupposed an increased consciousness by the proletariat that its rights had been violated. Isolated opposition to the war could contribute powerfully to this awareness. Absolute neutrality was not the negation of the nation, "but affirmative, and to the extent that it will be absolute, also creative of a new form of nation in which the proletariat will find the recognition of all its rights."[20]

On the issue of the war Tasca was close to his old opponent Bordiga. The latter, however, operated from the premise that the war was a fatal product of capitalism in decline and that the proletariat had no association with the conflict except to prepare for the coming collapse of the bourgeois system. Tasca worked within the context set by Salvemini and other pro-war radical intellectuals and sought to respond to their arguments that the war might aid the proletariat by creating the basis for a more modern democracy or for a future revolutionary worker elite. Tasca seemed not to share, either then or in the future, the illusions of the revolutionary Left about the easy and imminent collapse of the bourgeois order.[21]

MILITARY SERVICE AND MARRIAGE

The outbreak of the war dispersed the Turinese socialist group. Tasca, Togliatti, and Terracini were called for military service almost immediately.

Only Antonio Gramsci, whose physical condition kept him from military duty, remained active in socialist politics. Tasca spent much of the war far from the front and near his home; yet despite this proximity to Piedmont, he took little part in active politics. Years later both Piero Gobetti and Alfonso Leonetti would hold this inaction against him, attributing it to fear on the part of Tasca that he might be sent to the front. There are, however, other explanations for Tasca's political inactivity. On 23 March 1916 he announced in a letter to his mother that he was going to marry Lina Martorelli, the sister of his close friend Renato. In March 1917 his first child, Carlo, was born, and these new responsibilities placed a burden on Tasca's precarious finances. In a letter to Ottavio Pastore, written after his marriage, Tasca asked for a loan and described his difficult economic situation. He also asked to see his old friends, if not for active politics, at least to renew old ties.[22] The years of military service were not entirely lost, however. Freed from political life, Tasca completed his thesis on Giacomo Leopardi and French Enlightenment philosophy in 1917. But, on the whole, the years of the war provided a strangely quiet prelude in Tasca's personal life to the frenetic pace of the period from the end of the war to the March on Rome.

2

Tasca and the Italian Revolution

The end of the war closed the period of international conflict but brought to Italy four years of bitter internal strife. The fragile Italian economy faced the problem of sustaining high levels of war production with weak internal demand. The price of imported raw materials soared when the Allied controls were removed. Italy's balance of payments was in serious deficit, and state expenditures far outstripped revenues. During the war the government had been forced to call upon peasants and workers with promises of a new deal in the postwar period. The introduction of universal manhood suffrage in 1913 necessitated that these promises for land reform and a better standard of living be honored to prevent massive defections from the established order.

The conservative political class was ill-equipped for the post-1918 revolutionary crisis. Italian liberals had never organized a party structure on the basis of universal manhood suffrage, although an electoral reform law had been passed in 1912 and one national election held in 1913. Neither the new middle class that had been created by the industrial and agricultural boom of the first decade of the twentieth century nor the older elites had modern political organizations to compete for the allegiance of a democratic electorate. Social conflict, on the rise before the war, exploded in 1919. Spurred on by wartime promises, discontented peasants began to seize land in parts of central and southern Italy. Militant unionized workers and peasants in the north were determined to press ahead with their demands for more political and economic power. With conservative Italy on the defensive, the middle-class parties divided and weak, and the economic crisis feeding the discontent of the masses, Italy seemed to be on the brink of revolution. Many observers on both the Left and Right felt that the entire structure of Italian capitalism was nearing collapse. The Socialists, especially, believed that their moment of triumph had finally come.

Unlike most other European socialist parties, the PSI avoided a major split over the issue of support for the war effort. The advantages that the party derived from this unity proved elusive, however. Party unity during World War I was maintained by the policy "neither adhere nor sabotage," which avoided conflicts over basic issues. Such a passive stance guaranteed that the party would not divide because of social patriotism or support for the war, but harmony was achieved in part because censorship and government controls made normal political activity impossible. At the end of the war, issues that had been swept under the table were bound to reemerge with increased force just when ideological and practical unity was most necessary to take advantage of the opportunities created by the war.

A number of factors combined to push the PSI's center of gravity to the left by 1918. International events, beginning with the socialist conferences of Zimmerwald and Kienthal in 1915 and 1916 and culminating in the Bolshevik Revolution, gave new weight to the revolutionary antiwar position. Internal social and economic pressures that led to the food riots and strikes of August 1917 in Turin made the prospect of large-scale protest more immediate. By the end of the war the Reformist faction within the PSI had lost much of its support among the masses, and the majority was divided among various revolutionary and Maximalist currents. Ideological confusion persisted. The Reformists believed that conditions in Italy were not ripe for revolution. In alliance with the middle class and peasants, they pressed for a series of constitutional and economic reforms that would lay the basis for a modern democracy. Led by skilled politicians such as Filippo Turati, they were untainted by social patriotism and determined to remain within the PSI. The Reformists had a base in the unions and in the parliamentary delegation from which to do battle. They also stole a march on the revolutionary factions by cleverly giving nominal support to the Bolshevik Revolution and to the Third International.

Behind the PSI's facade of unity was a radical disagreement over theory and practice that set Right against Left within the party and splintered the revolutionaries themselves. Maximalism had always been an elusive ideological position, more a mood of intransigent rejection of the Italian state and a belief in the inevitability of a violent revolutionary outburst than a coherent doctrine. Moreover, the Maximalists viewed revolution as a process that developed according to determined historic laws. Thus, the party did not "make" the revolution, but rather it prepared to inherit the fruits of the violent upheaval that would destroy the old society: "Not to take power until the proletariat is capable of exercising its dictatorship; but not to commit itself in the struggle for the dictatorship before the struggle shifts in favor of the proletariat." In short, many Maximalists believed that although the power of the bourgeoisie was crumbling, the role of the party was to stand aside, to prepare for the future, and, above all, to do nothing that might offer a respite to the capitalist state.[1]

The extreme Left differed from the majority of Maximalists over the party's function during the period before the collapse of the bourgeois order. The Maximalists believed that the PSI could profitably engage in electioneering and sit in parliament in order to mobilize the proletariat and sabotage the state, whereas the far Left called for total abstention from electioneering and from participation in parliament. Instead, the party should organize the proletariat entirely outside the state for the coming violent insurrection. This position of "revolutionary abstentionism" was held by a relatively small minority led by the charismatic Amadeo Bordiga.

The most representative figure in Italian socialism was Giacinto Menotti Serrati, the editor of the *Avanti!* and de facto leader of the party. Serrati placed an enormous value on party unity. He believed that events would carry Italy toward revolution, but that the experience of the Reformists in parliament and in the unions was vital for ultimate success. As long as the reformists accepted the overall aims set by the Maximalists, cooperation was possible. However, Serrati faced an inescapable contradiction in his position. He wholeheartedly supported membership in the new Third International, but this organization had as its basic premise the exclusion of the Reformists.

At issue was the meaning of Leninism in the Italian context, in 1919 an unknown. The various factions of the party read the success of the Bolsheviks differently. Serrati understood Bolshevism as internationalism and faith in the revolutionary potential of the proletariat, but not as Leninist party organization. He felt that Leninism could be made to conform to the practice of Italian Maximalism.[2] Antonio Gramsci, influenced by the libertarian Lenin of *State and Revolution*, sought an Italian equivalent for the soviets. Bordiga believed that the Leninist model of the party was the core of Bolshevism. Already before 1919 he had supported the idea of a radically different party from the open and democratic PSI. The success of the disciplined and centralized Bolsheviks offered a concrete model of a revolutionary elite.[3]

The electoral question was far from academic in 1919. The life of the prewar parliament was at an end, and new elections were scheduled for late 1919. It was vital that the PSI decide in what way it would use the mass following that it had gained at the end of the war. A certain kind of party, the traditional model of the pre-1914 socialist Second International, was organized for activity within a liberal or parliamentary system of open politics, whereas the Bolshevik or Bordigan model, although not ruling out tactical participation in elections, was not organized with this factor in mind. Thus, the issue of participation became a test of ideological correctness in terms of the Bolshevik model.

TASCA AND THE FORMATION OF THE ORDINE NUOVO GROUP

The return of Tasca, Terracini, and Togliatti from military service reunited them with Gramsci, who had edited the *Grido del popolo* during the war and in 1918 was working on the Piedmontese edition of the *Avanti!* Gramsci, now twenty-eight, had matured in his commitment to socialism during the war; Tasca and Terracini were resuming their political careers. Only Togliatti, who had remained on the margin of the socialist movement before 1914 and who had gone furthest in supporting the war, was about to turn a new page.

The revolutionary climate of 1918 and 1919 made it urgent that the young Piedmontese revolutionaries find a way of participating in political life and of influencing the debates taking place within the PSI. The idea for a socialist periodical that would help create a new cultural and political outlook originated in the pre-1914 *La voce* and *L'unità* of Salvemini, and in the new French periodical *Clarté* of Romain Rolland and Henri Barbusse. These were the models that Gramsci and Tasca had in mind. *Clarté*, especially, sought to link avant garde culture with the emerging revolutionary political order in Europe.[4]

The first issue of *L'ordine nuovo* appeared on 1 May 1919. Tasca raised the money for the venture from his contacts in the union and cooperative movement and from the Martorelli family.[5] As a result, his ideas and interests shaped the first issues of the new periodical. The sharp differences that were to divide the editors did not exist in these early days. Tasca, Gramsci, and the others were all culturalists to the extent that they wished to use *Ordine nuovo* to help form a new proletarian consciousness by mediating between the revolutionary working class and the intellectuals. The editors also agreed in their desire to break with the past practices of the socialist movement.[6]

As enthusiastic admirers of the Bolshevik Revolution, the editors of the *Ordine nuovo* adopted a resolutely internationalist perspective. Yet, in 1919, they understood the Bolshevik experience only through a wall of censorship. The Russian example served more as an inspiration for increased militancy than as a complete model of political organization.[7] Like Serrati, Tasca believed that the litmus test for membership in the new International movement would be past opposition to the war, rather than present or future issues. In this regard he was typical of the majority of Italian Socialists who adhered to the Third International without a precise idea of the implications of membership for the future.[8] In 1919 the new

International symbolized a break with a socialist past that had been unable to stop the carnage of the Great War. The Russian Revolution opened a new epoch: "The Third International does not merely signify a modification of the Second; it is a different reality, completely new, because in it the single groups already live in function of the International."[9]

Although Tasca and Gramsci founded *Ordine nuovo* with a common purpose, Gramsci focused much more quickly on a few new issues. Tasca tended to emphasize the same positions he had espoused in 1915. In an early editorial, "Cultura e socialismo," he sounded themes of 1912 when he defined culture as people's capacity to understand the world, their place in society, and their relationships with others. Despite the ferment of the moment Tasca still placed the revolution at the end of the process of education, whereas Gramsci gradually became convinced of the possibilities inherent in revolutionary spontaneity.[10] Tasca was also a traditionalist in his belief that the political revolution had priority over all other changes. No fundamental alterations in the organization of labor could be undertaken before the political revolution was completed.[11]

THE CONGRESS OF BOLOGNA, OCTOBER 1919

Almost naturally, Tasca was drawn to the politics of the PSI and the union movement, just as Gramsci was attracted to the emerging factory council movement. Differences over basic options on the road to revolution meant that each man would take a different stand on the important question of abstention versus participation in the elections of 1919 that would be one of the major subjects for debate at the PSI's Congress of Bologna.[12]

On major issues Tasca was close to Serrati and the "maximalist electionist" faction. At the provincial socialist congress on 31 August 1919, Tasca introduced a motion favoring participation in the elections. He also urged support for this position in both the *Ordine nuovo* and the Piedmontese *Avanti!*, while emphasizing that the real revolutionary struggle would occur outside parliament.[13] He shared the majority's reluctance to split the party by forcing out the Reformists. In classic Maximalist fashion Tasca called for waging the immediate struggle for economic and political gains and for the creation of new institutions of proletarian rule. His sharpest disagreements were with the revolutionary intransigents, led by Bordiga, who forced the party into a needless debate on elections. The extreme Left, he felt, misread worker psychology by rejecting participation in elections at a time when the workers were able to use their vote for the first time.[14]

IN SEARCH OF A POLITICAL BASE

Tasca's positions at the Congress of Bologna set him at odds with many of his future comrades in the Communist party. His political support lay in the labor movement, rather than in the party or factory councils. He became secretary of the Turinese Camera del Lavoro from May 1920 to August 1922 and a member of the administrative council of the Alleanza Cooperativa. In both of these positions, Tasca worked closely with the traditional union bureaucracies and inevitably increased his isolation from the other editors of the *Ordine nuovo*.[15] Thus, he was far more an orthodox Maximalist than was Gramsci, who looked almost exclusively to the novel forms of struggle created in Turin and sought to build his political base on them. By the end of 1919 Tasca and Gramsci had split over both party policy and the council movement.

THE FAILURE OF THE STRIKE MOVEMENT IN TURIN

The conflict between Gramsci and Tasca over the council movement came to a head in the spring of 1920, when Tasca effectively left the *Ordine nuovo* group. In September 1919 elections were held at Fiat for the new shop steward committees (commissioni di reparto). The labor militants and the *Ordine nuovo* group then discussed ways to make the shop steward committees for each division true factory councils representing all the workers of the factory. In early November the Metalworkers Union (FIOM) voted to accept the idea of the councils.[16]

Events in Turin made the debate over the councils somewhat academic even as it was taking place. The turning point came in March 1920, when the metalworkers struck, ostensibly over the issue of standard versus daylight savings time. The strike rapidly became a struggle over the enhanced powers of the shop stewards, who were the driving force behind the factory council movement. The strike was led by the local *commissari di fabbrica* who dominated the local branch of the FIOM. On the other side, the industrialists were determined to end the council experiment, which they had never recognized in a collective contract. Their short-run aim was to stop meetings between the *commissari* and the workers within the factory and to force a return to the simple internal commission, which was restricted to the terms of the collective agreement. The strike was notable for the determination of the radicalized workers to act outside the syndical bureaucracies. It began as a sit-in at Fiat, then spread to all metal and mechanical workers, and finally became a general strike in Piedmont, where it merged with a parallel strike of agricultural workers. Both the reformist leadership of the Confederazione Generale del Lavoro (CGL) and the Maximalists of the national PSI were excluded from the planning and execution of the strike.[17]

During the strike the *Ordine nuovo* group and the local section of the PSI supported the *commissari di reparto* and their strike committee (*comitato d'agitazione*). It became clear by mid-April, however, that the strike would be defeated unless it spread beyond Piedmont. On 19 April the National Council of the PSI met in Milan. Tasca and Terracini were dispatched to represent the Turinese. Terracini, expressing the views of the *Ordine nuovo* group, called for the extension of the strike on the national level and criticized the party for its passivity and for its subservience to the reformists in the General Confederation of Labor.[18]

Tasca's position was somewhat different. He had worked in Turin to extend credit and supplies to the strikers in his capacity as an official of the ACT, but by mid-April he concluded that the strike had been defeated. Sensing that the Turinese were totally isolated in the PSI's Consiglio Nazionale, Tasca practically admitted that it had been a mistake but warned that, if the workers failed in Turin, all the talk about revolution would be fruitless. Thus, the national leadership of the PSI should intervene with the government to force a settlement or, if that failed, issue a call for a national general strike.[19]

But Tasca failed to find middle ground between the extreme Left in Turin and the Maximalist majority within the PSI. The leaders of the PSI and of the CGL ignored the suggestion that the appeal should be directed at the government and, in the event of a negative response, should be followed by a general strike. On 20 April Lodovico D'Aragona, the secretary general of the CGL, accepted the proposals advanced by the industrialists to end the strike, isolating the radical shop stewards along with their allies in the local PSI section.

The outcome of the April strike convinced Gramsci that the traditional union structure and the Maximalist leadership were dead weight on the workers. Tasca's ambiguous position between the two camps made the battle with Gramsci inevitable. During the May meeting of the Turinese section of the PSI, Tasca introduced a motion critical of the handling of the strike. Then at the congress of the Camera del Lavoro on 25–27 May Tasca's report on the councils caught his friends by surprise. Despite his disagreements, he had been expected to back the Left; instead he supported the union bureaucracy. Gramsci accused Tasca of betrayal and of selling out to ensure his election as secretary of the Camera del Lavoro. In Tasca's defense, however, it must be pointed out that he had made his disagreement with the radical faction clear for some time. The program that he offered to the executive committee of the Camera del Lavoro reflected his long-standing desire for compromise and unity: close attention to the political context of economic agitation, avoidance of partial and uncoordinated strikes that only exhausted the workers, closer ties between blue- and white-collar workers and between workers and peasants, and finally integration of the councils into the unions.[20]

THE DEBATE OVER THE FACTORY COUNCILS

At this point the dispute between the editors of the *Ordine nuovo* could not be ignored. Gramsci opted wholeheartedly for the councils in his search for an Italian equivalent of the soviet. In choosing the factory councils he unified the process of making the revolution and constructing a new society. These two phases were separated by both Bordiga and Tasca, as well as by the majority of Maximalists. In Gramsci's eyes the essence of the revolution was the creation of new institutions. The proletariat would obtain power with the instruments it created during the struggle and would use them as the basis of the new society.[21] After mid-1919 Gramsci began to attack the incapacity of unions and cooperatives to reflect the real revolutionary aspirations of the workers. Only a radical break with the past could accomplish this objective. It was essential to gain control of the productive process but this was impossible through the traditional union, which had been in most cases excluded from direct access to the single factory.[22]

A completely new organization, designed for control of the productive process, was necessary. Such an organization could only be the factory council that developed from the older internal commissions of shop stewards formed before World War I to oversee the execution of the collective contracts within the factory. These new organizations had to be freed from dependence on the unions and put on an entirely new basis. To this end, each unit within the factory would elect representatives to a council. These delegates would unite with other workers until the entire enterprise was represented in a general factory council. This body would then challenge management for control of production.[23] Gramsci also relied on a new stratum of leadership that would be created outside both the party and the trade unions. He tentatively accepted a suggestion that unorganized workers within the factory have a vote in the elections for the councils. Such a move would have made them clearly distinct from the unions and would have increased the likelihood that the councils would not reproduce the existing syndical bureaucracy.[24]

Tasca disagreed with Gramsci on almost all points at issue. In his alternative, the council movement would be integrated into the trade union structure by giving organized workers a greater role in the elections to the executive committee of the factory council. The weight of unorganized workers would be effectively limited and the councils made more accountable to the union leadership. Tasca argued that the factory councils were inadequate as future instruments of governance because the problems of controlling a vast system of capitalist finance and distribution was too complicated for them. Instead, the councils should become the basis of the unions, an arrangement that would have the practical advantage of spreading the council movement beyond Turin, but at the cost of completely submerging them in the unions.[25]

During June and July, Gramsci and Tasca engaged in a bitter debate over the councils. Tasca was accused of playing to the most conservative instincts of the workers, of setting back the educational efforts of the *Ordine nuovo* almost to the starting point, and of allowing takeover of the new worker institutions by the established syndical bureaucracy.[26] Tasca responded quite correctly that the councils could never stand alone. Like Serrati and Bordiga, he believed in the primacy of political organs and in the need for a territorial organization for the future soviets.[27] There was, he felt, no basis to Gramsci's distinction between the unions, products of the capitalist system, and the councils outside that system. In bourgeois society both operated under the same rules, just as both would become quite different in a future communist society. Tasca was convinced that unions would play an essential role in such a society and that producer cooperatives represented a real expansion of worker control under capitalism and merited the same level of importance as factory councils. The ideal would be to integrate the councils into the unions, but, if he had to choose between them, Tasca left no doubt of his loyalties to the unions. This position was far more realistic than that advocated by Gramsci, but it had one great weakness. Outside revolutionary Turin the unions and cooperatives were controlled by reformists and moderates who did not share Tasca's enthusiasm for the revolution. Moreover, the factory council movement was genuinely popular in the auto and metal-working factories of Turin. It was on this avant garde that Gramsci counted.[28]

The last act of the revolutionary era of 1919–1920 came with the factory occupations of September 1920. More dramatic, although less important than the April events, it was the final wedge between the revolutionary Left and the center of the PSI. The crisis temporarily reunited the *Ordine nuovo* group. Tasca, as secretary of the ACT, was again in charge of credit and supply for the strikers. He also created within the framework of the Camera del Lavoro a purchasing and supply committee for the workers. Once again, however, the strike failed. The collapse of revolutionary hopes ended any prospect for continued unity of the PSI, as all factions engaged in endless recriminations. The only remaining question centered on the nature of the rupture that all knew to be inevitable.[29]

THE CONGRESS OF LIVORNO

If the failure of the Italian revolution rendered inevitable the split within the PSI, the form that rupture would take was still unclear up to the moment of the Congress of Livorno in January 1921. Only Amadeo Bordiga was absolutely certain of his objective: a break far enough to the left to ensure a compact and ideologically coherent Communist party. In October 1920

neither of the two main factions in the Turinese revolutionary Left was certain that this outcome was desirable. Terracini, Togliatti, and Tasca of the
Comunista Elezionista group and Gramsci of Educazione Comunista
were somewhat more flexible toward the Maximalist center of the party,
but they agreed in November to set aside past differences to work for the
formal constitution of a revolutionary faction within the PSI. On 29 November at Imola such a communist faction was created on the basis of
Bordiga's call for a radical purge of the PSI.[30]

As Umberto Terracini recently pointed out, the revolutionary Left at
the Congress of Livorno was motivated by an overwhelming desire for
clarity after two years of compromise with the Reformists and Maximalists.
Bordiga's intransigence, commanding personality, and moral rectitude
made him the central figure in the drama. Only later did his absolute
rigidity in matters of doctrine and strategy become an inconvenience. In
1921 it seemed a needed corrective to past and present confusion.[31]
Nonetheless, it was expected that the Reformists would withdraw from the
party, leaving the Communists in alliance with the bulk of Serrati's Maximalists. However, the tactical ability of the Reformists, Serrati's attachment
to party unity, and the rigidity of the Third International in refusing to modify its conditions forced the split much further to the left than had been
anticipated by everyone but Bordiga.

Tasca found himself in that group of socialists who hesitated until the
last minute. Politically, he was close to, but not part of, the "circular" group
of Antonio Graziadei and Anselmo Marabini who, between the meeting at
Imola and the Congress of Livorno, pressed for the formation of a Partito
socialista-comunista d'Italia. These Left Maximalists, mainly from Emilia,
were determined to find some middle ground between Serrati and the
Third International. Tasca, who had been associated with similar attempts
at compromise, was referred to by Bordiga as a *"massimalista realiz-
zatore"* but not a communist.[32]

Three factors drew Tasca to the new party: his willingness to expel the
Reformists; a desire to overcome the paralysis within the PSI by putting the
movement on a new basis; and, most important, a desire to stay within the
Third International. Despite his inclination to the new party, Tasca's adherence remained somewhat ambiguous. He did not attend the Congress
of Livorno and sought a mediatory role. He made it clear that the split at
Livorno was imperfect and needed correction.[33]

THE COMMUNISTS AND THE CGL

The first major test for the new Communist Party of Italy (Partito Comunista d'Italia [PCI]) came at the congress of the General Confederation of
Labor in Livorno in February 1921. This event also marked Tasca's emer-
gence as a member of the PCI. The Reformist leaders of the CGL hoped to

capitalize on their earlier success by forcing the Communist minority out of the confederation. The Communists, including Bordiga, were determined not to lose contact with the mass of workers inside the CGL. Thus, Tasca, who believed in an alliance with the Left Maximalists, was ideally suited to argue the case for the new party. During the congress Tasca took the initiative in criticizing the Reformists for reducing the revolutionary opportunity to "a miserable bureaucratic procedure."[34] Although the communist faction remained a minority, its position was less weak than had been feared. The Socialists defeated the Communists by 1,435,873 to 432,564 votes, but the results from the Camera del Lavoro were much closer: 598,941 for the Socialists and 293,428 for the Communists. Tasca's own Turinese Camera del Lavoro provided a strong majority for the Communists.[35]

TASCA'S CRITIQUE OF LIVORNO

By the end of 1921, Tasca presented a clear alternative to Bordiga's leadership. Its central premise was that the Communist party had to recapture the Socialist party's mass base by reaching an understanding with those Maximalists who sincerely wished to rejoin the Third International. Only then could a representative Communist party emerge. Unlike Bordiga, Tasca did not believe that an amalgamation of the Socialist masses ignoring the party leaders was possible. In his capacity as the major spokesman for the party on labor issues, Tasca worked to put forward his ideas on the united front.[36]

The majority of the PCI viewed Tasca as a liquidationist who threatened Bordiga's party of an intransigent revolutionary elite. But Bordiga was at odds with the International on relations with the PSI. At the third congress of the International in June 1921, the postrevolutionary climate in Europe and the first steps toward the New Economic Program (NEP) in Russia made themselves felt in the debates. There was a shift from the Twenty-one Conditions to a call for a united front tactic with the European socialist parties. The PSI, which had never withdrawn its application for membership in the Communist International (Internationale Communiste [IC]), was openly courted.

THE CONGRESS OF ROME

The change of strategy of the International began a process that eventually undermined Bordiga's leadership of the PCI and threatened to set the entire party against the International. The second party congress in March 1922 revealed a deep split between the right wing of Tasca and Antonio Graziadei and the vast majority of the party, which included all of the future leaders (Gramsci, Terracini, Grieco, and Togliatti). The Right was not, strictly speaking, an organized faction, however. Graziadei was a prominent economist and lawyer, whose open sympathy for the style of traditional socialism made him an anomaly in the PCI. The backbone of the faction was union officials, who tended to be more moderate in their politics. But, except for the small Right opposition, the heart and soul of the new party belonged to Bordiga.[37]

Differences between the majority and minority emerged clearly from the precongress debates. Bordiga rejected any front with the socialists except on terms that constituted virtual surrender by the PSI. In contrast, Graziadei argued that, just as socialism had emerged from bourgeois radicalism, communism was a similar outgrowth of socialism. Hard feelings were natural after such a rupture, but momentary bitterness ought not to preclude future cooperation between the two movements.[38]

The representative of the International took an intermediate position but was critical of the Italians for refusing to bring their party in line with the IC's policy of a "united front" with the socialists. Tasca's and Graziadei's optimism about the possibility of winning over a substantial majority of the Socialist party held far more appeal to the International. Tasca believed that a correct policy by the PCI would facilitate a split between Reformists and Maximalists within the PSI.[39]

THE UNITED FRONT IN PRACTICE: THE ALLEANZA DEL LAVORO

At the Rome party congress, Tasca appealed for a broad united front with the Socialists to meet the Fascist danger. He favored antifascist coalitions like the Alleanza del Lavoro (Labor Alliance). The Alliance was formed in February 1922 by the CGL, the syndicalist Unione Italiana del Lavoro, the anarchist Unione Sindacale, the Sindacato Ferrovieri, and the Lavoratori del Mare to fight the seemingly irresistible Fascist onslaught. The PCI, however, opposed the Alleanza del Lavoro from the start. It insisted that the alliance not bind the political parties and attacked the reformist direction, but the Communists proposed little in the way of an alternative. Eventually, the Alleanza degenerated in political bickering. Despite his party's negative position, Tasca, as an official of the Camera del Lavoro of Turin, served as the Alleanza's local secretary. In that capacity he sought a common front of Communists and Socialists against the Fascists. He even thought that such an alliance might be broadened to include democratic Catholics and left liberals. The Communists in Turin made contact with the left wing of the Italian Popular Party (Catholic) and with some Giolittian liberals, but the attempt was blocked by the PCI leaders in Rome.[40]

In trying to bring the Socialist left into the PCI, Tasca was not, as his opponents charged, a liquidator of the Communist party. He was as firm as Bordiga in defending Communist positions within the Camera del Lavoro in Turin against both Maximalists and Reformists. Any united front would be on terms established by the PCI. His break with the Maximalists was sharpest on two issues: the need for a party with more centralized discipline and direction and his demand for a clear separation from the Reformists. The refusal of Serrati and his followers to end their ties with the right wing of the PSI had been a principal reason for Tasca's adherence to the PCI in January 1921.

Throughout these years, when the tide of revolution seemed at its strongest, Tasca represented a balanced position between the older forms of worker organization and the new proletarian ideals and institutions of postwar Italy. Far more realistic than most of the leaders of the Communist party, he was aware of the need to maintain contact with the mass of workers outside the party and with the other parties of the Left. The defeat of the revolution at the end of 1920 made this contact even more important. But the PCI, led by Bordiga, moved in the opposite direction. As 1922 drew to a close, however, developments within the Socialist party offered the best chance to realize Tasca's ambition to redimension the split that had occurred at Livorno.[41]

3

Tasca, the Third International, and Unity of Action

In late 1922 the Italian Left was torn by a double crisis that was only in part caused by the triumph of the Fascist party on 29 October 1922. A month earlier the fragile tie holding the Reformists and the Maximalists together finally snapped. At the PSI's Congress of Rome, the Reformists broke off to form their own Unitary Socialist Party (Partito Socialista Unitario [PSU]). The crisis in the Socialist party had an immediate impact on the already troubled relationship between the PCI and the Third International. The break between the Reformists and Maximalists satisfied one of the key demands set by the International for admission and a merger with the Communists. More than ever the IC considered the moment ripe for fusion between the PCI and two of the three major currents within the PSI: the followers of Serrati who incarnated the old Maximalist tradition and a group of pro–Third International socialists headed by Fabrizio Maffi, Ezio Riboldi, and Costantino Lazzari. The new right-wing faction of the PSI, which was still forming under the leadership of Arturo Vella and Pietro Nenni, was hostile to any merger between the PSI and the Communists.[1]

The question of fusion was particularly acute because, once the Socialist party renewed its application to enter the IC, any merger had to be undertaken before Serrati could reconsider or before opposition to such a move crystallized within the Socialist camp. Forced by a clear order from the International, Bordiga was in the distasteful position of administering a policy that he considered disastrous. He made it clear that the PCI would accept only individual memberships and would not negotiate with Serrati's Maximalists or the Third Internationalists (terzini) of Maffi and Riboldi.[2]

The central issue was a choice of fusion with the bulk of the PSI (minus the Nenni-Vella Right), with certain factions, or with individuals on a case-by-case basis. The first two alternatives would have meant the end of Bordiga's conception of the party. The leadership of the PCI realized that it was on a collision course with the IC. The Bolshevik leader Karl Radek emphasized that the Italians were totally isolated within the International's Executive. Umberto Terracini, who represented the Italian Communist party at the International, wrote from Moscow to confirm that the IC was financing the Terzini group within the PSI. Togliatti, who was closely allied with Bordiga at this time, felt that none of the present leaders of the PCI could undertake fusion with the PSI and rejected the option of giving way to Tasca and Graziadei, who could. Togliatti differed from Bordiga only in his refusal to break with the International on the issue.[3]

THE CONGRESS OF THE INTERNATIONAL, NOVEMBER–DECEMBER 1922

Two delegations represented Italy at the fourth congress of the IC, which met from 5 November to 5 December 1922. The PSI sent Serrati, Giuseppe Romita, Giovanni Tonetti, and Fabrizio Maffi to plead its case for admission. The Communist delegation included Bordiga, Gramsci, and Tasca. From the beginning, the proponents of fusion clearly had the ear of the IC leadership. Tasca played a major role in the work of the Italian Commission, which dealt with the question of a merger between the PSI and PCI. On 13 November he presented a plan that became the basic document for all future negotiations. It suggested that the agreement be worked out in Moscow rather than in Italy, that a common party Directorate be created immediately, and that both sides agree to the convocation of a congress for fusion before calling separate party congresses. Tasca's project excluded Vella and Nenni from the new party and reserved a majority on all committees for the Communists. His sense of urgency was based on an accurate reading of the situation within the PSI. Unlike Bordiga, Tasca realized that the crisis of the PSI was transitory and that the Socialists had to be merged within the IC before they regained their clear sense of identity.[4]

A mixed commission of Socialists and Communists was established under the auspices of the International to work on Tasca's proposals. Gramsci, Tasca, and Mauro Scoccimarro represented the PCI. Serrati, Romita, Maffi, and Tonetti were the Socialist delegates. Spurred on by the International, this committee developed the terms for the creation of a new Partito Comunista Unificato d'Italia to emerge from a fusion congress scheduled for March 1923. The expectation was that Serrati would carry the bulk of the PSI with him, but he was arrested in February, shortly after his return from Moscow. His opponents within the Socialist party, organized now in a Committee of Socialist Defense, took advantage of Serrati's absence to win a majority against fusion. By March it became clear that immediate fusion had failed. As a temporary expedient, Tasca proposed forming a close alliance between the two parties until a new majority for fusion could be re-formed by Serrati and the Terzini.[5]

FRICTION WITHIN THE PCI

Bordiga's obvious satisfaction at the failure of negotiations with the Socialists only increased his difficulties with the IC. To mollify Moscow, the Central Committee of the PCI was enlarged in March 1923 to include Tasca and Graziadei from the Right and Mauro Scoccimarro and Camilla Ravera of the majority. Togliatti and Scoccimarro joined the party executive. But these were mere cosmetic changes, as Ruggiero Grieco admitted. Only Tasca's faction was sufficiently detached from the split at Livorno to follow the directives of the International.[6]

Bordiga and his followers were not prepared to admit defeat or to accept blame for past failures. Togliatti launched a series of attacks on the PSI, which he described as counterrevolutionary and responsible for the failure of fusion. As for the Right minority within the PCI, Terracini referred to them as "vile." For his part, Tasca contended that responsibility for the breakdown of fusion had to be shared equally by Nenni and Vella and by the leaders of the PCI, who gave only lip service to the directives of the IC.[7]

INTERVENTION BY MOSCOW

The split within the PCI had a temporary, unsatisfactory resolution at the meeting of the Enlarged Executive of the IC in June 1923. At the Moscow meeting the "United Front" tactic in Italy, Germany, and England was a major topic of discussion. Bordiga led the Italian delegation, which included the major figures of the party. Only Bordiga, however, was determined to press his case to the limit. The others of the majority were unwilling to create a crisis with the International, and Gramsci began to consider the possibility of a new leadership combination that would exclude both Bordiga and Tasca. Until this was accomplished he sought to avoid open confrontation with the International, while doing little or nothing to carry out its policies on fusion with the PSI.[8]

Within the Italian delegation Tasca was isolated, but support for his position came from the leadership of the International, Radek and Zinoviev, who were unsparing in their criticism of the PCI. Potentially more interesting was the alliance between Tasca and Maffi of the Terzini. One of the fears expressed earlier by the Bordiga group was that, although the fusion agreement called for a new party executive with four Communists and three Socialists, the Tasca minority would probably vote with the Socialists. The common front presented by Tasca and Maffi did little to allay these fears. Both blamed the leadership of the PCI for the failure to achieve even a pact of alliance with the PSI and pointed to Bordiga's insistence on only individual membership as the central difficulty. According to Maffi, such terms could not be put to a party of thirty-two thousand members without creating suspicion and bitterness.[9]

Tasca delivered a scathing indictment of Bordiga's leadership for the failure to achieve either fusion or a political alliance with the Socialists although 43 percent of the Socialist membership favored the Third International at the last congress of the party in April 1923. He proposed that the Communists offer to the Socialists an alliance between the two parties and their respective youth organizations and request full freedom for the PSI's Terzini faction to work for fusion. Unless the PCI acted rapidly, Tasca warned, the PSI would survive; even if it did not, the Communists would never gain as much as they might have from a policy of cooperation and eventual fusion.

Most interesting of all was the context in which Tasca placed the future PCI-PSI bloc, as the nucleus of a broad antifascist front from the Communists on the Left to the Catholics and petty bourgeoisie on the Right. Such a front was necessary for the long-range struggle against the Fascist regime, which was likely to stay in power for a prolonged period: "What constitutes the novelty of fascism is its combat apparatus, organized in a political party and in control of the state. It is precisely this apparatus which will allow fascism to maintain its domination for some future time before the economic contradictions which it has unleashed undermine the foundations."[10]

TASCA AND THE "MIXED EXECUTIVE"

Tasca and Maffi called on the IC to give the minority control of the PCI and to admit the PSI as a "friendly party," but Togliatti ultimately persuaded Tasca not to press his case that far. The International created a mixed Executive for the PCI. Tasca and Giuseppe Vota represented the Right; Bruno Fortichiari (an ally of Bordiga who refused to serve), Scoccimarro, and Togliatti were held over from the old majority. The new Executive was paralyzed from the beginning by factional fighting. In a letter to Gramsci and Scoccimarro, Togliatti called the imposed settlement unworkable. Gramsci's response must have been disappointing because he too began to express reservations over the nature of the split that occurred at Livorno.[11]

Relations with the PSI gave rise to further friction between Tasca and Togliatti. Although the prospects for ousting the Nenni-Vella group from control of the PSI were slight, Tasca urged a policy of continual pressure coupled with direct appeals to the socialist masses, support for the Terzini, and inclusion of one of their representatives on the Executive of the PCI. Togliatti was adamant that the majority had no intention of proceeding along those lines.[12]

It was soon apparent that neither side accepted the new mixed Executive. At the meeting of the Central Committee on 9 August Terracini attacked the Right for trying to take over the party in Moscow. Tasca responded that the IC made him share power only because the base of the party would never understand such a drastic change imposed from above. The dispute was not between the majority and minority, but "between those who have the will to apply the tactics of the International and those who do not." The arrest of many of the members of the Central Committee in September marked only a momentary lull in the battle.[13]

THE COLLAPSE OF FUSION NEGOTIATIONS

The principal issue in the dispute, the nature of the relationship between the PCI and PSI, became increasingly academic by August 1923. The leaders of the PSI were determined to maintain the autonomy of their party and even to avoid any real alliance with the Communists. They refused even to allow the Terzini to form an organized opposition within the PSI. In early August the PSI expelled Serrati, Maffi, Riboldi, and their followers for attempting to publish a pro-fusion periodical, *Pagine rosse*. Revocation of these expulsions became yet another bone of contention between the two parties.[14] The Socialists also rejected a Socialist-Communist labor alliance designed to wrest control of the Camera del Lavoro in Milan from the Reformists. Thus, Tasca's argument that the PCI leadership bore a large part of the responsibility for the failure to arrive at fusion was only partly valid.[15]

Tasca seemed uncertain about the way to proceed with the Terzini. He preferred that they work for readmission to their own party and opposed the creation of an intermediate party between the PSI and PCI. He correctly judged that the Terzini would act in the labor movement as a bridge between the Communist and Socialist workers, but as time went on, he doubted their political capacities. Tasca wrote occasionally for the *Pagine rosse* but was unable to advance his objective of winning the readmission of the Terzini into the PSI.[16]

Tasca was willing to go further than any other Communist in meeting the demands of the PSI that any alliance on the Left include all parties from the PCI to the PSU (reformist). But his model of the United Front differed substantially from that of the Socialists. The basis for any broad Left alliance had to be a close pact between the Maximalists and the Communists to provide a dynamic center around which all other components could rally. (Ironically, Tasca's proposals in 1923 were similar to those of Nenni in the late 1930s that Tasca bitterly opposed.) Tasca also indicated that he believed that there could be but one party of the proletariat and that the ultimate goal of any alliance was fusion. Thus, Togliatti was correct when he complained to Terracini that Tasca wanted the liquidation of Livorno. Tasca aimed at a Communist party somewhere between the old mass-based and open PSI and Bordiga's revolutionary elite. The ultimate failure of Tasca's alternative was due in no small part to the increasing severity of the Fascist dictatorship, especially toward the Communists, which made normal political life impossible. The PCI had to wait until after 1945 to realize a party like that Tasca envisaged in the early 1920s, and Togliatti would create it.[17]

THE ELECTIONS OF 1924 AND TASCA'S ATTEMPT AT A UNITED FRONT

By early 1924 differences between Tasca and Togliatti on the question of the Terzini diminished. Both rejected proposals that the Terzini form an intermediate party. Neither man viewed the Terzini as anything more than a weapon to be used against the Nenni-Vella wing of the PSI, and Tasca began to consider renewing a direct approach to the PSI as the course more likely to succeed. This change in tactic was prompted by the Fascist government's decision to call elections for the spring of 1924. These elections, the last relatively free vote until after 1945, were held under the provisions of the Acerbo law of 1923, which assigned two-thirds of the seats in parliament to the electoral list that won a plurality of the ballots. Thus, unity among the Left opposition was vital, if the proletarian parties were to have any chance to compete. Tasca, who never abandoned his hope of reviving the United Front, proposed setting common policy with the PSI and even extending that alliance to the PSU. Togliatti never viewed the initiative as more than a ploy, so the PCI acted from the beginning with ambiguity. On 24 January the Communists offered to both the PSI and PSU a broad alliance that went beyond electoral strategy and simultaneously announced that it intended to participate in the elections. The tone of the letter, a kind of fait accompli that prejudged the question of participation in the elections, doomed the negotiations from the start.[18]

Togliatti later said that he allowed Tasca to take a leading role in the negotiations to sour the latter's relations with the Socialists. In fact, at the first meeting with the PSI on 26 January, when Tasca, Graziadei, and Gennari pressed for a broad alliance of the two parties, the Socialists countered by insisting that the Reformists be included in any pact. Tasca then attempted unsuccessfully to rephrase the original Communist conditions in terms acceptable to the PSI and PSU, even conceding that the Reformists would not have to abandon their parliamentary strategy. In the end, negotiations failed, and all three parties presented candidates in the elections.[19]

The failure to form an electoral bloc left Tasca with few alternative suggestions. He still blamed the failure on the lack of a unified policy within the PCI: "Under these conditions of uncertainty and of an absence of a clear realistic tactical vision, I also consider that it is impossible to continue to lead the party." Thus, a frustrated Tasca sounded the death knell of the mixed Executive imposed by the IC. Tasca's criticisms were shared by Jules Humbert Droz, the delegate of the IC, who sought to resolve the impasse by elevating Tasca to sole control of the party, a prospect totally unacceptable to the majority.[20]

TASCA'S EXCLUSION FROM GRAMSCI'S NEW "CENTER" GROUP

Antonio Gramsci had long realized the dangers to the leadership cadre of the PCI that were inherent in the rift with the International. Togliatti remained close to Bordiga; Gramsci, however, foresaw the necessity for a clear break with the past. As Paolo Spriano has pointed out, Gramsci took to heart the destruction of the Bulgarian Peasant and Communist parties in 1923 after they failed to unite to prevent the fall of the Radical government of Stamboliski. The defeat of the attempted revolution in Germany in October 1923 strengthened Gramsci's resolve to reexamine the problem of the United Front and the prospects for a broader coalition against the Fascists.[21] Under this new optic, Tasca seemed less of an enemy even if he remained too close to Social Democratic positions on many issues. Gramsci hoped to draw several leaders of the Right minority, including Tasca, into his new leadership group. Most importantly, he now agreed with Tasca that Bordiga had created a party of bureaucrats without strong ties to the masses.[22]

Gramsci attempted to persuade Togliatti and the others to soften their resistance as the important meeting of the Central Committee of 18 April approached.[23] But Tasca showed no sign of compromise and, in fact, toughened his stand by stressing that the members of the new majority refused to admit their past errors during their period of alliance with Bordiga and still agreed with the ex-leader on most issues. Perhaps Tasca hoped that his resignation threat in February might have provoked the intervention of the Comintern. He made no secret of his belief that the mixed Executive could no longer function and that Gramsci's emerging leadership combination was totally artificial. In a report to Mátyás Rákosi of the International's secretariat at the end of April, Tasca sounded unreconciled to defeat. Although he admitted that Gramsci could probably reach an accommodation with the IC, he rejected any role in the new leadership and continued to organize the Right minority for the party conference at Como in May 1924.[24]

THE COMO CONFERENCE

At the Como conference each of the three party factions presented theses. On the Left, Bordiga justified the past policies of the party from 1921 to 1923. Those of the Center, signed by Egidio Gennari, Alfonso Leonetti, Camilla Ravera, Mauro Scoccimarro, and Togliatti (but not Gramsci), attempted to break with Bordiga while preserving his policies. The views of the Right minority were presented by Tasca and signed by Giuseppe Berti, Aladino Bibolotti, Dante Cappelli, Giorgio Carretto, Nicola Cilla, Carlo Farini, Cesare Massini, Gustavo Mersù, Ottavio Pastore, Giovanni Roveda, Mario Piccablotto, and Giuseppe Vota. The background of the signatories reveals that the Right had its base in the syndical and cooperative movements. Tasca and Bibolotti were associated with the Alleanza Cooperativa Torinese; Vota was the leader of the Woodworkers Union (FILIL); Roveda had been in the FIOM; and Massini was a leader of the rail workers.[25]

The theses accused Bordiga of turning the party into a closed faction with rigid barriers excluding the rest of the working class. Tasca also attacked Bordiga's refusal to consider fascism as more than an extension of the interests of the capitalist bourgeoisie. A more profound analysis of the meaning of its lower-middle-class mass base would move the party well beyond the simple slogan "fascism=bourgeoisie=social democracy." The Communists had to interpret their call for a worker and peasant government as a long-term goal and allow for the intermediate step of an antifascist constituent assembly that would be elected by universal suffrage.[26]

The final voting on the various theses reveals something of the true feeling within the party. Voting in favor of Bordiga's position were one member of the Central Committee, four interregional secretaries, thirty-five federal secretaries, and one representative of the youth federation. Togliatti's document had the support of four members of the Central Committee, one interregional secretary, and four federal secretaries, whereas the Right had the backing of four members of the Central Committee, one interregional secretary, and five federal secretaries. The soul of the party still belonged to Bordiga, even if the levers of command were firmly in Gramsci's hands.[27]

THE FIFTH CONGRESS OF THE INTERNATIONAL

Tasca's hope to appeal to the International was dashed by the Fifth Congress of the Comintern. Much had changed since 1923. Preoccupations with Trotsky forced Zinoviev and Stalin to shift leftward. Possible social democratic allies in the United Front once again became the left wing of the bourgeoisie. Most of the prominent leaders of the western parties, such as Ruth Fischer and Ernst Thälmann of the German Communist party and Suzanne Girault and Albert Treint of the PCF, were identified with the Left. As a consequence, Togliatti was spared the necessity of justifying his past resistance to the International.

At the congress, which met from 23 June to 4 July 1924, all three factions of the Italian party were represented, but only Bordiga's left wing continued to express clear opposition to the new leadership of the PCI. Finally acknowledging defeat, Tasca offered support, but not collaboration, to the Center. The accommodating attitude surprised Togliatti. Tasca made little effort to attack the new leadership even when it might have hurt the Gramsci-Togliatti group: "The stand which Rienzi [Tasca] tends to take and which he has taken here is that of a spectator. . . . It is not to be excluded that his conduct is also due to reactions which you know, fatigue and distaste for positions of clear responsibility."[28]

After a year as co-leader of the PCI and spokesman for the Right minority, Tasca emerged with remarkably little. Despite his advocacy of an essentially correct policy, which sought to overcome the split in the proletarian movement as rapidly as possible, he was unable to move the party. His faction soon dissolved. The question of the Terzini was resolved by the Comintern in favor of fusion with the PCI. Tasca had failed to alter the state of cold war between Socialists and Communists. His only achievement was the exclusion of Bordiga and his followers from the new Central Committee and Executive. On the former, the center received nine seats, the Right four, and the Terzini four. The new Executive included Gramsci, Togliatti, and Scoccimarro for the Center, Mersù for the Right (Tasca declined to serve), and Maffi for the Terzini. Perhaps recognizing that the heart of the PCI still belonged to Bordiga and that he could never become its leader, Tasca became resigned to the new Center group. There was also a good deal of psychological insight in Togliatti's comments about Tasca's unwillingness to carry on the battle. Tasca had staked his hopes for leadership on the policies of the IC on the United Front. For the first, but decidedly not the last time, he would be caught short by a shift in Comintern policy.[29]

ON THE SIDELINES

Tasca's last years before leaving for exile in 1926 were spent out of the center of party politics. He refused all posts of responsibility in the party and devoted his energies to finishing his law degree at the University of Turin.[30] Tasca gave some indication of his isolation and discouragement in a letter to Piero Gobetti:

> When I left an official position with the party, I did not have any precise plans, especially about replacing the lost income in the family budget. For the rest, many aspirations, crazy plans, flirting with possibilities which seem, after so many years, to take on real substance. Taking courses at the university was

and is more a door open to the future than a solution to present problems to the extent that the crunch at the end of every month forces me to accept any sort of work. . . . My political position and my convictions enormously limit the range of resources; consequently within these limits I do not have much choice and I have to push myself to the point of exhaustion in terms of financial and human resources. I have arrived at a state of resigned discontent and to avoid useless regrets I try to avoid all circumstances which call me back to what I have been separated from and for the foreseeable future excluded.[31]

Tasca emphasized that his differences with the leadership of the PCI brought his career to a standstill. His situation was complicated by a wife who did not share his political convictions and by a growing family. His son Carlo and daughter Elena were born in 1917 and 1919 and a second daughter Valeria was born in 1926. The combination of personal pressure and political discouragement go far to explain Tasca's withdrawal and even his curious advice in November 1926 to dissolve the party at the time of the promulgation of the full Fascist dictatorship.

THE MATTEOTTI CRISIS AND THE CONSOLIDATION OF THE DICTATORSHIP

The PCI also faced great obstacles in these years. The outrage that swept Italy after the murder of Giacomo Matteotti, the secretary of the reformist Partito Socialista Unitario, at the hands of the Fascists in June 1924 seemed to offer hope that Mussolini might be toppled. Unfortunately, this momentary euphoria dissipated during the summer of 1924 and disappeared completely on 3 January 1925, when Mussolini, once again secure, challenged the opposition to oust him. In June 1924, when the crisis was at its peak, the PCI joined the coalition of opposition parties on the premise that they would take militant, direct action against the Fascist government. When the leaders of the opposition opted for a purely legal and passive strategy, the Communists went their own way. Relations with the PSI, which remained wedded to the strategy of the legal opposition, continued to deteriorate throughout 1924 and much of 1925. Communist strategy, as outlined by Togliatti in August 1924, was to stress the objectively bourgeois character of social democracy and to try to undermine the PSI's mass support.[32]

Tasca's views on party policy offered few practical alternatives to those of the center, but his attitude reflected a pessimism and passivity that put him at odds with the activist traditions of the PCI. Tasca had always been quite cautious in his choice of tactics. This conservatism had been at the heart of his differences with Gramsci over the factory councils in 1920. He consistently favored working within existing syndical organizations even after the formation of the PCI. Now, with the pressure from the dictatorship increasing daily, Tasca again urged caution. He felt that the failure to bring down the Fascist government would profoundly discourage the masses. As a result, the PCI could only assume a defensive position and wait for economic conditions to provoke a crisis within the regime. Throughout 1925 he cautioned the party to avoid exposing the proletariat to Fascist retaliation.[33]

PROBLEMS WITH BORDIGA

Tasca's sporadic opposition was not the major internal problem that the PCI faced in 1925. More important was the persistence within the party of a strong pro-Bordiga faction. At the meeting of the Central Committee on 11–12 May, Gramsci made it clear that he viewed Bordiga as the chief obstacle to the party's political and ideological development.[34] But the struggle within the PCI, although still rooted in Italian reality, began to be subsumed in the struggle for control of the Russian party and of the International between Trotsky and the duo of Stalin and Bukharin. Despite some differences, Bordiga sided with Trotsky, whereas the majority moved cautiously toward his opponents. Both internationally and within the PCI the struggle against factions took on new meaning. Bolshevization of the PCI, which meant the transformation into a party based on factory and neighborhood cells, became also a struggle against factions and a demand for increased discipline and adherence to the directives of the Comintern. In general, Tasca backed the measures taken against the party Left, but his warning at the Como conference that the Center faction that had made itself into the party would now make the party, which still belonged to Bordiga, into a faction took on new meaning.[35]

THE LYONS THESES

At the end of 1925 the leadership of the PCI developed a series of theses that were to form the basis for discussion at the Third Congress of the party. This congress, scheduled for late 1925, had to be postponed until January 1926 and held in Lyons rather than in Italy. The Lyons theses represented Gramsci's last major contribution before his arrest in November, and they remained party policy until 1934. These theses were original in their analysis of fascism as a broad bourgeois coalition extending from the large industrial and agrarian interests to the small farmers and urban lower middle class. Although fascism had developed an extremely dynamic mass-based regime, its long-term stability was dubious because of the difficulty in satisfying the various components of the Fascist coalition. Thus, Italy was in a period of preparation for revolution.

The Lyons theses moved the party to the left by accepting the bourgeois nature of social democracy. The Socialist parties helped extend the influence of the bourgeoisie over large numbers of workers. The PCI would have to weaken this influence to unblock the revolutionary process and to create its own worker-peasant alternative.[36] However, Gramsci avoided the excessive tactical rigidity of the past. His analysis of fascism accepted the reality of the relative stabilization of capitalism that had occurred after 1923 and emphasized longer-term revolutionary aims. Opposition to the Lyons theses came from Bordiga and his followers, who challenged Gramsci's analysis of fascism and the very ability of the Center to consider itself representative of the party.[37]

At Lyons Tasca continued his debate with the old *Ordine nuovo* group. Gramsci and Togliatti had called for the organization of the unions at the factory level into *comitati d'agitazione* (syndical defense committees). Tasca was extremely skeptical about the possibilities of introducing such an innovation in a period of repression. This relatively narrow dispute touched on a larger issue, however. Tasca accepted Gramsci's tentative theory of the relative stabilization of capitalism, but he drew from it very different conclusions: "The Italian situation in the short term is marked by the relative immobilization of the masses and, if a change for the better takes place, it will be to the extent that fascism must use ever greater means of pressure to maintain this immobilization." The best tactic for the party was to emphasize immediate economic demands under the banner of traditional unions such as the FIOM. The *comitati d'agitazione* had no tradition and little appeal to the workers. Instead of repeating the mistakes of 1920, Tasca urged the party to build up the unions before moving to new organs.[38]

Tasca also presupposed that the left wing of social democracy could make an acceptable ally in the struggle: "I do not accept the conclusion of the political program which denies that social democracy is the right wing of the worker movement and which makes it instead the left wing of the bourgeoisie. If the latter alternative were so, the united front tactic would be absurd." Even if bourgeois influences were working through social democracy, it still kept its proletarian character: "And that is especially true where social democracy represents a historic outcome of the whole worker movement, as in the case of the English Labour party."[39]

Despite differences in emphasis, the rapprochement between Tasca and the Center was bolstered by the outcome of the Lyons congress and the meeting of the Enlarged Executive of the Comintern in February 1926, where Bordiga sought to reverse the new policy line of the PCI. Reacting to Bordiga's attack, even Togliatti began to modify his views on the Socialists in a direction already taken by Tasca.[40]

Nonetheless, Tasca was still useful as a symbolic opponent. The Gramsci-Togliatti leadership always balanced its strictures against the Left with a ritual critique of the Right, and Togliatti blocked Tasca's nomination to all positions with the International.[41] Tasca protested against the tendency to create a mythical Right opposition with Tasca as its leader. He believed that the leadership was deliberately distorting his views in order to isolate him. Shortly before Gramsci's arrest, Tasca wrote to him that their differences were small when compared to the common ground that they shared in their analysis of fascism. Both men agreed on the importance of fascism's lower-middle-class base. They also concurred that the policies of the industrialists and the government would eventually alienate this lower-middle-class support: "The conclusions which can be drawn from that point not to a period of democratic-republican petit bourgeois rule but to a regime of the monarchist and plutocratic nationalist right." Under those circumstances a durable relationship between the proletariat and the petty bourgeoisie would be viable.[42]

Already in 1926 Tasca had arrived at two propositions that would be the backbone of his study of fascism. He was convinced that the Maximalists made a tragic error in believing that they could paralyze the state without having a well-prepared revolutionary strategy. Moreover, he believed that only a gradualist and long-term strategy to dissolve the social base of the regime would be effective in toppling Mussolini's government:

> I suggest that among the causes which provoked the fascist reaction in Italy be listed the policy of the Maximalists which consisted in immobilizing the bourgeoisie (or convincing themselves of such immobilization) with the consequent creation of a stalemate in the working of the state machinery without seriously considering the problem of taking power.[43]

Such views, if carried to their logical conclusion, placed Tasca well to the right of his party and closer to a classic Social Democratic position and raised once again the basic ambiguity of Tasca's adherence to the PCI and to the Third International. Despite his relative isolation in the party and his failed attempt to become the leader of the PCI, Tasca offered the best and most coherent strategy for fighting fascism. He continued to seek some alliance with the majority of socialists. His position during the electoral campaign of 1924 was sabotaged by both his fellow Communists and the Socialists' bad faith. Moreover, Tasca, earlier than others on the Left, came to a clear understanding of the nature of fascism and of its long-term potential to survive. He never believed that the battle would be short or victory easy. Unfortunately, neither his ideology nor his political positions were shared by the other members of the PCI. Only the tradition of free debate and tolerance within the party allowed Tasca to remain in the Communist movement. The suppression of normal political activity by the Fascist regime helped conceal Tasca's profound differences with the majority of his party, but the changed conditions of the late 1920s would force them into the open and make his continued membership impossible.

4

Tasca and the PCI in Exile

The end of the Communist party's legal existence came suddenly and brutally in late October and November 1926. Gramsci, Terracini, Scoccimarro, Bordiga, Maffi, and Roveda were among the prominent officials arrested. Togliatti was in Moscow; Grieco, Paolo Ravazzoli, Alfonso Leonetti, Camilla Ravera, and Pietro Tresso remained free. Tasca had been briefly detained in October but escaped and hid in the home of Serrati's widow. His concern about the vulnerability of the party organization grew as the extent of the crackdown became known. Briefly, he even considered the possibility that the PCI might follow the example of the other parties and dissolve its organization within Italy. Although he seems to have convinced Grieco of the wisdom of this course, the idea was killed by Camilla Ravera and Luigi Amoretti when they met with Tasca on 10 November.[1]

Shortly after this meeting, Grieco and Tasca were sent to Paris to report to Togliatti. In January 1927 Grieco announced that Verri (Tasca), Ercoli (Togliatti), and Garlandi (Grieco) would form the new PCI secretariat in exile. A month later Tasca, Leonetti, and Tresso were co-opted into the political office of the party, and in March it was decided to publish *Lo stato operaio*, a new periodical of politics and theory under Tasca's direction.[2]

As the party painfully reorganized, three issues emerged at the center of debate. The first involved the prospects for economic and social stability within the Fascist regime; the second dealt with the tactical consequences that might be drawn from the analysis of fascism. The final issue concerned the construction of socialism in Soviet Russia and the relationship of the Italian party to the various factions struggling for power in the Soviet state.

FASCISM AND THE STABILIZATION OF
THE CAPITALIST SYSTEM

In 1927 and 1928 Tasca offered the most elaborate Italian explanation of fascism as a variant of Bukharin's "third stage" of postwar capitalism. In its grasp of the realities it remains superior to any other by an Italian Communist in the same period.

Bukharin argued that the capitalist system progressed through three stages after World War I. The first was an acute revolutionary crisis that culminated in 1920 and 1921 but ended in defeat for the workers in 1923. The second phase was marked by the reconstruction of the productive system of capitalism. In Europe capitalism regained the offensive, although revolutionary tension shifted to the colonial periphery. Finally, in the third period, capitalist reconstruction, measured in quantitative and qualitative terms, exceeded prewar levels. The increase in capacity was due in part to the tremendous technical progress made in certain core areas, such as the United States, to expansion of cartels and trusts on an international scale, and to the interpenetration between these industrial and financial empires and the state apparatus. Bukharin termed these developments "state capitalism." The revolutionary process was stalled in the core areas of capitalism, but it had made major gains in Russia and would continue on the periphery. Furthermore in the core areas the contradictions of capitalism that had led to the outbreak of revolution after World War I would not go away but would gradually intensify. However, in the short run, there would be no general crisis that would lead to revolution.[3]

TASCA'S ITALIAN MODEL

Tasca considered the Italian case to be a variant of this general process of stabilization in the "third period." Italy, predominantly agrarian and short of raw materials for its industry, was forced to use openly terroristic instruments of repression. He disagreed, however, with the Soviet economist Evgeni Varga, who wrote that Italy had not substantially modified its agrarian character. Tasca stressed that Italy had made considerable progress in production of synthetics, rubber, and electricity, even if, in relation to other countries, she was still behind. Reduced competition in the advanced sectors of the economy was pronounced, yet technological progress and moves toward rationalization resulted in a vast underused productive capacity. Italian industry was caught in a fundamental contradiction. Unable to meet the challenge of modern international competition, industrialists turned inward to carve out shares of the market through cartels and high tariffs. Rather than trying to develop a mass market, they imposed colonial wage levels on Italian workers. To succeed, Italian capitalism needed a system of political control such as that offered by fascism.[4]

Thus, Italy was an especially brutal variant of the pattern of capitalist stabilization by means of state capitalism. These characteristics became pronounced in 1925 and 1926, when Count Giovanni Volpi di Misurata became Minister of Finance. Volpi favored a high degree of coordination between the state, industry, and banking. Financing the process of cartelization and concentration demanded large amounts of capital. Tasca noted that one of the difficulties of the Italian economy was that it did not generate sufficient capital, and the Italians were forced to look to American and English bankers. The revaluation of the lira and the deflationary policies followed by Volpi were designed to win foreign support.

On this issue Tasca engaged in a debate with the Anglo-Italian economist Piero Sraffa. Sraffa disagreed with Tasca's view that every act of the Fascist government was dictated by the immediate direct interests of the banks and industry. Instead, he considered Mussolini and Volpi to be following a policy of revaluation to win over sectors of the lower middle class who were hurt by inflation. Tasca argued that the Volpi period was a direct seizure of control over the state apparatus by industrial and financial interests. The first manifestation of this control was the use of the instruments of state credit in the revaluation program.[5]

The application of these policies was marked by intensification of the exploitation of labor, a high level of internal prices, increased fiscal pressure, and the development of armaments. Industry used the vast power over the work force and over the domestic market, granted it by the Fascist regime, to reinforce monopoly positions. The cost of deflation fell on the workers, whose wages dropped more than prices, confirming the tendency toward underconsumption and overproduction which could be relieved by increased armaments and a bellicose foreign policy.[6]

THE UNITED FRONT REVISITED

Despite the difficulties that Italian capitalism faced, the Fascist regime had broken and dispersed the worker movement. As a result, Tasca felt that the PCI ought not to isolate itself. Instead, it had to continue to work for a United Front, which might even be extended to elements of the petty bourgeoisie. Recent events seemed to favor resumption of such a tactic. In January 1927, after the reformist leadership of the CGL dissolved, the labor confederation, Bruno Buozzi, the militant antifascist leader of the metalworkers union, attempted to reconstitute the CGL in exile. On 20 February in Milan a number of Communist unions decided on the reconstruction of the CGL within Italy. Once this was done, two questions remained. What would be the internal CGL's relationship with the exile movement in Paris, and would it seek recognition from the Socialist Amsterdam or the Moscow labor international? Although both Tasca and Togliatti favored some accord with Buozzi short of totally merging the two groups, Tasca went further in urging inclusion of noncommunists in the internal CGL and the establishment of a relationship with both Buozzi in Paris and the Amsterdam International. He was also pessimistic about the possibility of autonomous action within Italy. For this reason, Tasca opposed basing the CGL on factory cells, an arrangement that would make it difficult for noncommunists to join. The PCI should, he argued, "actively seek the cover of mass movements within the factory."[7]

In April 1927 an Antifascist Concentration was constituted in Paris by the reformist Partito Socialista dei Lavoratori Italiani (PSLI, the former Partito Socialista Unitario [PSU]), the PSI, the Republicans, Buozzi's CGL, and the Italian League for the Rights of Man (LIDU). When the Socialists urged inclusion of the PCI in the Concentration, Tasca saw this as a moment to resume direct negotiations with the Maximalists for a "United Front." To achieve this end, he was even willing to accept Communist participation in the Concentration.[8]

Tasca and Togliatti differed on the extent to which Communists should seek the United Front and the changes in the party program that were needed to establish a framework for compromise. Togliatti made it clear that any return to the old constitutional system in Italy was out of the question. Nor could the antifascist opposition of 1927 repeat the error of the Aventine opposition of 1924 by separating the struggle against fascism from that against capitalism. Still, the form of the postfascist regime was unclear. The transition to a proletarian revolution could be seen as proceeding in a single stage after the fall of fascism or an interim period could be envisaged. Gramsci came to see the latter as more likely, and the party adopted a cumbersome, ambiguous slogan to accommodate it: "a republican assembly elected on the basis of worker and peasant committees." Tasca accepted this formula as the lesser evil but preferred changing it to appeal more directly to the lower middle class, which he felt would play a large role in any postfascist solution.[9]

TASCA AND THE PCI'S NEW LEFT

On the need to broaden the appeal of the PCI and on a number of other issues, Tasca clashed with the party's younger and more radical members led by Luigi Longo, the secretary of the Federazione Giovanile. On 20 October 1927, Longo wrote to the Ufficio Politico that it had been a mistake to separate short-term economic demands from the political aspirations of the PCI. The struggle could not become an economic war against employers but had to embrace the entire capitalist state structure that manifested itself in fascism. The "Republican Assembly" slogan only confused the masses with its ambiguity. Instead, the PCI should call directly for the dictatorship of the proletariat and a "worker peasant government" without worrying about potential bourgeois allies or intermediate forms. In place of the existing policy of caution, the PCI should adopt an aggressively revolutionary strategy within Italy even at the risk of exposing the party to Fascist reprisals.[10]

Longo's letter reinforced the alliance between Togliatti and Tasca that had developed in 1927. Togliatti was willing to envisage a United Front strategy during the transition to full proletarian power. He also accepted some of Tasca's reasoning on capitalist stabilization. Disagreements remained, but they involved peripheral issues. Togliatti felt that Tasca's caution might reduce the party to total impotence within Italy. Both he and Grieco had sought middle ground between Tasca on the Right and Longo on the Left, but circumstances in 1927 and early 1928 drew them closer to the former than to the latter. Thus, when Togliatti responded to Longo's criticism, he defended policies that reflected Tasca's decisive contributions.[11]

There is no doubt, however, that Tasca went much further than either Togliatti or Grieco. He warned that the bourgeoisie could separate its interests from fascism under certain circumstances and felt that the PCI would do well to prepare for a future struggle with the bourgeoisie over the postfascist regime. Nor did Tasca believe that the Communists would automatically inherit the Social Democratic following. There were no signs in 1927 of a radicalization of the masses or indications that the Communists had succeeded in undermining the base of the Socialist parties. He urged the party to abandon its "Republican Assembly" slogan in favor of a simple call for a "Socialist Republic" that had been accepted by the Socialists and rejected by the PCI. Instead of concentrating on mere slogans, the party had to seek the leadership of the largest possible antifascist coalition.[12]

Tasca's conception of a broad alliance of social forces centered around the proletariat and led by the PCI not only called for a substantial ideological reorientation but also a completely different idea of the party from that held by Togliatti and the other ex-Bordigans. Here again, we can see better the limitations of Tasca's alliance with Togliatti and Grieco, who had come quite far from their original loyalties but were unwilling to follow Tasca back to Social Democracy.

THE OUTSIDER AS POLITICAL LEADER

Tasca's psychology was completely unsuited for life as a Communist militant. He seemed never to be at home in clandestine political activities or in the Byzantine politics of the Third International. Tasca took positions with remarkable consistency and rarely wavered on points that he held dear.

The theory of fascism and the strategy that he developed to combat it were formed in the mid-1920s and held until World War II. His increasingly subtle analyses were often quite accurate but tended to run against the PCI's historic activism. Later Tasca would find himself in a similar situation within the Italian Socialist party when he opposed Pietro Nenni's activism. Tasca approached the revolution with the eye of a historian; Togliatti, his equal in intelligence and subtlety, was more capable of blending theory and practice. Tasca, the moralist, never could.[13]

Thus, even when he was most integrated into the leadership, Tasca seemed isolated. Camilla Ravera recalled a conversation with him when he expressed doubt that he had been destined for clandestine work. He certainly felt the loss of his family, which remained in Italy. The first to start a family, he was forced to leave his wife and children in Turin and now found himself alone. This rupture must have been all the more painful because it repeated his own experience as a young boy raised by a single parent after his mother's departure. To some extent Tasca's isolation was cushioned by a sense of commitment to the party and to the International. Like the other Communists, Tasca had little contact with other Italian exiles. Although the community of Italian political exiles was a small one, the policies set by the Comintern in these years made normal relations with other political groups difficult and forced the Communists into a closed world. As a soldier of the revolution, Tasca's salary arrived through the Soccorso Rosso, which also aided his family. But the strain of being an outsider even while within the party took its toll and might explain why he decided to resume writing his diaries in 1927.[14]

THE PCI AND THE SOVIET PARTY

The total dependence of the PCI on the International placed the Italians in a delicate position. Although the Italians had a high degree of cohesiveness and a tradition of free debate, events maturing in the IC threatened the margin of freedom for the PCI. In 1927 the struggle between the Trotsky-Zinoviev and the Stalin-Bukharin groups reached new levels of asperity. Most painful was the problem of China. To the dismay of Bukharin and Stalin, in April 1927 Chiang Kai-shek abruptly turned on the Communists who had been allied in a United Front with the Kuomintang. This clamorous defeat, coupled with the breakdown of the Anglo-Russian Trade Union Committee, opened Comintern policy to attack by Trotsky and made it more urgent than ever to complete his political destruction. At the eighth Plenum of the Comintern's Executive in May 1927, Zinoviev was refused permission to participate in the debates. Stalin tried to induce the Italian delegation to subscribe to a condemnation of Trotsky without seeing the document. To his credit, Togliatti refused. In October Trotsky and Zinoviev were excluded from the Central Committee of the Soviet party, and a month later they were expelled from the party.

The success of the Stalin-Bukharin alliance against the Trotskyist opposition proved its undoing. By 1928 Stalin began to dissociate himself from Bukharin and to move leftward toward positions held by the Trotskyist opposition. In light of the rapid changes in Comintern politics, any rupture of unity within the leadership of the PCI might prove dangerous. The implied menace of Longo's Left opposition in 1928 was that it offered alternative leadership to the Comintern should the occasion arise. Togliatti and Tasca had aligned the PCI with Stalin and Bukharin on the issues of NEP and "socialism in one country," but no provision had been made for an eventual split between the two Soviet leaders.[15]

TASCA AND BUKHARIN

Of the major leaders of the PCI in 1927 and 1928, Tasca identified most closely with Bukharin. As early as 1923, he returned from a trip to Russia full of enthusiasm about the NEP as an example of balanced industrial and agricultural growth.[16] In May, June, and November 1927, Tasca published three articles in Lo stato operaio defending the NEP as the only reasonable way of achieving socialism.[17] State supervision took the place of direct state control in a system that offered maximum flexibility both in means and in the balance to be achieved between industry and agriculture. The only alternative was development directed against the peasants, a permanent revolution that would become permanent civil war.[18]

The alliance between the urban proletariat and the middle and poor peasants within the framework of the NEP would lead the rural masses to socialism. Tasca's understanding of Bukharin's program was not that the wealthy peasants would benefit, but that the state would work for the general good of the rural masses. Accumulation of an economic surplus must be built on the progress of rural society: "Industrialization of agriculture cannot be understood only as the introduction of machines and electricity into existing agricultural technology, but also as the development of industrial activities connected with agriculture." Tasca criticized Trotsky, as he would later attack Stalin, for rejecting the constraints of an essentially rural society.[19]

Tasca's diary notations indicate both firm support for Bukharin and a growing preoccupation about the bureaucratic tendencies that he detected in the Soviet state. What was revolutionary in the early days of the revolution now took on an official, ritualistic tone. Tasca found himself in a dilemma: he strongly disapproved of the Trotskyist opposition, yet he feared for the disappearance of critical debate that was the real basis for unity. In the classic Leninist view of unity, "every critique is at the same time self-criticism, every opposition is collaboration." But what if this theo-retical conception of unity proved insufficient to hold the party together? Then conformity, bureaucracy, and ritualistic behavior might be the only ways to achieve agreement, and the party would have no defense against them: "The dangers of bureaucracy are greatest where organism and associations lack the power to resist: the old ones because they have lost the capacity and the newer ones because they have not yet formed such powers of resistance."[20]

THE PARTY CONFERENCE AT BASLE

At the PCI's conference, held in Basle at the end of January 1928, Tasca continued to enjoy the support of both Togliatti and Grieco. Togliatti ex-pressed general approval of Tasca's management of *Lo stato operaio*, but, as Ernesto Ragionieri has pointed out, there was no real closeness between the two men. Togliatti's reluctance to become entrapped in Tasca's passive strategy became evident at the conference. During the de-bates Tasca defended his gradualist approach by stressing that the narrow base of the Italian economy made satisfaction of the various elements in fascism's bourgeois coalition difficult. Thus, exploitation of discontent by emphasizing economic issues was the tactic best suited to the situation. In his most provocative statement yet, Tasca proposed the notion that fas-cism could possibly become a costly burden for the industrial class (*go-verno caro*). Such an eventuality might lead to a split between the regime and many of its capitalist backers and offer increased leverage for the pro-letariat in the postfascist struggles.[21]

The Left of Longo, Pietro Secchia, and Giuseppe Dozza strongly ob-jected. They suspected that the conference had been called in part to le-gitimize the Tasca-Togliatti alliance, and they were in no mood to be ac-commodating. The Left proposed to the party a completely different set of policies based on the conviction that the masses were ready for insurrec-tion and that extreme activism (attacks on jails, sabotage) was in order.[22] Togliatti's response to the Left and to Tasca revealed an unwillingness to be tied closely to either perspective. He accepted Tasca's short-term analysis but refused to reject out of hand the possibility of a rapid radi-calization of the masses. Both Grieco and Togliatti disagreed with Tasca's new emphasis on the distinction between capitalism and fascism.[23]

In the following weeks, however, Togliatti indicated that he still ac-cepted the need for a United Front tactic in the unions and in countries where the social democrats were strong. He admitted that in the Italian case the Fascist suppression had made compromise between the so-cialists and the regime impossible and even foresaw that a socialist-communist alliance might extend into the period of transition from capitalism to the dictatorship of the proletariat. All of these attitudes put him much closer to Tasca than to Longo.[24]

THE SIXTH CONGRESS OF THE COMMUNIST INTERNATIONAL

The alliance between Tasca and Togliatti held through the Sixth Congress of the International in Moscow from July to September 1928, but a number of events were converging to destroy Tasca's position both within the PCI and in the International. The rupture between Bukharin and Stalin came in 1928; at the beginning of the year, economic difficulties led the Soviet government to adopt harsher fiscal measures toward the peasantry. Bukharin and Rykov agreed to them as temporary measures against the richer peasants but not as a break with the basic approach of NEP. Stalin pushed for more extensive requisitions of grain to alleviate supply shortages caused by confusion over future policy and peasant reluctance to deliver grain at nonmarket prices.

By May and June the split between Bukharin and Stalin became too great to be healed. Stalin's shift to the Left over NEP had its counterpart in increased hostility to social democracy and collaboration with noncommunist parties. Differences over the United Front became a debate over the nature of the "third period," which had been defined by Bukharin as the stabilization of capitalism by the application of technological advances, reorganization into national and international trusts, and the introduction of state capitalism through the interaction of government and business. The third period was a continuation of the relative stability of 1923–1926, but it was increasingly menaced by the contradictions between productive capacity and the narrowness of domestic markets. Bukharin predicted increasing imperialist conflict that would eventually bring the period to an end. Stalin radicalized this notion of the third period by stressing a much more immediate revolutionary crisis. Capitalism was on the brink of a true breakdown. A militantly revolutionary policy, an end to united fronts, establishment of a separate communist union organization, and increased discipline within each party were necessities. Thus, Longo and Secchia were much more in tune with Stalin's thinking on these issues than were Tasca, Togliatti, and Grieco. The PCI attempted to correct course in midyear. Paolo Ravazzoli and Grieco redefined social democracy in terms almost bordering on "social fascism."[25]

The Sixth Congress of the International pushed the Communist movement further to the left and complicated the internal equilibrium of the PCI. Togliatti, Tasca, Grieco, Longo, and Ravera were among the Italian delegates. The position of the Italian delegation, "Le osservazioni al 'Progetto di programma della Internazionale comunista,'" was drafted by Togliatti with Tasca's assistance. Tasca also represented the PCI on the program committee, where he defended party policy. His personal position was clarified in a joint statement by Tasca and August Thalheimer. The leaders of the right wing of the Italian and German Communist parties expressed their support of Bukharin's economic program and of the United Front tactic: "In our opinion the united front is a permanent tactical option until the party brings it about within its own ranks and its own sphere of influence."[26]

The Sixth Congress was the last relatively free meeting of the Third International. It marked the shift from an era of competitive leadership to the supremacy of Stalin. For Tasca the congress was decisive. From 1926 to 1928 on every major issue he had taken a position on Russian and international questions that was close to that of Bukharin. In Moscow for the congress of the International, Tasca's loyalty to Bukharin hardened. It was one of those commitments that, once made, Tasca would not under any circumstances abandon. It would prove his undoing because shifts in the balance of power in the Comintern and within the Soviet party inevitably had to manifest themselves in the PCI. Although it was not clear to the Italians from their vantage point in Paris, Stalin had achieved a position that allowed him to crush all forms of opposition. Only the hardliners among the young Communists (Longo and Secchia) were entirely comfortable with the new alignment. Tasca was the most exposed. In one way or another, the other leaders, including Togliatti, were caught in the middle and would have to scramble to survive.

Tasca's Expulsion and the Stalinization of the PCI

One of the most important decisions made by Togliatti at the congress of the International was to leave Tasca in Moscow as the PCI's representative on the Comintern secretariat. A more unfortunate choice could not be imagined. Togliatti was certainly aware of the changes that were taking place in Moscow. To send Tasca, the leader most tied to Bukharin and most rigid in his views, was strange. Tasca recalled that Togliatti even stressed that he stay in contact with Bukharin, "the only one who thinks." Ignazio Silone believed that Togliatti sent Tasca to get rid of him. At the time Silone suggested Pietro Tresso, a more leftist choice who might have prospered better in Stalin's Moscow. Togliatti himself apparently preferred to remain outside the Comintern bureaucracy during this delicate period because he rejected a position with the Western European Bureau (WEB) in Berlin.[1]

Yet it does not seem likely that Togliatti would have deliberately run the risk of a conflict between the PCI and the Comintern by sending a man whom he knew in advance would not be able to work with Stalin; there were far easier and less dangerous ways of getting rid of Tasca. Moreover, there was every indication that Togliatti wanted to continue working Tasca into the leadership. Their differences notwithstanding, the two-year collaboration had been profitable for both. Certainly, the Comintern did not look with disfavor on the nomination when it included Tasca in the top leadership of the Secretariat. Thus, it is likely that Togliatti and Tasca shared a common outlook toward the problems that had arisen at the congress and that the differences emerged later.[2]

Regardless of Togliatti's motivation, the choice was unfortunate because, once in Moscow, Tasca reacted predictably. He would neither change his views nor bend to Stalin's will. By refusing to yield to the new orthodoxy, Tasca underlined just how far the PCI had strayed. He became a stick with which the Italians could be beaten back into line. Tasca's expulsion opened a prolonged period of purges leading to the imposition of a Stalinist discipline over the PCI.

THE GERMAN QUESTION

The series of events that had such a tragic impact on Tasca and his party began as a result of the struggle within the German Communist party (KPD) between Ernst Thälmann, Stalin's man at the top of the party, and the right wing of August Thalheimer and Heinrich Brandler, both closer to Bukharin. Thälmann had been caught protecting a subordinate, Wittdorf, who had stolen party funds. The Right seized the scandal to pass a vote of no confidence in Thälmann. Immediately, the issue involved more than the survival of one leader: Stalin's prestige in the German party and in the whole International was on the line. Fully realizing what was at stake, Stalin decided to force the KPD's Central Committee to back down and to discipline the right wing instead. Togliatti, who had learned of the complications on a visit to Berlin, warned Tasca on 6 October to approach the issue with caution.[3]

The fact that Thälmann had been imposed on the KPD by Stalin was sufficient to arouse Tasca's hostility, but the menace to Thalheimer and through him to the entire Bukharinist Right inside and outside the Soviet state forced Tasca into open opposition to Stalin. Until 21 October, however, Tasca managed to achieve some discretion, but the underlying tone was ominous: "I will act with the maximum of prudence compatible with the duty not to accept unlimited complicity with methods which I deem harmful to the development of our movement. . . ."[4]

The problem with Tasca's good intentions was that the German question involved too many others. The KPD under Thälmann had completely rejected the United Front tactic and adhered to the theory of social fascism. Still, at a meeting of the Comintern secretariat, when Jules Humbert Droz openly criticized Stalin's position on the KPD, Tasca sought compromise by supporting Thälmann as leader while opposing expulsions on the right and calling for a change of policy. He complained to the PCI on 4 November that "the political atmosphere had a crushing force. To resist it one had to realize that the interests of the revolution, perhaps for the foreseeable future, were at stake." In this same letter Tasca made the fatal link between the German and Soviet power struggle. He reported optimistically that Bukharin and Rykov were determined to mount a strong counteroffensive against Stalin's policy, which they considered "crazy."[5]

TASCA'S GROWING PESSIMISM

Tasca was torn by conflicting emotions: He could not believe that Stalin could prevail against the combined authority of Bukharin and Rykov. At the same time, he began to realize the extent to which the rules of the game had changed. Tasca's report to the PCI on 26 November revealed his unease for the future. Although Stalin seemed to accept a compromise on economic policy with Rykov and Bukharin, the Soviet leader was working actively to displace their supporters from all positions of power. Thus, any compromise could never last. Similarly, within the KPD, Thälmann's leadership was no longer an issue. Instead, the question had become the survival of the party's right wing. On 22 November Tasca had unsuccessfully proposed to the IC that it mediate a settlement within the German party to avoid expulsions and the creation of a new opposition Communist movement.[6]

Until the beginning of December, Tasca's reports caused no particular alarm in the PCI. Certainly Togliatti could not have approved of the way the KPD conducted its affairs, and he and Grieco seemed still to believe that the outcome of the battle within Russia was uncertain. But Tasca dangerously increased the stakes. To this point, he believed that he could resist Stalin on the German question as long as he did not take a position on the struggle within the Soviet party. On 5 December he wrote that he and Humbert Droz had still pressed for a compromise on the German question at the meeting of the Presidium of the IC two days earlier. Although Bukharin supported their efforts, Tasca was pessimistic about persuading the Comintern to take independent action: "In its make up and by the way it functions it has nothing in common with a true international command center." The IC was divided between professionals who sought only to survive and others who cared only about their own countries. Then he came to the heart of the problem:

> If the Russian delegation functioned as a true center of the IC, we would have one. But that is not the case, even though all important questions pass through it. Within the Russian party's Political Office, questions are treated as "internal" in the worst sense of the word. In this case light cannot come from the East. The man who directs or should direct the International [Bukharin] disagrees with the majority of the Political Office and that further complicates the whole system.[7]

There exists in Tasca's notebooks a draft letter, also written on 5 December, to the president of the IC in which Tasca asked to be replaced as soon as possible on the Comintern secretariat. Although he did not approach Togliatti at this time (perhaps the letter to the Comintern was not sent), Tasca clearly realized that his position in Moscow was impossible.[8] By early December he had become aware not only of his own defeat but of the collapse of all opposition. Thousands of militants were terrified to be on the wrong side: "They say, 'I have a family and little children whom I cannot condemn to starvation. . . .' Even when material questions are not at stake, only a small minority can resist the *ideological terror* which is directed at the 'problem maker. . . .'"[9]

Only on 14 December did Tasca discover that even within the PCI there might be a different view of the German question. He was sent notes from a conversation between Dozza and Sachs of the WEB in which they agreed that any "errors" of the Left were more than justified by the danger from the Right opposition of Thalheimer. Tasca refuted this point in a detailed letter. The real problem was the total blindness of the Stalinists, who dictated tactics on the basis of a supposed radicalization of the masses. In disgust, he finally asked to be replaced.[10]

TOGLIATTI'S CAUTIOUS SUPPORT

Togliatti understood that Tasca risked compromising the PCI on the German question when an orderly retreat was necessary. Moreover, Tasca raised other issues (the stabilization of capitalism, the nature of the third period, and the radicalization of the masses) on which Togliatti wished to take the middle ground. Togliatti did not know when he wrote to Tasca on 17 December that his representative had openly committed himself to an anti-Stalinist position. Togliatti's letter brought Tasca up to date on the policy of the PCI. The Central Committee had met twice, the second time in the presence of Manuil'ski, who had been sent to persuade both the Swiss and Italian parties to take a firmer line on the German question. The Central Committee, however, took the middle ground by accepting the existence of a rightist danger but by also criticizing the internal situation in the KPD and increasing factionalism in the IC. Togliatti also accepted Stalin's contention that the right of Bukharin and Rykov represented petty bourgeois pressures on the Soviet state, but he warned against a simplistic transposition of Soviet questions to the IC. Regarding Tasca's status, Togliatti was reassuring: "About your conduct we are in general in agreement with it. Perhaps if we had been in Moscow instead of you, we might have put certain things differently but in substance we approve the line which you have followed until now." Tasca could only draw the conclusion that his position on the German question and other major issues was not substantially different from that of his party and that Manuil'ski had failed in his mission. But reading Togliatti's letter more closely, one sees two major reservations: Togliatti, perhaps unrealistically, was determined to separate conflicts within the Russian party from those of the IC; more importantly, he was willing to accept Stalin's position on Russian questions as a trade-off for greater flexibility for the PCI. Tasca contradicted both of these premises by linking the German and Soviet issues and by firmly committing himself to Bukharin.[11]

On 19 December an official of the Soviet Youth League attacked Tasca and intimated that Gino Amadesi, the Italian delegate to the International Youth movement, was not in agreement with Tasca. Simultaneously, Stalin attacked Humbert Droz and Tasca and moved that the former be officially condemned for his positions. Tasca abstained on that vote, but not without first confronting Stalin with the accusation that he was violating the rules of the IC.[12] A few days later, Tasca once again defied Stalin by presenting a hostile motion on the KPD. Thus, Togliatti's letter of 17 December must have been a great relief, and Tasca's failure to read between the lines may be understandable. Manuil'ski had just returned, claiming that he had convinced the PCI to support the IC on the German question. Tasca jumped to the conclusion that this was not the case.[13]

THE PCI ALTERS ITS POSITION

The Manuil'ski mission does not seem to have been decisive in undermining Tasca's position; rather, the cumulative effect of his rupture with the Stalinist leadership of the Russian party and the linkage between Russian and international questions was. Togliatti's letter of 27 December went a long way toward disabusing Tasca. The party leader singled out Tasca's report of 14 December as evidence that he had departed from party policy on the United Front and the German question. Tasca was asked to return home to meet with the Central Committee.[14]

When the resolution of the Central Committee, expressing full support for the IC on the KPD just as Manuil'ski had predicted, arrived, Tasca finally understood the new circumstances. But he still felt betrayed, as his report to the party on 30 December showed: "In general, however, I do not believe that the 'rightist danger' represents, as they pretend to believe, the central problem of the International, or, if it is, it is true in the sense that our political incapacity does not allow us to stop the shift of the masses toward social democracy." Tasca also argued that only internal party democracy could guarantee a healthy relationship with the masses. These were positions that the Italian party had always accepted, and its shift meant to Tasca that his comrades did not fully understand the issues.[15]

Tasca's last days in Moscow were spent preparing a detailed report to the party on the work of the International. On 15 January, just two days before his departure, Tasca and Humbert Droz visited Bukharin. His description of the visit is a graphic example of the climate of fear that gripped Moscow: "One walks with coat collar up and hugging the walls like conspirators in order to pierce the *cordon sanitaire* which surrounds our comrade. During the conversation every so often the secretary, Zeitlin, gave the alarm; from the window one could make out suspect shadows which moved and we planned how to leave without 'scandal.'" Bukharin reiterated his critique of Stalin's economic policies, describing them as a war waged by part of the proletariat against the peasantry, but he was pessimistic about the probability of survival of any opposition to Stalin within the Soviet party. This final meeting with Bukharin, whom Tasca admired more than any other Russian, certainly strengthened Tasca's resolve to carry the opposition's views to the Italian party.[16] This decision, however generous and well motivated, proved fatal to his case with the rest of the party because Tasca seemed to base so little of his argument on issues related to Italy.

From Berlin Tasca reported to the PCI that the central issue had become Stalin's methods of control over the Russian party and over the International: "The entire situation gravitates around Stalin. The IC doesn't exist, nor does the Soviet party. Stalin is 'lord and master' and controls everything. Is he up to such power? Is he capable of carrying such tremendous responsibility? My answer is clear: Stalin is unimaginably below it . . . . Between Lenin and Stalin there is an abyss, not of quantity but of quality."[17]

TASCA'S REPORT TO THE CENTRAL COMMITTEE

Tasca's presentation to the Central Committee on 28 February 1929 was decisive for his political career. Giuseppe Berti has argued that Togliatti, far from receiving Tasca with hostility, did his best to persuade him to make a formal declaration of error and not to break with the IC. This course was not entirely altruistic because Togliatti feared that Tasca might well bring down the entire leadership of the party and pave the way for a transfer of power to the Longo-Secchia group. By going ahead with his report, Tasca rejected Togliatti's advice and made his eventual expulsion inevitable.[18]

Ignazio Silone recalled the fear within the party that they would be drawn into a major conflict with the IC on international and Russian questions without fully understanding all the issues and being unable to take the question to the party members: "At that time, even those of us who agreed with Angelo Tasca and were his friends committed the error and the failure of nerve by abandoning him and condemning him."[19]

Tasca's long and dense report treated two subjects: the problems facing the International and the construction of socialism in the Soviet state. Tasca broadened his critique of the IC's handling of the German problem into a sweeping attack on the whole range of Comintern tactics. It contained nothing new, except that it gained force as a coherent presentation. He argued that policy ought to be made on a case-by-case basis to avoid simplifying the third period as did Stalin. Not every leftward push by the working class was a true radicalization of the masses. In fact, Tasca saw a clear gap between the subjective consciousness of the proletariat and the objective economic situation.[20]

Tasca's minimalization of the crisis of capitalism dictated his choice of tactics. Competition with the Socialists should be intense but not carried out in a way that would weaken the entire Left and confuse the workers. Communists had to remain within the traditional union structures and turn the United Front to their advantage.[21] The real problem came not from the Right but from a false radicalism: "The ideological positions of social democracy . . . have roots of such complexity in the working class which we must recognize in order to disentangle." But the key is to have leadership capable of appealing to the entire working class.[22] A sectarian party will of necessity be sectarian in its relationship with the masses. Discipline was vital, but, as Lenin put it, true discipline arose from experience and could not be arbitrarily imposed by Stalin.[23]

If Tasca's critique of the International was tolerable, his report dealing with the Soviet state was not. Tasca made it clear that the break with NEP was a tragic mistake. The problems that by 1927 demanded policy adjustments—the failure of agricultural production to keep pace with industrial needs and a low marketable surplus—might have been dealt with within the framework of NEP. At the Fifteenth Party Congress in December 1927 the Bolsheviks decided to increase the pace of industrialization, enlarge the scope of state planning, and emphasize collectivization of agriculture. In January 1928 the government issued emergency decrees that entailed harsher measures against the kulaks and confiscation of hoarded grain. Stalin was given the task of administering the decrees and did so with extreme ruthlessness that exceeded the intentions of Rykov and Bukharin, who called merely for some controls over the kulaks, partial collectivization, and more emphasis on capital goods production in industry. In September 1928 Bukharin published his "Notes of an Economist," which attacked Stalin's industrialization policy as essentially that of the Trotskyist opposition.[24]

Tasca's report to the PCI was a presentation of the Bukharinist point of view on the break with NEP: "When they had the first positive results of the policy and with them the first inevitable inconveniences, they judged the former to have been already enough and sufficiently consolidated, while the attention of the party was ever more fixed on the symptoms of a strengthened new rural bourgeoisie." [25] However, Stalin not only attacked the richer kulaks, but also the middle and small peasants, and threatened to compromise all Soviet agriculture. Any kulak danger was marginal in Russia, where even the so-called rich peasants would be considered members of the middle peasantry in Italy. In fact, the poverty of the peasantry in general acted as an obstacle to the development of an internal market and put all industrial growth in danger.[26]

Tasca recognized that Stalin had a potent argument when he contended that the Soviet regime had to industrialize in case of war with bourgeois Europe, but, even here, NEP had certain advantages in winning the support of the peasant population; in case of war, this support might be as important as a munitions factory.[27]

The harmonious resolution of this fundamental conflict of interests between urban and rural Russia was a test case for socialism. It was, Tasca argued, a question of balancing the increased cost of capitalism in terms of war, the useless destruction of wealth, and the misery of the workers against the temporary suffering involved in the first stages of a new socialist society: "This destruction is permanent and organic in the capitalist system and infinitely greater than that inevitable, contingent destruction produced by the installation and first phase of the dictatorship of the proletariat." The attraction of the Soviet model was that it could create a society that would justify the initial sacrifices. Stalin's effort to plunge Soviet society into vast misery seemed a monstrous distortion of true socialism.[28]

REACTIONS TO TASCA'S REPORT

The Central Committee that received Tasca's report was divided into several factions. Togliatti, Grieco, and Camilla Ravera had shared responsibility with Tasca but now were determined to distance themselves to preserve the continuity of the leadership group. Secondino Tranquilli (Silone) condemned Tasca but took little part in the debates. The "three"— Leonetti, Tresso, and Ravazzoli—who were to be expelled the following year were not a coherent group. Ravazzoli shared Tasca's critique of the International's syndical policy. All disliked some of the practices of the Comintern, but, most of all, they were convinced that Togliatti and Grieco were as guilty as Tasca. Finally, Longo, Secchia, and Dozza criticized the leadership along Stalinist lines. On one issue, however, all could agree: Tasca focused an inordinate degree of attention on Russian questions.[29]

In his response to Tasca, delivered on 2 March, Togliatti had the delicate task of separating himself from Tasca without engaging in a wholesale attack on the past. He was well aware that his leadership was under considerable scrutiny. Togliatti argued that Tasca's views on the third period placed him on the side of the German Right and led him into a series of tactical errors on the United Front. He also considered Tasca's critique of Stalin's policies to be excessively ruralist. Although severe, Togliatti's response indicated that the party wished to conclude the affair as rapidly as possible. The Central Committee voted unanimously (except for Tasca) to condemn the report. Tasca then unsuccessfully offered his resignation from the Ufficio Politico. He was, however, replaced by Grieco in Moscow.[30]

Tasca's position remained ambiguous after March. He was still one of the prominent leaders of the PCI, and the party, much as it had with Bordiga, seemed in no hurry to take action other than verbal sanctions. But the pressures on Tasca were great. In mid-February he noted in his diary: "Tonight (February 12–13) I committed suicide. Of course I only dreamed it but with a clarity of detail, that on awakening I looked at my wrists to see the stigmata. Why did I want to die? No special reason: weariness. I had that morning a long talk with the secretary of the party and I was left with a trace of nausea." Tasca was moreover well aware of the difficulties that the party would face if it accepted his report.[31] He seemed eager to withdraw from the limelight and explained to Camilla Ravera that it was useless to keep him in the Ufficio Politico to maintain control over him because he had no intention of breaking discipline.[32]

Despite good intentions on both sides, the crisis could not be long delayed. Ravera recalled that the contents of Tasca's report began to circulate among other parties, constituting a direct threat to Togliatti's leadership. Tasca's refusal to participate in the Ufficio Politico was understood by the rest of the party as less than complete acceptance of policy. All factions—Togliatti, Tresso, Leonetti, and Dozza—joined on 6 June to demand Tasca's open acceptance of the new leftward course. Togliatti referred to Tasca's position as "evidence of political and ideological failures." Tasca bitterly noted in his diary "that what is tragedy in the central committee of the Russian party repeats itself as comedy in ours."[33] Pressure from the Comintern was also mounting for a decision on Tasca. Moscow treated him differently than it had Humbert Droz, who was equally guilty, because the PCI presented a special problem. By forcing the Italians to take a strong position against Tasca, it might expose any hidden sympathy for his position.[34]

For his part, Tasca was determined not to retreat. Not only did he think that he was correct on the issues, but he also felt that he was struggling against a system that was detrimental to the PCI. The most he would do was accept silence imposed by the Comintern on certain issues.[35] Stalin made it clear at the X Plenum of the IC in July 1929 that Tasca's modus vivendi with the PCI was insufficient and that only a show of public self-criticism would save him from expulsion; these were the terms presented to Grieco and Togliatti. On 12 August Tasca wrote to Fanny Jezierska, a member of the Comintern secretariat and a long-time friend of many Italian leaders, that he would not accept the conditions set by the IC: "For my part I have decided to sign nothing more than a pure and simple disciplinary submission. . . ."[36] But much more was to be asked. He informed Jezierska that the terms of his continued membership were presented on 24 August and included public disavowal of his past positions, a press campaign against opportunism, active approval of all future decisions of the IC, and complete rupture of all relations with the Right opposition in the Soviet state and in the International.[37]

Thus, the meeting of the Ufficio Politico on 28–29 August could only end in Tasca's expulsion. Of more interest was Tresso's (Blasco) refusal to accept Togliatti's distinction between his own views and those of Tasca. Tresso and, to a certain extent, Leonetti argued that Togliatti had been in substantial agreement with Tasca and was now trying to protect himself. Longo, formerly of the Left opposition, came to Togliatti's defense. The break with the past was well underway.[38]

On 30 August Tasca offered to modify many of his views on the Russian situation but refused to repudiate his rejection of social fascism, the third period, and the United Front. The pressure for some gesture must have been extreme. His diary notation for August described the frightening nature of his isolation from the party, but his belated willingness to compromise on Russian questions was not enough.[39] On 4 September Tasca wrote to the Comintern and to the Segreteria of the PCI that he could not accept the conditions imposed. The Central Committee then expelled him from the party and named Leonetti to handle the transition.[40]

Clearly, without the intervention of the Comintern, Tasca's dispute with the PCI would have been handled without his expulsion. Berti believed that Togliatti had wanted to keep him in the party. Tasca certainly never considered the PCI to have been the problem, although he criticized his comrades' lack of courage in opposing Stalin. His battle was with the IC, which set the terms for his capitulation. He stated his position on the Comintern in a letter to Boris Souvarine on 16 September:

> But in reality it was a matter either of becoming an active accomplice in their policies or leaving the IC. I could only opt for the second horn of the dilemma, even though I was without any other prospects. Apart from that I confess to you that even if they had not put such impossible conditions, it would have cost me to remain in the IC under the "new course."[41]

Tasca had represented within the PCI a link with the old socialist traditions. He had always considered the party part of a vast Italian Left that it aspired to lead. His point of view, often in the minority, had been an important part of the intraparty debate over policy and tactics. With his expulsion both Tasca and the PCI lost. Tasca started down a long road that would lead him to increasingly negative positions. For the PCI the loss was equally great. Although Togliatti had little choice, short of resigning and turning the party over to Longo and Secchia, but to bend to Stalin, he would have to wait until after World War II to take the course that Tasca outlined for him. Moreover, an even longer time would be needed to restore the tradition of debate within the PCI as it had existed during the 1920s. The abandonment of this tradition was never complete, even in the darkest moments of Stalinism, but it was sufficiently weakened to cost the party the allegiance of many intellectuals who might have made a major contribution after 1945.

Congress of Third International, Mosca 1928. *Back row*: Grieco, Tasca, Willy Münzenberg, unknown, unknown, Chiarini. *Front row*: Togliatti, Marcel Cachin, Henri Barbusse.

PART 2
THE SOCIALIST,
1930–1938

Marxism Revised: Tasca and *Monde*

Angelo Tasca emerged from the Communist movement into a France in intellectual and political turmoil. The impact of the Great Depression was about to ravage the French economy. The rise of Hitler posed new and, in the end, insoluble foreign policy problems. The immensity of these changes overloaded a brittle political system, which was much like an automobile with no accelerator but with wonderful brakes, and created a profound psychological and moral crisis that would change the meaning of "Left" and "Right" for many of the French. A large section of the Socialist movement, influenced by Henri De Man, the major theorist of the Belgian Workers' Party (Parti Ouvrier Belge [POB]), and by Marcel Déat of the SFIO sought to redefine socialism in non-Marxist terms. First, they broke from the objective basis for socialism, which Marx had attempted to establish, in favor of the psychological and ethical motivations that weighed on each individual. Second, they rejected Marxist internationalism to stress planning within the national framework as a way out of the depression. Finally, they accepted a large part of the Fascist critique of liberal democracy and argued that socialism would have to compete with the Fascists on their own terms to win the allegiance of the middle class.[1]

Tasca's ideological development from 1930 to 1938 must be placed in the context of this process of revisionism within France. His own outlook predisposed him to the neorevisionist critique. Tasca had always emphasized the need to reach beyond the proletariat to form political alliances against fascism. Moreover, he had never accepted the determinist mentality that predominated among Italian Maximalists. His Marxism had tried to find a balance between subjective consciousness and the material and environmental conditions that shaped social classes. "Culturalism" was the process by which individuals developed an ethical framework and perspective that would make revolution possible. As we have seen, Tasca's positions aligned him much more closely to traditional, even non-Marxist, social democracy than to either maximalism or communism. Once outside the PCI, what was latent in his thought became fully realized, but now his attitudes were dictated by the French political crisis and not by Italian events. The same process that would carry De Man, Déat, Adrien Marquet, and Paul Marion on the road to collaboration during World War II was also at work in Tasca's case. Although he never followed them to their final Fascist destination, he did come to lose faith in liberal, parliamentary democracy as practiced in Third Republic France.

Tasca was also intimately involved in the other aspect of the ideological crisis of France on the eve of World War II. If the abandonment of Marxism in the search for new means of winning over the nonproletarian electorate inspired a large number of socialists, anticommunism powerfully reinforced and shaped this neorevisionism. The socialist movement became polarized between those who looked to the Communists and to the Soviet Union on the Left for allies against fascism and those whose hostility to the USSR and the Communist party could never be overcome. Anticommunism and neorevisionism would unite many socialists, including Tasca, under the banner of Vichy.

But this was all in the future when, at the end of 1929, Tasca took the first steps from his past as a Communist militant. The years between 1930 and 1934, when he rejoined the Socialist party, marked a turning point in Tasca's life. His understanding of Marxism changed in significant ways and with it his belief in socialism. His marriage dissolved, and the ties that he maintained with Italy were weakened. Out of these multiple crises came a new life, henceforth centered on France.

THE PUBLIC RUPTURE WITH THE PCI

Tasca's expulsion from the PCI in September 1929 left him still psychologically a communist. He hoped to remain silent about the expulsion but was under no illusions about the campaign that would be waged against him.[2] The truce was broken on 13 October with an article in *La vie prolétarienne* attacking Tasca as an opportunist and giving the official version of his expulsion. Inevitably, the news began to spread in the exile press, and these reports forced Togliatti to respond by denying that Tasca had ever had any real importance within the PCI except as "a vain little professor." Togliatti's article brought a rejoinder from Tasca, who recalled that for over two years he and Togliatti had worked closely in the leadership and went on to say that "the servility and the demagoguery, which caused the sudden change of policies, forcefully defended until yesterday, threaten to reduce to impotency the future political work of the Communist party. . . ."[3]

Tasca's diary notations indicate that he well understood the reasons for his expulsion:

> On my return from Moscow a comrade, a member of the secretariat of the PCI, explained for me the sudden conversion of Ercoli etc. to the demands of Stalin: "We must yield on Russian and international questions in order to salvage the Italian policy of our party. If not, Moscow won't have any hesitation about putting together a left leadership group with a few boys from the Lenin school."

But Tasca understood that Stalin would be satisfied with nothing less than total surrender from the Italian party.[4]

POLITICAL ISOLATION

During the months following his expulsion, Tasca hoped that the Right opposition to Comintern policy might coalesce into a movement of substance. To Fanny Jezierska he urged the formation of an independent Communist party in Germany and in France, where there was little hope of reforming the existing Communist parties. Jezierska, more aware of the difficulties, believed that a complete rupture with the KPD would lose for the Right all worker support. Tasca also briefly considered the publication of a political review with Boris Souvarine and other French dissidents, but, here again, nothing came of the idea.[5] At about the same time, Tasca rejected overtures from Maximalist friends to rejoin the Italian Socialist party.[6]

PERSONAL CRISIS

Tasca's isolation was deepened by personal tragedy as well. His marriage to a woman who remained in Italy with his children created problems, but his total immersion in his work with the PCI and the Comintern tended to reinforce the marital status quo. With his expulsion the situation changed. The loss of his Comintern salary meant that Tasca's ability to support his family was greatly diminished. He now began to hope that Lina and the children might come to live in France.[7]

On that score, however, the news from Italy was anything but favorable. In January 1930 the economist Piero Sraffa, who visited Lina on Tasca's behalf, wrote that she had changed and warned that renewing a common life might be difficult. Tasca, however, was determined to press ahead with a reconciliation: "Dear Lina, often I felt the weight of a life, for which I am so unsuited, in a furnished room and the searing need for a loved one near by, to escape from a terrible loneliness. Separation has been for me even in this regard a tremendous experience, almost a revelation."[8] But, throughout 1930 and 1931, Lina made it clear that she had little hope that they would ever live together again: "If I were still the Lina of four or five years ago, I would be more trusting and even my absolutely frigid feelings would not frighten me." She offered only the vague hope of a meeting in Monte Carlo, where Tasca's mother still lived. Tasca, unable to convince Lina to join him or to begin a totally new life without her, continued to move from one temporary expedient to another. At year's end he noted sadly in his diary: "The tragedy of my life moves toward catastrophe and I have no other defense than paper, and I write and write until exhaustion, until nausea. . . ."[9]

Perhaps the closest Tasca came to revealing his feelings about his marriage was in a letter to Cécile Beitzman, a woman with whom he had a sentimental relationship that waxed and waned with his hopes for a reconciliation with Lina:

> Love had been for me, when I knew it, the discovery of an unknown country, that political battling led me to ignore. I have had for my wife, who introduced me to it, a profound gratitude so that the need for and the gifts of tenderness which had built up in me left me strongly attached to her. I never had a family—my father had to take the place of everyone else—and I found it only with my wife and children.

He recalled that his political commitments made a normal family life impossible: "My wife has never been able to understand how I could sacrifice to that degree. She doubted my love because I 'preferred' politics to her."[10]

Finally, in 1932, Lina came to Paris, but the attempt at reconciliation failed miserably. In late 1932 or early 1933 Lina sought to return to Italy with the three children. To facilitate her voyage she may even have passed information to the Italian embassy, and the Fascist regime, hoping to embarrass a prominent enemy, offered a scholarship to his son. Tasca managed to keep the younger daughter, Valeria. Carlo and Elena returned to Italy with their mother, and Tasca would see them again only after 1945.[11]

The trauma of these years deepened certain of Tasca's psychological characteristics. One of the dangers of clandestine political work is a necessary compartmentalization of life, a necessarily rigid separation between an individual's legal and hidden activities. Even the question of names becomes complicated. Tasca recalled that once he failed to recognize a name that he was using as he crossed the Swiss border and was temporarily detained by the police. In fact, during his years in the PCI Tasca used at least four names: Rienzi, Serra, Baule, and Valle. Expulsion and a return to a completely legal life-style did not mean an end to this double existence. Instead, it reinforced the compartmentalization. He continued to use pseudonyms—A. Rossi, André Leroux, three stars, and Lynx—and to divide his world into closed compartments. He separated his Italian and French political activities, his cultural and political interests, his collaboration with Vichy from his work in the Resistance. Friends in one area had little idea of what he was doing in other parts of his life. Inevitably, certain interests suffered and contradictions abounded. One of the most serious was the displacement of Italy by France in his order of priorities.

CULTURALISM REVISITED: BARBUSSE'S *MONDE*

Adjustment to France was not easy, however. Tasca lived a precarious existence from October 1929 to April 1930.[12] Apart from friends such as the Arabist Charles André Julien and his wife and the Mesnils, Tasca gravitated to a small group of dissident communists who sought to maintain their commitment to revolutionary activity outside, but still close to, the Communist party. This group, which included the writers and critics Georges Altmann, Augustin Harbaru, Léon Werth, and Paul Louis, collaborated on the cultural-political weekly *Monde*. The director was Henri Barbusse, whom Tasca had known from the days when Barbusse and Romain Rolland published *Clarté* and Tasca worked on *Ordine nuovo*.[13]

In 1927 Barbusse, a prominent member of the French Communist party and literary editor of *L'Humanité*, launched *Monde* after a trip to Moscow for a Congress of Revolutionary Writers. After discussions with the French party, it was agreed that *Monde* should not be an official publication but should serve to rally noncommunist sympathizers to the Soviet cause. This independent role was reflected in its editorial board, which included Albert Einstein, Maxim Gorky, Michael Karolyi, Miguel de Unamuno, Miguel Ugarte, and Upton Sinclair. Barbusse recalled that a Soviet even suggested the rightist Drieu la Rochelle as editor, but at that he drew the line. Instead, he gathered a number of communists and former communists of all varieties: Georges Altmann, who was still a member of the PCF in the late twenties; Augustin Harbaru, who had been affiliated with the Belgian party; the Trotskyists Paul Louis and Daniel Guerin; and Socialists Lucien Laurat and Magdeleine Paz.[14]

Tasca joined the staff of *Monde* in spring 1930 with vast ambitions for using the review to develop a new program for the revolutionary Left. His idea of a critical, independent publication above any single party was bound to clash with those of Barbusse and the PCF. Wisely, Tasca expressed his increasingly negative view of the PCF only in his diaries and private letters. Although he was extremely hostile to Stalin, he remained loyal to the ideal of the Soviet revolution and still considered Lenin to have been the ideal revolutionary.[15]

THE STRUGGLE AGAINST FASCISM

Tasca's hostility toward Comintern policy stemmed in part from his estimation of the Fascist danger. On this subject he showed no hesitancy
about expressing himself in *Monde*. Carrying on the tradition of sophisti-
cated analysis that had been associated with the PCI, Tasca explained that
fascism was not just another term for reaction or violence. He called for a
systematic study of fascism in terms of its ideology and organization, especially the armed paramilitary formations at the service of the single
party and the distinctive lower-middle-class social base of the movement.
Even after the direction of the Fascist movement was taken over by large
capitalists, the petty bourgeoisie determined the choice of methods: "We
might define this method as 'a reactionary struggle against the working
masses by the weapons forged by the masses.'" The aim of the Fascists
was to pit other social groups against the workers to isolate the proletariat:
"Fascism is not the immediate and direct dictatorship of capital. It is, at
least for an entire decisive period in its development, a dictatorship of
capital resting on the support of a part of the middle and lower bourgeoisie and even on a small section of the workers." [16]

Tasca believed social fascism to be absolute folly: "the most urgent
task of the worker parties in Germany is to make the maximum effort to
separate the still gelatinous mass base of National Socialism. To win the
middle classes and the Hitlerian workers is *precisely the strategic aim of
the movement*." [17] But the conflict between Socialists and Communists in
Germany made this course impossible. Fanny Jezierska reported to Tasca
on the negative impact of KPD propaganda during the September 1930
elections in which the Nazis jumped from 12 to 107 seats. In return he
noted bitterly: "If I had been a voter in Germany, I would have voted for the
list No. 1 [SPD]." [18]

TOWARD A MARXIST HUMANISM

As Tasca began to search for an alternative to Comintern policy, he turned
back to Marx to understand the nature of the reformist-revolutionary split.
Marx, he argued, had no definition of reformism: "The ideas of Marx and
Engels on the abolition of the state imply in no way that one must arrive in
power without using the institutions of bourgeois democracy to the degree that circumstances permit. . . ." Tasca still accepted Engels's view
that, although parliamentary strategy was valid, the final struggle was likely
to be violent. Thus, classic reformism erred by shunning all violence and
by obscuring the proletariat's responsibility for the construction of the alternative to capitalism. [19]

The justification for partial reforms was to provide a minimum of material support for class consciousness, but the demands of the workers must be framed in a way that showed the incompatibility between their true needs and the functioning of the capitalist system. Reforms were revolutionary when they pushed the system to the limit. Everything depended on the framework within which the reforms were placed.[20]

Tasca insisted on the objective nature of the Marxist vision of history. It was one of the great conquests of Marx to create a truly dynamic theory of environmentalism. Tasca, who came to Marx by way of a study of eighteenth-century materialist thought, was convinced that the laws of economic and social development could be turned to the service of human liberation. If Marx and Engels erred, it was only in making the connection between economic crisis and proletarian revolutionary consciousness too immediate.[21]

Robert Owen was one of the first to see that revolutionary consciousness could be transformed by the rise of the factory system. Marx drew from early socialists such as Owen and Fourier his understanding that certain problems were of such vast proportions that they became a collective experience. Although he would change his views later, Tasca was convinced in 1930 that the fundamental alterations in society could not occur in single individuals but would have to be on the level of an entire class.[22]

Marx and Engels set forth in objective terms that the interests of the proletariat became those of all humanity and that awakened class consciousness became the motor force for change. In Marx the terms *human*, *proletariat*, and *universal* were equivalent. Marxism was a new humanism, which offered a solution for the basic problems of capitalism. Tasca still insisted that he rejected any revisionism that tended to undermine the objective or scientific basis for socialism by reducing it to social psychology or individual morality. This was the crux of his critique of Henri De Man, Marcel Déat, and Henriette Rolland Holst when *Monde* sponsored a debate on "La crise doctrinale du socialisme" in 1930.[23]

THE KHARKOV CONGRESS

Thus, during his years with *Monde*, Tasca remained well within the Marxist tradition, but his reputation and the ongoing critique of Comintern tactics made him an obvious target for criticism from the PCF. Barbusse's *Monde* could remain a temporary refuge only as long as the French Communist party and the Comintern were willing to tolerate a high degree of heterodoxy. A turning point came in November 1930 at the Congress of the International Union of Revolutionary Writers, held in Kharkov in the Soviet Union. This congress marked the beginning of Stalinization of the arts and the official adoption of "socialist realism" as an international proletarian art form. The avant garde fell out of favor. Surrealists such as André

Breton, Paul Eluard, and René Clavel were expelled from the French Communist party. Only Louis Aragon took up the new orthodoxy and remained the PCF's leading literary figure.

Barbusse, however, made no move after the Kharkov congress to bring *Monde* into line. He even protested the PCF's veto of Georges Altmann as a representative to the congress, and *L'Humanité* responded by accusing Barbusse of allowing *Monde* to publish anti-Soviet propaganda.[24] When the Communist party insisted that its official representative be a member of the editorial committee, Barbusse with the strong support of his staff defended *Monde*'s independence. He did, however, attempt to curb some of the magazine's more unorthodox positions. Tasca was refused permission to launch an inquiry on the United Front. Sensing perhaps the growing pressure, Tasca offered his resignation in February 1931. A compromise was reached under which Tasca promised to use Communist writers whenever possible on political articles, although the Trotskyist Paul Louis would continue to write the "Semaine politique" column. Barbusse also entered into negotiations with the PCF to induce Gabriel Péri to join the editorial board, but he failed to persuade either Péri or any other of the PCF's leading writers to join unless they were given full control. Thus, throughout 1931 and much of 1932 the precarious status quo continued at *Monde*.[25]

By 1933 tension had reached such a point that *Monde* had to be reorganized. Five issues that made the review's continued independence impossible arose: a long series of articles by Tasca on "Marxism in 1933" in which he set forth a clearly reformist theory of Marx; sharp differences with the PCF and the Comintern about the United Front tactic; fallout from the Kharkov congress; the Victor-Serge case; and the increasingly precarious financial condition of *Monde*.

MARXISM IN 1933

Tasca's revision of Marx finally brought him to an openly social democratic position. He now divided the career of Marx and Engels into two distinct periods, with the revolutionary years of 1848–1850 as the turning point. During the first part of their career, under the influence of Blanqui and the Chartists, Marx and Engels developed a theory of capitalist crisis, the dictatorship of the proletariat, and the notion of permanent revolution. After 1848 they turned their backs on the past to develop a theory of revolution built on the universalized conquests of the bourgeoisie. As the development of capitalism enlarged the basis of class consciousness, the proletarian revolution became associated with the coming to power of the vast majority of the population. In this context, the struggle for liberal democracy took on meaning as a way of deepening the proletarian consciousness and as an end in itself. Tasca argued that by the end of their lives Marx and Engels abandoned the idea of the dictatorship of the proletariat. Taking the place of the violent conspiratorial tactics of the pre-1848 period was a theory based on the hegemony of the proletariat in a vast movement for human liberation.[26]

Tasca changed his mind about whether Marx and Engels could conceive of a conquest of power through republican and democratic institutions. He insisted that Engels was aware of the changed balance of power within the modern state that had been created by the modern military and bureaucratic system. As proof, he cited the preface to *Class Struggles in France* (1890) and the letter to Lafargue of 3 August 1895 to show that Engels allowed the possibility of using universal suffrage in a revolutionary way.[27] In any case, the battle had to be waged in alliance with other classes. As Engels wrote to Turati in 1894, the proletariat should seek an alliance with the radicals and republicans in Italy to achieve full bourgeois democracy.[28]

Tasca looked to Jean Jaurès to bolster his theory of "revolutionary opportunism." Jaurès, who consistently rose in Tasca's estimation during these years, was singled out for his realism and openness to alliances with the peasantry and lower middle class and for his warnings against the dangers of statism and bureaucracy that menaced socialism. Tasca no longer believed that socialism would automatically eliminate arbitrary power and protect the individual. In fact, state control of the means of production only increased the dangers of bureaucratization: "It is inevitable that the take over by the state of the means of production leads to an inflation of the bureaucratic apparatus. One must ensure that this fact does not negate the specific advantages of the socialist economy." The conflict between the individual and society was inherent in all systems, but, if correctly understood, would be resolved more readily under socialism.[29]

THE UNITED FRONT AGAINST FASCISM

Tasca concluded his series on Marxism by offering some practical suggestions for fighting fascism that brought him into direct conflict with the Comintern over the United Front.[30] In these years since his expulsion from the PCI his views had evolved to the point that he had even broken with Fanny Jezierska, his old friend and Right oppositionist within the Comintern. They agreed that only a United Front could stop Hitler, but Jezierska assigned more of the blame for failure on the social democrats. By the end of 1931 she realized that Tasca no longer belonged to the Communist opposition and had passed over to social democracy. On 3 February 1932 Jezierska wrote of her continuing faith that only the Communist movement offered a hope for a new society: "I will never be able to find a place in the social democratic ranks because I am convinced that their policies will never lead to revolution."[31] Unlike Jezierska, Tasca lost faith that the Communist parties could ever be redeemed. His alternative at the end of 1931 was to call for an international United Front based on a Paris-Berlin-Moscow axis to stop Fascism. The foreign and domestic policies of each of the parties on the Left would be directed to the formation of a vast antifascist front.[32]

Throughout 1932 Tasca watched as the Socialists and Communists continued in their old ways. He guessed correctly that the Papen-Schleicher combination in Germany would not last and that Hitler might ally with the conservatives just as Mussolini had to gain power. With the fall of the Socialist bastion in Prussia in July, Tasca lost hope that the situation could be salvaged without a complete change of policy by the Communists: "But, as the Hitlerians clearly want to conquer the Reich and to modify or suppress its constitution, the vote of the Communists represents a direct support to Fascist demagoguery and, above all, to that red hot antisemitism which is in the process of corrupting the deepest layers of the German people."[33]

After the victory of Hitler in January 1933 Tasca relaunched the idea for a Paris-Berlin-Moscow United Front of socialists and communists and gained the support of Barbusse and the socialist Georges Monnet. For years Tasca had argued that a socialist domestic policy would be worthless without a strong internationalist commitment in foreign policy: "The demands for nationalization of such or such industry, for control of the banks, for the development of 'social services' play a part in a national program, whose socialist character can be destroyed in one blow if this program is not totally integrated in international policy." Tasca hoped that Stalin might finally rally the USSR to his Paris-Berlin-Moscow front now that he realized the tremendous danger that the USSR faced.[34]

FRICTION WITH THE PCF

Tasca's views on these and related issues were bound to cause friction between *Monde* and the PCF. His criticism of the Communist party's rejection of any alliance with the SFIO during the 1932 elections led the PCF to a demand for a complete purge of *Monde*.[35] It was impossible to overlook this open rejection of the social fascism on the pages of a supposedly pro-Soviet periodical. Tasca's entire position conflicted with the Comintern policy of "United Fronts from below," in which the Communist parties launched direct appeals to the socialist masses while bypassing the leadership. This latter approach was embodied in the appeal that Barbusse and Rolland launched in spring 1932 for an international congress against war in response to the Japanese invasion of Manchuria. The first meeting was held in Amsterdam in August 1932 and was followed in June 1933 by a second gathering at the Salle Pleyel in Paris. The Socialists were invited to join the Amsterdam-Pleyel peace movement on terms already set by the Communist party.[36]

FALLOUT FROM KHARKOV

The consequences of the Kharkov Writers Congress were eventually felt by the staff at *Monde*, when the Comintern sought to mobilize more effectively the writers and artists of the International Union of Revolutionary Writers (Union Internationale des Ecrivains Révolutionaires [UIER]) behind the Kharkov theories of "proletarian realism." Naturally, the more militant and dogmatic policies of the UIER had an impact on France, where its affiliate, the Association of Revolutionary Writers and Artists (AEAR), was purged of its original sponsoring group (Aragon, Barbusse, Breton, Luis Buñuel, Paul Eluard, Man Ray, and Rolland). Apart from the avant garde, one of the main targets for attack was "populist" literature, which was leftist without adhering to precise political guidelines. Paul Nizan, one of the PCF's cultural watchdogs, called for the elimination of the "gauchistes" elements. *Monde* was singled out for criticism as an example of political and cultural eclecticism.[37]

In this context *Monde* held a debate on "proletarian literature" to mark the first anniversary of the Kharkov meeting. Tasca presented a report in which he argued that there was simply no way to translate dialectical materialism into literature as demanded at Kharkov: "Dialectical materialism is a way of understanding and of transforming reality. It is a revolutionary instrument par excellence. To call the proletarian artist a dialectical materialist means simply that he must be a revolutionary, a militant." There was, however, no way to cram this experience into a single literary form.[38]

On 7 December 1931 at another debate sponsored by *Monde* the representative of the AEAR attacked both *Monde* and Barbusse personally. This was followed by further criticism of Georges Altmann and Rossi (Tasca) in *L'Humanité*. *Monde*'s response came in the form of a theoretical defense of its position that the role of "proletarian literature" was to understand the historical mission of the proletariat and to support its social demands. Revolutionary writing had to explore the crisis of the bourgeoisie and to present proletarian life authentically, but such a commitment had to develop according to each artist's sensibilities. *L'Humanité* and the AEAR responded by calling *Monde* counterrevolutionary and bourgeois. At that point Barbusse yielded some ground. In April 1932 *Monde* published an issue on proletarian literature and followed it with a series on industrialization in the USSR that reported progress in glowing terms.[39]

THE VICTOR SERGE CASE

The dust had hardly settled when another controversy arose, over the arrest of the writer Victor Serge in the USSR. Victor Serge had been born of Russian parents in Brussels and had been raised in Western Europe. Originally an anarchist, he converted to the Bolshevik cause and moved to the USSR, where he was caught up in the Stalinist repression after 1930. Tasca had had occasional contact with Victor Serge over the years and was aware of the circumstances under which he lived in the USSR. After his arrest Victor Serge managed to smuggle letters out of the Soviet Union to various friends such as Tasca and Magdeleine Paz who began a campaign for his release.

Victor Serge's appeal contained an impassioned attack on Stalinism: "For many years the revolution has entered its reactionary phase. . . . It is no secret that socialism has within itself the germs of reaction. At the present moment we are increasingly in the presence of a caste-bound, absolute totalitarian state, drunk with power, for which man counts not at all." [40] Tasca, obviously, could not publish Victor Serge's letter in *Monde*; instead, he turned to *Le Peuple*, the paper of the Belgian Workers party, to which he contributed irregularly. Tasca demanded that the Soviets free Victor Serge and recounted his life history: "The only crime of Victor Serge is a 'crime of opinion,' of nonconformism. I consider the freedom to criticize as one of the most precious assets of the socialist revolution." [41]

Eventually, the Victor Serge case was discussed in June 1935 at the International Writers Congress for the Defense of Culture. Despite the efforts of the Soviet delegates to exclude it from the agenda, Gaetano Salvemini, Magdeleine Paz, and others spoke in his favor. After Gide and Rolland intervened directly with the Soviet government, Victor Serge was released. [42]

THE BREAK WITH BARBUSSE

As Tasca's importance at *Monde* increased, the probability of conflict with Barbusse rose proportionately. In January 1932 Tasca was placed in charge of the political and economic departments of the magazine. For the balance of that year his relations with Barbusse remained delicate but friendly, and Tasca's diary comments reflected a consistent, if not uncritical, admiration. [43] The vulnerable point in Barbusse's relationship with Tasca and the rest of his noncommunist staff was *Monde*'s precarious financial position. The French Communist party naturally refused to assume the burden of the review without full control. Efforts were made to find secure alternative funding. Georges Monnet, a prominent socialist, and the Left radical (and future Vichyite) Gaston Bergery were brought into the administrative council in 1932 but to no avail as *Monde*'s losses mounted.[44]

As financial difficulties increased in 1933, Barbusse became increasingly critical of Tasca's handling of political issues, and Tasca retaliated by threatening to resign. The crisis reached its climax after Barbusse's return from a trip to the USSR in the summer. In a letter to all the editors, Barbusse announced pay cuts. Tasca, who had been managing the review after the departure of the editor Léon Werth, claimed that he would lose everything under the new system of payment by article rather than by regular salary. Barbusse responded by stating that since Tasca had already resigned, the point was moot. Tasca appealed to the Syndicat des Journalistes, but, by the time his appeal was heard, Barbusse had turned *Monde* over to the French Communist party. Tasca, who was told that he could return if he were willing to work under the new regime, then formally resigned in November 1933 with a month's severance pay.[45]

Tasca's experience at *Monde* illustrated the difficulty of carving out a viable independent position on the revolutionary Left. The unremitting hostility of the Communists to former members and the violence of the press campaigns mounted against them were actually designed to force the ex-Communists to the Right. Tasca attempted to resist for a time, but his own attitude toward Marxism began to alter once he was outside the Communist movement. Finally, as Tasca began to apply his views on fascism to practical issues, an additional source of friction developed between him and his former comrades. Tasca completely rejected the negative politics of both the German and French Communist parties and stressed the importance of enlisting the proletariat in an alliance with other social classes. On all of these issues, Tasca drew closer to the socialist parties of France and Italy. His transition from the Communist movement was over, and the logical step in a return to active politics was a return to the Socialist camp.

7

Tasca's Return to the PSI

It was significant that, as the situation at *Monde* deteriorated, Tasca put out feelers to the French and the Belgian Socialist parties rather than to the PSI. In May 1932 he wrote to Léon Blum, stressing the need for a common Socialist foreign policy based on the Paris-Berlin-Moscow formula. Tasca argued for the primacy of foreign policy, which might even demand a change in the historic socialist refusal to participate in governments: ". . . I believe that the Socialist party should not hesitate to accept the co-responsibility for a policy of economies at home, without fearing Communist demagoguery, if participation in power will permit it to seriously influence the foreign policy of France. . . ." [1] He expressed the same ideas in a letter to Emile Vandervelde of the Parti Ouvrier Belge (POB): "Either socialism succeeds in finding a solution to the world crisis or all humanity will regress a century. We must have, in each country, a crisis program, a program for governing by which the working class will obtain the support of the non-capitalist classes, a program which would have to be oriented to foreign policy." [2] Domestic policy and ideological orthodoxy took second place to the need for national unity.

Thus, Tasca was quite close to De Man and the neosocialists when the crisis of *Monde* forced him to seek alternative employment. He approached *Le Peuple*, the paper of the Parti Ouvrier Belge, Salvemini, Henriette Rolland Holst in Holland, and the American radical Scott Nearing, but without success. Marcel Déat offered a possibility of work with the Socialist parliamentary group, and the radical Bertrand de Jouvenel mentioned a documentation service that he hoped to organize. Nothing concrete was forthcoming, however, and Tasca was able to care for his small daughter only through the help offered by the Julien family. By August 1933 he was desperate when offers came from Vandervelde and from *Le Populaire*. Tasca accepted the latter position in early 1934.[3]

PONTIGNY

A decisive factor in Tasca's development toward social democracy and neoreformism was his participation in the seminars at Pontigny. Each summer the Third Republic's left-wing intellectual establishment met at an old Cistercian abbey at Pontigny in Burgundy. Regulars at the gatherings were André Siegfried, Roger Martin du Gard, Paul Valéry, Leon Brunschvicg, and André Maurois. The idea for Pontigny grew out of the Union pour la Verité, which had been founded around the turn of the century by Paul Desjardins. Desjardins, whose intellectual mentors were Kant, Pascal, and Montaigne, had been associated with the Catholic modernist movement but was, above all else, devoted to free inquiry. In 1910 he created the Entretiens d'Eté at Pontigny as a framework within which the participants could exchange views without the pressure of ordinary politics. His own outlook was internationalist, a cross between the radicalism of the Third Republic and reformist socialism. By the 1930s the meetings at Pontigny became a sounding board for the new theories on planning and the need for an ideological reorientation of the socialist movement proposed by De Man and others.[4]

Among the Italian exiles, Tasca, Carlo Rosselli, Nicola Chiaromonte, and Andrea Caffi found their way into this center of French politics and culture. Charles André Julien felt that Pontigny exerted a profound influence on Tasca's evolution from Marxism. He attended the sessions at Pontigny in 1932 or 1933, and during the latter year he spoke on antifascism. Significantly, in 1934 both Tasca and Carlo Rosselli participated in the session dedicated to socialist planning at which De Man, Sir Stafford Cripps, and other prominent social democrats spoke. Tasca's presentation of Marx as humanist coincided perfectly with the overall aim of the conference to provide a new, non-Marxist basis for socialism.[5]

TASCA AND CARLO ROSSELLI

The fact that Tasca and Carlo Rosselli shared interests in the problems discussed at Pontigny offered the basis for further cooperation between the ex-Communist and the founder of the Giustizia e Libertà (GL) movement. GL was precisely the sort of movement to attract Tasca if he ranked a return to Italian politics among his top priorities.

Carlo Rosselli was one of the most original and dynamic of the new generation of antifascist leaders. Like so many others, Rosselli was drawn to radical politics by the historian Gaetano Salvemini, but Fascist violence, which culminated in the murder of Matteotti and the consolidation of the dictatorship, turned Rosselli to active participation in the Socialist party. He helped Filippo Turati flee Italy in 1926 and was himself arrested soon afterward. Along with Emilio Lussu and Fausto Nitti, he made a daring escape in 1929 from Fascist imprisonment on the island of Lipari. Once in Paris, Rosselli, convinced that the old parties of the Left could no longer serve the antifascist struggle, decided to launch a new movement, Giustizia e Libertà, intended to offer a new beginning to the Left. Neither the verbal extremism of the Maximalists nor the passive strategy of the reformists appealed to Rosselli. Unconstrained by ideological rigidities, Rosselli sought to fuse a revived liberalism and a humanist socialism into an ideological alternative to both fascism and classic Marxism. For this reason Rosselli was almost alone among the major leaders of the Italian Left in expressing interest in the neosocialist movement of Déat. He also chose for his book *Socialisme libéral* the publishing house of Georges Valois, the ex-syndicalist, ex-Action Française militant and founder of the French Faisceau movement, who was on the way back to the Left and specialized in publishing Left dissidents. Like Tasca, Rosselli was involved in the process of revisionism in France as well as in Italy. Unlike his fellow exile, however, Rosselli was primarily an activist and an anti-Fascist democrat who never allowed himself to follow Déat and De Man down the slippery road from neorevisionism to fascism.

In 1927 the traditional leftist Italian political parties, which had regrouped in Paris, formed an umbrella organization called the *Concentrazione Antifascista*. It included the Italian Socialist Party, the reformist Partito Socialista Unitario dei Lavoratori Italiani (PSULI), Buozzi's General Confederation of Labor, the Republicans, and the Italian League for the Rights of Man (Lega Italiana dei Diritti dell'Uomo [LIDU]). Ideologically, the Concentrazione Antifascista was reformist rather than revolutionary. *La Libertà*, its weekly newspaper, was edited by one of the most respected leaders of the PSULI, Claudio Treves, who favored alliances between the Socialists and other bourgeois antifascist forces.

When Rosselli launched Giustizia e Libertà, he proposed to the Concentrazione that it make the basis of its organization more centralized, with a unified organization within Italy. These ideas were rejected by the other parties in 1929, and the new GL movement remained outside the Concentrazione Antifascista until mid-1931, when it reached a compromise with the other parties. Under its terms, GL was designated as the representative of the antifascist alliance within Italy; in exchange, a member of the PSI and one from the CGL would be included on a five-member committee to direct activities within Italy. The major objections to GL's proposals had always come from the Socialist party, but the PSI had just merged with the reformist PSULI in July 1930. The withdrawal of its Maximalist left wing in protest against the merger shifted the balance within the now-unified PSI somewhat to the right and allowed it to approve Rosselli's project.[6]

Around the time GL joined the Concentrazione, Tasca was advising his friend and fellow ex-Communist Riccardo Boatti to consider GL as a possible solution to renewed political militancy. Somewhat earlier, in March 1931, Tasca had promised to collaborate on Rosselli's *Quaderni di Giustizia e Libertà*: "Our theoretical differences are mainly over the post-fascist period. I fear that political success, when it comes, will change you too rapidly into conservatives, while Italy will need leaders who will have the necessary daring to liquidate the terrible negative legacy of fascism." [7] An editorial note in the June 1933 *Quaderni* described Tasca and Gramsci as the most interesting personalities to emerge from the Communist movement and expressed hope for further collaboration with Tasca. In fact, Rosselli completely agreed with Tasca's attack on the "static and conservative class-based policies" of parties like the SPD and on the need for the working class "to transcend its own class limits." Both Tasca and Rosselli were convinced of the necessity to reach beyond the working class to form broader alliances against fascism. [8]

TASCA BETWEEN GL AND THE PSI

Tasca might have gravitated to GL, but a return to the PSI was much more compatible with his association with the SFIO. Membership in a party, such as the PSI with its longstanding ties to the SFIO, far outweighed the advantages of belonging to the innovative but maverick GL movement. Moreover, despite his calls for innovation, Tasca was a traditionalist with strong loyalties to the historic organizations of the working class. Thus, although his intellectual orientation made him more at home in GL, a combination of practical and sentimental factors weighed against that choice.

It is likely, however, that Tasca would have maintained his loose relationship with GL if external events had not intervened to force a clear choice between it and the PSI. Relations between the Socialist party and GL had never been good. Rosselli's movement threatened at any time to infringe on territory that the Socialists considered their own. In 1932 GL launched its *Quaderni*, aimed not only at Italy but also at the exile community, and it adopted a program that advocated a republic based on the working classes, more social and economic content to traditional democracy, land reform, and some nationalization. [9]

As long as the Socialists chose to view GL and its new program as bourgeois-radical in character, it could ignore the obvious competition between the two organizations. Membership in the Concentrazione was reaffirmed by the PSI's congress in Marseilles in April 1933, but the political situation was changing rapidly. The death of the two historic leaders of reformist socialism, Filippo Turati in 1932 and Claudio Treves in 1933, removed the party's two most respected moderates and left the more radical Pietro Nenni in charge of the party. The defeat of the German Socialist party dealt another crushing blow to the whole reformist strategy and removed a moderating force from the international socialist movement.

THE BREAK-UP OF THE CONCENTRAZIONE ANTIFASCISTA

Relations between Giustizia e Libertà and the Socialist party, already poor by the end of 1933, were worsened by an incident in early 1934 that directly involved Tasca. Rosselli involved Tasca and a few other militants from GL in a project for a new antifascist paper, *Il Giornale degli operai*, which would appeal to workers within Italy but would be published outside the framework of the Concentrazione Antifascista and the traditional union structure. Giuseppe Faravelli, a reformist socialist newly arrived from Italy who was close to both Tasca and Rosselli in 1933, warned that it should not be seen to compete with the CGL's paper, *L'Operaio italiano*, in France and Belgium. Rosselli and the others disregarded these warnings, and the new paper appeared only once before it collapsed in the face of violent opposition from Bruno Buozzi, who judged Rosselli to have infringed on his territory.[10]

Almost simultaneously with the arguments over the *Giornale degli operai* came Emilio Lussu's article "Orientamenti" in the February issue of the *Quaderni*. Lussu had been a member of parliament from Sardinia, a leading antifascist who was imprisoned and then escaped from Italy with Rosselli and now was prominent in the GL movement. He called on his organization to adopt a much more overtly socialist program. The veteran socialist Giuseppe Emanuele Modigliani, who succeeded Treves as the leader of the old generation of reformists, immediately charged that GL wanted to eliminate the PSI and accused Rosselli of violating the compromises that allowed GL to act as the representative of the Concentrazione in Italy.[11]

By March 1934 the PSI was rapidly moving to establish its own organization within Italy and to break with GL. The Socialists sought the support of Tasca, whose influence with ex-Communists such as Paolo Ravazzoli, Riccardo Boatti, and Ignazio Silone was great. The leader of the PSI, Pietro Nenni, wrote to Tasca on 14 April, shortly before the final rupture of the Concentrazione on 5 May, to urge him to join the party. He noted that Tasca had been behind Boatti's request for membership and might also influence Ravazzoli. Tasca, who still looked on the PSI with distaste, responded that he was not yet ready to join a party but would be willing to write for the *Nuovo Avanti*. As yet, Tasca was undecided about his future with GL and discouraged by the prospect of its rupture from the PSI.[12]

The end of the Concentrazione could not be postponed. On 6 April

Rosselli resurrected his old idea of transforming the Concentrazione Antifascista into a kind of superparty. Nenni demanded that unless GL limit itself to its role under the agreement of 1931, the Socialists would no longer delegate their activities within Italy to GL. He insisted that unity among the various socialist factions could be achieved within the PSI and not through a new organization like GL: "At bottom we have an attempt to suppress our proletarian party and to englobe it in a movement which would take on a nonsocialist veneer." [13] Or, as Nenni bluntly stated in the August issue of *Politica socialista*:

> The process of self definition in GL can have but two consequences: either the identification or the rupture with the Socialist party. . . . In fact, there is only one socialism, that which is class oriented, proletarian, internationalist, Marxist, which is embodied in the traditional parties of the working class and in the two worker Internationals. Outside of this, there is chaos. [14]

Rosselli's decision to turn GL into a political party was decisive for Tasca. He wrote to Rosselli that GL's importance was precisely that it was not a party: "Giustizia e Libertà had larger frontiers than the Concentration and those more ample frontiers were needed, I continue to believe, in order to have the maximum return from antifascist activity. Giustizia e Libertà ought to have been an alliance of political groups in which various socialist currents would have found a place. . . ." Within the broad movement formed by GL, the PSI would have been the most important element. Tasca refused to support GL as a rival socialist party, however. He informed Rosselli that the PSI had asked him to join but that, as yet, he had responded negatively. [15]

Rosselli considered Tasca to be mired in contradictions. On the one hand, he seemed to argue that GL should not abandon its unique role in the antifascist movement but should become itself a revised version of the Concentrazione. On the other hand, Tasca constantly called for a new beginning but without the will to break with the past. Rosselli concluded:

> So, now that we are being frank, allow me to express in synthesis my judgment on the Socialist party as it is presently constituted: along side a lot of tired, conservative deadwood, stuck in totally out of date formulas, it contains a not very numerous nucleus of workers and artisans of value; but its leadership, almost without exception, is corrupted by insincerity, by profound political demagoguery, and above all by a progressive skepticism which makes a mockery of any effort at renewal. . . . [16]

Unmoved, Tasca wrote to Faravelli on 18 May that he had agreed to write a regular column about foreign policy for the *Nuovo Avanti*. Publicly, Tasca disputed GL's claims to represent the new socialist generation and accused Rosselli of the same mindless activism that he had fought in the PCI before 1929.[17]

Personal relations between Tasca and Rosselli were affected by these political differences. In this case the culprit was Faravelli, a notorious gossip, who repeated to Tasca remarks that Rosselli had made in a moment of exasperation. Yet, beyond personal matters, it was doubtful that Tasca and Rosselli could have collaborated for long. There was little room in Tasca's outlook for spontaneity; he thought in terms of education and the slow formation of cadres for a future battle. Rosselli was the liberal counterpart of Longo and Secchia, who believed that the establishment of a presence in Italy was vital for the antifascists. The leaders of GL, Rosselli above all, placed a premium on action. These differences were revealed in a letter from Tasca to Lussu. GL, he noted, might have become the nucleus of a new party but "the vanities, the forced idleness and the impatience of emigration pushed you to move too fast and to attempt with your forces alone a task for which all the preconditions are missing: a clear ideology, precise political positions, expert leaders, ties with the masses." Tasca's inadequacies as a leader of a party in exile are all revealed here. He viewed political action as a classic battle, not as modern guerrilla warfare. The routine of a completely legal party such as the SFIO was much more to his taste.[18]

UNITY OF ACTION

The rapid advance of fascism in Europe that culminated in the Nazi victory in Germany in January 1933, in the 6 February 1934, anti-Republican riots in Paris, and in the destruction of the Austrian Socialist movement left the strategies of both the Socialists and Communists in shambles. Belatedly, the Comintern reviewed the policy of "social fascism." Attempts at a "united front from below," such as the Amsterdam-Pleyel movement, were inadequate to protect the USSR in the growing climate of tension in Europe. The turning point in Communist tactics came in June 1934, when the PCF offered a Unity of Action pact to the SFIO. Negotiations proceeded rapidly between the French parties, who signed an agreement on 27 July 1934.[19]

Togliatti proposed similar negotiations with the PSI at the meeting of his party's Ufficio Politico on 12 and 17 July. The Communists judged that their offer would receive a favorable hearing, with the possible exceptions of Buozzi, Modigliani, and the vice-director of the Nuovo Avanti, Pallante Rugginenti.[20] In response, Nenni nominated Buozzi, Giuseppe Saragat, and himself to negotiate with the Communists. After a first meeting in late July at which the Socialists reached substantial agreement on a document presented by the PCI, the Nuovo Avanti announced on 28 July that the phase of the United Front was at hand. Only a slight note of old hostility lingered: "The Italian Communists say they want 'unity of action' at all costs. We want, however, that degree of unity of action which, in the present condition of our country is possible to achieve: we want it on the basis of absolute loyalty and of doctrinal and functional autonomy which we cannot renounce without giving up the reason for being of our party. . . ." Despite these reservations, the Consiglio Generale of the PSI on 31 July set terms that were very close to those offered by the PCI.[21]

Some difficulties did arise. Nenni preferred a general document, and Buozzi and Saragat were reluctant to accept any organizational obligations. Luigi Longo scornfully noted that the Socialists merely wanted a pact that would shelter them from attacks by the Communists and distinguish them from their ex-partners in the Concentrazione. Longo's strategy, however, recalled some uncomfortable parallels with the old united front days: "Our concessions must be compensated for by a fraternization and common action at the base. . . ."[22]

On 6 August the two parties agreed on an outline for a pact that established a mechanism for consultation on specific actions to be taken against the danger of war, in favor of the liberation of political prisoners, and on behalf of the political and economic demands of Italian workers. Both parties agreed to press for an understanding between the two Internationals. Finally, each would maintain independence in matters of ideology, propaganda, organization, and recruitment.[23]

TASCA AND UNITY OF ACTION

Tasca wrote to Nenni the next day to inform him that he had no objection in principle to Unity of Action, but his practical reservations were evident: "the Communists propose to obtain the same objectives of the 'united front from below,' that is the destruction of the socialist organization, but with new means." He shared his reservations with Faravelli, who with Modigliani and Giovanni Faraboli, the secretary of the Toulouse federation, represented the leaders of the opposition to Unity of Action.[24]

Tasca wanted the Socialists to press for the inclusion of a demand for the restoration of democracy in Italy with no mention of a workers' state during the first period after the fall of fascism. The Communists countered with their own formula, "the demand for all the democratic liberties of the working peoples." Nenni found that proposal acceptable but pressed the Communists to compromise on the more ambiguous "demand for all popular liberties." Unsatisfied, Tasca appealed to Pallante Rugginenti, who often moderated between party factions. Rugginenti sided with Tasca and used the occasion to urge him to join the party as a counterweight to Nenni:

> We all know the qualities and the defects of Nenni. He has an egocentric and improvising personality. It is necessary to control him. It's not a matter of surrounding him with party policemen, but with collaborators of a certain political and intellectual authority so that in this collaboration he feels the limits of his mandate and of his possibilities. One cannot carry out this control with any authority from outside the party. In Saragat, in Joseph [Faravelli], in me, in Buozzi, and even in Modigliani you have guarantees.[25]

In the end, the opposition to Unity of Action forced Nenni to make a number of polemical points against the Communists in a declaration published along with the pact on 17 August. The PSI attacked the past theories of social fascism and placed the blame for conflict on the PCI. The Communists protested that the French parties had no such limiting document, but it was the price that the opposition exacted to have any pact at all.[26]

TASCA AND NENNI

It was unfortunate that from the beginning Tasca was placed in the role of Nenni's nemesis. Conflicts in style were immediately apparent. In a letter to Nenni, written two days after the pact was signed, Tasca criticized both the procedure used and the substance of the pact: "I fear that we are continuing the old Italian tradition which led us to adhere to the Third International and to the Twenty-one Conditions in three lines in a vague motion and then to work for months and years to eliminate the equivocations and to destroy what had been improvised." Tasca warned that Unity of Action was simply a tactic of the Communists, who counted on the Socialists' poor organization and slowness to react to take advantage of every situation. Yet, even Tasca was forced to admit that Unity of Action was the only way to increase the base of the proletarian parties and to give new impetus to antifascism.[27]

The relationship between the two leaders would never be an easy one. Impulsive, improvising, instinctive, bored by theories, Nenni was the opposite of Tasca, with his massive library and archive, his carefully weighed opinions, and his proclivity to wait rather than act. Yet they shared a common passion for work, and both were well connected to the French political world. Nenni had worked as a journalist for *Le Soir*, and Tasca was now writing for *Le Populaire*. They were not enemies in 1934 and would not have an open conflict until much later, but they were not fated to get along. Nenni's style of leadership grated on Tasca's nerves. Tasca believed that Nenni had led the PSI too rapidly into Unity of Action, even if he agreed that the policy was necessary. To Tasca, Nenni represented the continuation of the Maximalist tradition within Italian socialism that had been responsible for the disastrous decisions made between 1919 and

1922. There was also a fundamental difference in their attitudes toward the Communist party. Nenni believed in Unity of Action and was willing to make sacrifices for it. Past polemics with the PCI, even the accusation that he had been a founder of the Bolognese fascio, were considered by Nenni part of the political game. Tasca's relationship with the PCI was entirely different; his expulsion had been brutal and the experience at *Monde* little better. Tasca's sense of personal hurt reinforced his belief that Nenni was too willing to concede on matters of principle. Sooner or later the two men would break over the issue of Unity of Action.[28]

TASCA AND THE CENTRO SOCIALISTA INTERNO

The alliance with the Communists strengthened the determination of the PSI to place greater emphasis on work within Italy, where the Communists and GL heretofore had had a monopoly. In February 1934 the PSI had been badly embarrassed when Emilio Caldara, the former Socialist mayor of Milan, appealed to Mussolini to allow an internal loyal opposition to the corporative system. Both Tasca and Saragat felt that the Caldara case revealed the need for improvement in the party cadres within Italy.[29]

The clandestine socialist organization emerged from the network of GL and was the product of dissatisfaction with the interclass orientation of Giustizia e Libertà. The center of activity was Milan, where Eugenio Colorni, Bruno Maffi, Lelio Basso, Lucio Luzzatto, and Roldofo Morandi represented a new generation of socialists, unburdened by past defeats. Many of them, like Morandi, were somewhat suspicious of, but not deeply hostile to, the Communists. They sought above all to impose a more incisive proletarian direction to the PSI. The young socialists in Italy wanted a renewed party as a rallying point for the various socialist currents that found the PCI too sectarian.[30]

In the summer of 1934 the PSI formally organized the Centro Socialista Interno (CSI), to be directed by Giuseppe Faravelli. Faravelli, Tasca's closest friend in the party, had begun his career with the Camera del Lavoro in Milan. He joined the reformist PSULI and worked illegally against the regime before fleeing to Italy in 1931. Faravelli combined strong anticommunism with a vital interest in Italian affairs. On both of these points he found himself in opposition to Nenni, whom he viewed as too internationalist, too inclined to favor the Communists, and too neglectful of Italian affairs in his role as editor of the *Nuovo Avanti*. Faravelli backed the militants of the CSI on the need for a publication that would reach into Italy and had attempted to launch *Politica Socialista* in 1933 to compete both with the Communists' *Lo stato operaio* and GL's publications.[31]

Faravelli enthusiastically greeted the possibility that Tasca might work with the PSI. They agreed on most important issues, although Tasca's position on Unity of Action was somewhat more nuanced than the outright hostility of Faravelli. Both men were at odds with the CSI, which tended to favor a more proletarian-oriented policy. They attempted to encourage any latent hostility toward the Communists in the clandestine party in the conviction that the future of the PSI did not lie in the direction of an alliance with the Communists, but in building a rival organization to the PCI within Italy. Consequently, they insisted that the CSI avoid contacts with the Communists until the Socialist network became fully operational.[32]

Tasca and Faravelli hoped to use *Politica socialista* to influence the development of the CSI. Tasca would have liked to make the review into the theoretical journal of neoreformism, a sort of rival to *Lo stato operaio*, but he received no support from the party leadership. Faravelli and Tasca protested to Nenni and Rugginenti. The latter was sympathetic but wanted a commitment from Tasca to join the party in order to balance Nenni's influence.[33]

THE DECISION TO JOIN THE PSI

Tasca's anomalous status in the PSI became increasingly inconvenient, as he was drawn more deeply into party politics. In December 1934, when Carlo Rosselli attempted to force the renegotiation of the Unity of Action pact to include GL, Tasca took a leading role in formulating the PSI's hostile reaction to the idea. Although one might have expected him to approve of Rosselli's call to abandon a strict proletarian stance in favor of an interclass alliance against the Fascists, Tasca was convinced that GL aimed to supplant the PSI and was determined to thwart the effort. He even called GL's policies elitist and Mussolinian, provoking an angry response from Emilio Lussu, who had just resigned from the leadership group of GL because it would not move further leftward. On 1 March 1935, Lussu wrote that the PSI could never renew the Socialist movement, as it often proclaimed it wanted to do: "Moreover it proclaims it through Tasca, who, let it be said with all seriousness, is among those who most needs to be renewed. Not only that, but Tasca, as everyone knows, is not even a member of the Socialist party."[34]

Lussu touched a sore point. Tasca had responded to repeated requests that he become a member of the party by arguing that it was not really necessary that he join. But it was increasingly evident that there were no alternatives to the PCI but GL and the PSI. Having rejected GL, Tasca had little choice. He shared this problem with a group of ex-Communists who hovered around the PSI. Silone, Ravazzoli, and Boatti gravitated toward socialism along with Tasca, whereas Pietro Tresso and Alfonso Leonetti, who had been expelled in 1930 along with Ravazzoli, tried to stake out a position further to the left. All of them faced the difficulty of conducting an active political career outside the established parties. Moreover, GL was an untested exile grouping that had no guarantee of finding a base within Italy.

The expulsions of Silone and the "three" (Tresso, Ravazzoli, and Leonetti) from the PCI differed from that of Tasca because they did not touch on Soviet policy but concerned the role that the Communist party would play in Italy and differing estimations of the impact of the economic crisis on the regime. Despite the differences, all the expulsions, including Tasca's, marked the imposition of Stalinist discipline on the PCI.[35]

Differences persisted among the ex-Communists, as Tresso indicated in a letter to Pasquini (Silone). Tresso objected to the fact that although Togliatti and Tasca held the same positions between 1926 and 1929, Togliatti escaped without paying any price. Thus, the expulsions of the "three" and Silone in the years that followed did not mean that they could ever consider the same political options once outside the party. Tasca, as Tresso correctly noted, had been for some time merely a social democrat.[36]

Tasca was bound to be disappointed in his desire to bring all the communist dissidents into the PSI. Tresso eventually joined the Socialist party at the same time as Ravazzoli, but more on the suggestion of Trotsky than of Tasca. Leonetti, who remained true to his revolutionary principles, could never find a home in the PSI. Ignazio Silone, whose expulsion from the Communist party was perhaps the most difficult of all for Togliatti on the personal level, turned away from active political commitments and began to work on the series of novels that would establish his reputation as a major figure in Italian literature. Tasca's most important recruit was Paolo Ravazzoli. Ravazzoli had risen within the ranks of the Milanese Communist party, had experience with union organization, and was engaged in the party's illegal network after 1926. His expulsion from the PCI was due to disagreements about exposing the illegal network to excessive risks. Once outside the party, Ravazzoli's life was extremely difficult. Unlike many others, he was of working-class background and had no profession to resume. He also lacked work papers and important connections and lived a hand-to-mouth existence until Tasca intervened with friends in the SFIO to regularize his status. Although Ravazzoli never shared Tasca's penchant for neoreformism, they did agree on a number of issues, ranging from a suspicion of Stalinist Russia to support for alliances between the PSI and bourgeois democratic parties.[37]

Tasca's own decision to join the PSI occurred almost simultaneously with those of Tresso and Ravazzoli and was made with little enthusiasm: "I did it because, for all practical purposes, I had no other choice. I remain convinced, however, that it would have been better to go on as before. . . . Entering the party I sacrifice something (which does not belong to me because it concerns the future of our movement) that I make a mistake in giving up." But membership in the party brought Tasca finally into the Direzione, where Faravelli and the others hoped that he would combat Nenni's headstrong policies.[38]

In the March issue of *Politica socialista* Tasca explicated his views on his new party. He made it clear that he considered the PSI's center of activity to be in Italy, where the primary task was the formation of cadres for the future struggle against the Fascist dictatorship. Relations with other parties would have to be governed by this policy. Consequently, the PCI was not a long-term ally and was certainly not to be courted within Italy. Instead, Tasca wished to draw the smaller socialist formations into the PSI. On all three of these issues he conflicted with Nenni, who placed much more importance on Unity of Action and whose attention was directed to the international struggle against fascism. With Tasca in the PSI the party conflict took on new life, and with the Unity of Action pact the stakes were considerably higher. The Communist party with its centralized leadership and rigid discipline made an uncomfortable ally for the more open and loosely organized Socialists. Tasca understood that the PCI's structure gave it a greater ability to maneuver politically. But neither he nor any of the other leaders of the PSI had an immediate answer to the danger that Unity of Action posed. On most issues the Socialists found themselves in a defensive and reactive position that sapped the party's vitality and presaged its political decline.[39]

8

Neoreformism versus Unity of Action

After the bitter defeats in Germany and Austria during the early 1930s, many socialists sought to relaunch their movement on a new basis. Although they did not propose to abandon the core of social democracy—the open organization of the party, a conditional commitment to democratic and parliamentary practice, and a refusal to impose a rigid orthodoxy on the socialist movement—they faced two quite different strategies to combat the rise of fascism. The first, neoreformism, advocated policies that would allow an alliance with the lower middle class by breaking with doctrines of class struggle and proletarian militancy in favor of moderate reforms in the context of a national plan. Implied in neoreformism was the abandonment of any integral socialist society and, especially, any change through revolution and the dictatorship of the proletariat. The second alternative was more radical; it argued that fascism would be defeated by increased proletarian unity based on a Communist-Socialist United Front alliance. Such an alliance by its very dynamism would carry with it a large part of the lower middle class. Integral to the second alternative was a stress on both the defeat of fascism and the socialist revolution that would inevitably follow.

Both alternatives drew quite different conclusions from a similar viewpoint on the recent past. They agreed that the polarization between reformists and revolutionaries was outdated, that a different method was necessary to stop the march of fascism, and that the socialist parties had to find some way to liberate themselves from bourgeois economic thinking about depression and recovery.

The first major socialist leader to move along neosocialist lines was

Oswald Mosley, who presented his ideas on planning, rationalization, and economic nationalism to the Labour Party in May 1930. On the Continent the French neosocialists and the Belgian Henri De Man were the most noted representatives of the neoreformist perspective. They worked from the premise that the proletariat alone could never form a majority in Western Europe. Interclass alliances with artisans, peasants, white-collar workers, and shopkeepers were necessary even if they necessitated altering the program of socialism in fundamental ways. Specifically, both De Man and the leading Neosocialists, Marcel Déat and Adrien Marquet, argued that, since Marxism was already in crisis, it should be abandoned altogether. It could never win broad support with a narrow proletarian orientation, whereas there was every possibility of forging an anticapitalist alliance between the proletariat and the petite bourgeoisie along non-Marxist lines. Finally, both De Man and the Neosocialists argued in favor of a purely national framework for their new socialism, with anti-Marxism, anticapitalism, and nationalism as its building blocks.

The French Neosocialists—Déat, Marquet, and their followers—contended that the Socialist party should prepare itself for the immediate exercise of power. The crisis of capitalism and the rise of fascism made action urgent. Déat advocated a government between the Radicals and the Socialists and excluding the Communists, which would undertake a series of reforms, such as restoration of public order, restructuring of the economy along corporative lines, and a strong dose of nationalism. This "national" socialism would create a new social order that was neither capitalist nor Marxist. Déat frankly admitted that his program was designed to compete with the Fascists on their own ground: "Between fascism and us there is, in reality, a race against time." [1]

Despite his acceptance of part of Déat's program, Tasca's reaction to the Neosocialist movement was hostile. He sided with Blum against the Déat-Marquet minority at the time of the Congress of Paris in July 1933. The "Neos" shocked Tasca by their slogan "Order, Authority, Nation." Nor was he yet ready for the wholesale denunciation of Marxism in which they engaged. When they broke with the SFIO at the July congress, Tasca saw only dangers in Déat's ideas on economic autarchy, Marion's defense of the strong state, and Marquet's authoritarianism. Paul Marion was singled out for special criticism. Marion, who would be Tasca's boss at the Information Ministry under Vichy, had a career that paralleled Tasca's in strange ways. He joined the French Communist party in 1922 after taking a degree in philosophy at the university. Within the PCF Marion rose rapidly. He joined the party's Central Bureau in 1926 and was sent as a representative to Moscow between 1927 and 1929. As with Tasca, the period in the Soviet state led to Marion's break with the party in August 1929, almost the same month as Tasca's expulsion. Like Tasca, Marion then wrote for

Le Peuple, the paper of the Parti Ouvrier Belge, and was influenced by De Man, but at that point their careers began to diverge. In 1931 Marion joined the Déat group within the SFIO and wrote for the Neosocialist paper, *La Vie Socialiste*. Thus, notwithstanding the similarities in their reaction to events in the past, Tasca called Marion's ideas "un fascisme de gauche," which abandoned the essence of socialism: "By abandoning internationalism socialism will lose its essence, its progressive role."[2]

DE MAN'S PLAN

De Man's reformist alternative was somewhat different from that of the Neosocialists. He did not abandon Marx for a technocratic elitism, as did Déat. Rather, he came to believe that the inspiration for socialism was ethical and psychological rather than economic factors. Socialism was a moral reaction to the dehumanization of labor. Marxism, by subordinating ethical concerns to supposedly objective economic factors, lost touch with a large part of the working class, as well as the lower middle classes. In De Man's view, then, socialism had always been a system of values, an aspiration to a superior social order. It was less a doctrine of the proletariat than for the proletariat because the working class alone was incapable of making a revolution.[3]

De Man felt that socialism could not be sold on the old basis to the reformist working class and to the nonproletarian majority. To achieve their goals, the Socialists had to present a program designed for society as it actually existed. This meant starting with the national framework for a solution to the economic crisis and international tension.[4] Drawing on the experience of American mass production and Soviet planning, De Man argued that only systematic planning could restore control by the collectivity over the power centers created by modern industry and banking.[5]

If it could be shown that unbridled capitalism worked against the interests of both the proletariat and the lower middle class, De Man believed that a concrete socialist program that included planning and social control of production could link the anticapitalist sentiments of both classes and undercut any possible reactionary alternative. He assumed that the lower middle class was politically antiliberal and economically anticapitalist and antiproletarian. To win the support of this class, the socialists would have to offer both radical reform and a method that would not violate lower-middle-class sensibilities. Therefore he called for nationalization of only certain sectors of the economy, such as credit, coal, and electricity. Economic reform would be accompanied by political change. De Man called for a single legislative chamber, elected by universal suffrage but flanked by an economic council made up of representatives from industry, banking, and commerce. In this way the commissions that supervised the plan in each branch of the economy would have a consultative voice on the national level. His program also curtailed parliamentary power and re-inforced the executive.[6]

De Man's plan was accepted by the Parti Ouvrier Belge in December 1933. Initially, at least, it was less authoritarian than the program of the Neosocialists. Its major advantage was that it offered an activist policy of moderate nationalization, tax reform, and political restructuring that at-tracted interest outside Belgium among Dutch and Swiss socialists and in some sectors of the British Labour party and the French General Con-federation of Labor (CGT).

Tasca sympathized with De Man's effort to break out of old ways of thinking, especially with regard to the mixed economy and flexible plan-ning. He was following, but more slowly, De Man's retreat from revolution-ary socialism to theories of social harmony, and he certainly responded to De Man's emphasis on the humanistic basis for socialism. Two ele-ments in De Man's plan met Tasca's opposition, however. As with the neo-socialists, he still could not accept the Belgian's wholesale abandonment of Marxism nor the nationalist, semicorporative spirit that underlay the whole project.[7]

THE LEFT ALTERNATIVE

The other alternative open to the Socialist movement was far more radi-cal. Given the willingness of the bourgeoisie to abandon parliamentary democracy, there seemed little alternative but a return to a militant pro-letarian orientation and a recommitment to a revolutionary program of economic and social change. Trotsky thought that such a program might rally disillusioned elements of the lower middle class that were crushed by the depression. The program of the Socialist center and Left was his-torically pacifist and internationalist. There was also a strong repugnance against competing with the Fascists on their own terms. From Blum to Nenni to Trotsky there was the feeling that too much had been abandoned by De Man and the Neosocialists with no guarantee that their program would either bring about structural change within capitalism or win over the petty bourgeoisie against fascism.[8]

OPPOSITION TO UNITY OF ACTION

These were the alternatives offered to the PSI during the mid-1930s. Throughout the spring of 1935 attention focused on the forthcoming meeting of the party's Consiglio Nazionale, which would be the first since the Unity of Action pact. From his position in Switzerland, where he directed the CSI, Faravelli sought to generate resistance against any exten-sion of the United Front to Italy. In his letters to Tasca he stressed the distinction between "unity of action abroad" and the need for an autonomous policy for the CSI. Initially, at least, he had the backing of the Milanese socialist group, which was opposed to alliances with either the PCI or GL.[9] In line with this policy both Tasca and Faravelli wanted the *Nuovo Avanti* to devote more attention to Italian problems. Faravelli informed the CSI that there was a danger that work inside Italy would be sacrificed by Nenni to the needs of action abroad and that the *Politica socialista* would be starved in favor of the *Nuovo Avanti*.[10]

The opposition to Unity of Action had a nucleus around Faravelli, Ravazzoli, Modigliani, and Tasca. Absent from this combination was Saragat, who was convinced that the PSI needed the alliance with the Communists. Moreover Tasca's position was far less rigid than that of Faravelli. There was no alternative to the United Front or an even broader Popular Front alliance in France, where the Communists and Socialists were moving toward an alliance with the middle-class Left by mid-1935. Tasca was convinced, however, that Nenni was not driving a hard enough bargain with the PCI under the terms of Unity of Action.[11]

The Communist party was increasingly worried about skepticism within the PSI over Unity of Action. Nenni was seen as favorable to further cooperation, but the Communists knew that the opponents were waiting for any opportunity to sabotage the pact. They understood that one of the tactics used by the Socialist opposition was to contrast Unity of Action with "socialist unity." This was Tasca's alternative when he suggested that the effort to bring the Maximalists and the various communist dissidents into the PSI take priority over Unity of Action.[12]

UNITY OF ACTION AND THE DEFENSE OF THE USSR

From the Communist point of view, one of the major achievements of Unity of Action was the commitment the Socialists made to the defense of the Soviet Union. The Communists used this provision to try to limit unfavorable comment on Soviet policy by the Socialists on the grounds that any criticism weakened the USSR. The PCI was also aware that it had to combat deeply held pacifist sentiments within the PSI: "The Italian proletariat cannot be against all wars: the Italian proletariat is against Italian imperialist war but not against the Abyssinian populations who defend their own independence." Nor could the workers be opposed to a defensive war by the USSR. The *Stato operaio* appealed to those socialists who favored Unity of Action to work for clarification of these issues.[13] By June 1935 the Communists were concerned enough about the potential opposition to the pact that they lashed out against Tasca and the Trotskyists within the PSI as "renegades from the Communist party and betrayers of the proletariat." Grieco singled out Tasca's opposition to cooperation between the CSI and the Communist underground.[14]

THE CONSIGLIO NAZIONALE, JULY 1935

Communist pressure on the PSI was designed in part to spark the party's left wing to take a firmer stand in favor of Unity of Action at the meeting of the Consiglio Nazionale. The debates that preceded the socialist gathering previewed the issues that would paralyze the PSI's leadership during the 1930s and into the post-1945 period. Nenni stressed the need to develop the pact with the Communists into a true alliance. He also began to question the party's absolute adherence to pacifism on the grounds that the defense of the Soviet Union was vital for the proletariat. Modigliani, whose opposition to Unity of Action stemmed in part from the fear that it would lead the PSI into an ill-considered stand in favor of national defense, warned against an alliance with the PCI "with its eyes closed." Blasco (Tresso) urged the delegates to develop a way of defending the USSR without following the dictates of the Comintern.

Tasca sought the middle ground on the issue of the defense of the Soviet Union. He shared the criticism of the Soviet system expressed by Modigliani, Saragat, and Tresso, but he argued that the "USSR is still an open door toward socialism." It should be defended without falling into a "soviet mysticism." Thus, Tasca seemed closer to Nenni's more flexible position than to Modigliani's intransigent pacifism and Tresso's "integral defeatism." But, although Tasca supported Nenni on day-to-day policy, he joined the opposition in seeking to undermine the basis for Unity of Action by stressing the vast ideological differences separating the PSI and PCI. Even more worrisome from the Communist point of view was Tasca's election to the Direzione of the PSI. He would now be able to act more decisively to advance his views.[15]

The Communists gave the meeting of the Consiglio Nazionale mixed reviews. On the negative side were the efforts to limit Unity of Action within Italy. But, all things considered, Luigi Longo did not feel that Nenni had done badly. Unity of Action received such overwhelming approval that it became apparent that the opponents, such as Tasca and Modigliani, had much less support at the base of the party than among the leadership.[16]

The popularity of Unity of Action among the workers gave to the Communists a strong trump card. They also began to discern a potential split between Tasca and the CSI.[17] Tasca was extremely critical of the Milanese CSI's "infantilismo di sinistra." Although he supported the CSI's reluctance to ally with the Communists, he opposed its rigorous objection to interclass alliances with the bourgeoisie. For his part, Tasca offered quite a different orientation to the PSI:

> Middle classes meant the urban petite bourgeoisie, artisans, and, above all, peasants. The Italian revolution will be the outcome of the initial fusion of their movement with that of the working class. This fusion is based on real

mutual interest on the issues of fascism and capitalism, even if their respective reactions are not identical. . . . The nature and the duration of collaboration between the middle classes and the proletariat in Italy depends on our policy.[18]

UNITY OF ACTION VERSUS THE POPULAR FRONT

The shift of the Comintern to the strategy of the Popular Front came at the VII congress, held in July and August 1935. The entire Communist movement was allowed much more flexibility in dealing with political realities, and the PCI moved rapidly to apply the new strategy to Italy. Togliatti probably never felt that social fascism had been an adequate analytical tool, and now he moved back to a position closer to the one he occupied during his collaboration with Tasca. Unity of Action and the Popular Front were means of reaching the masses outside the Communist party:

> The new and important fact seems to me to be this: by means of formal "united front" accords with the leadership of the Social Democratic parties, some Communist parties have managed to establish permanent contact, not just with small groups of socialist workers, *but with the entire mass of workers who belong to the Socialist parties and are influenced by them.*

Henceforth the Communists would push for joint united front committees from the local to the national level. But Togliatti felt that the United Front had decided limitations in the struggle against fascism. The proletarian parties also had to reach out to the lower middle classes on a program that placed primary emphasis on the defense of democratic liberties. Togliatti couched this tactical shift in the context of the great debate over alternative strategies that faced the Left. He noted that socialists such as De Man sought to win middle-class votes by abandoning the revolution. Togliatti suggested that the Communists seize the leadership from the Socialists and redirect the antifascist alliance. Thus, the Italian Communists moved in two directions: They pushed to strengthen the United Front, while simultaneously calling for the extension of the antifascist alliance to include Catholics and even disillusioned Fascists.[19]

Nenni viewed the shift in Communist tactics with mixed emotions. He believed far more passionately in the United Front than did his French counterpart Léon Blum. Blum was more willing to substitute the Popular Front for Unity of Action in order to dilute the importance of the Socialist-Communist alliance. Nenni favored enlarging the scope of the pact with the Communists but was skeptical about applying a Popular Front strategy to Italy; nor did he wish to return to the old Concentrazione Antifascista under any form. With no Italian equivalent to the French Radical party in sight, only a proletarian solution to postfascist Italy was possible.[20]

When the Communists proposed to broaden the Unity of Action pact by including the Republicans, Rugginenti, supported by Nenni, Tasca, and Modigliani, responded negatively: "Unity of action with the Communists is viewed by us, or many of us, as tied to socialist organic unity. It is evident that the more the basis of unity of action is broadened, the further we move from the ends which we gave to the accord with the Communists."[21] But the Communists were determined to press ahead with the Italian Popular Front. Longo suggested that a successful alliance with the Republicans might influence the Maximalist Socialist party. Such a move, however, was bound to cause friction with the PSI, which considered relations with the Maximalists as an internal party matter.[22]

The Communists faced the fact that their strongest ally, Nenni, was the greatest obstacle to the formation of a Popular Front until further progress in strengthening Unity of Action occurred. Buozzi, Rugginenti, and Modigliani, with whom the Communists negotiated on the Unity of Action committee, were more favorable to the Popular Front but wanted to substitute it for Unity of Action.[23]

MOBILIZATION AGAINST THE WAR IN ETHIOPIA

The first opportunity to test the new Popular Front method came when the Communists proposed a congress to be held in Brussels in October 1935 to protest Italian aggression in Ethiopia. The Socialists immediately understood the idea to be a way of devaluing the bilateral Unity of Action pact in favor of an understanding with the middle class. Moreover the decision to call a congress revealed differences between the PSI and the PCI in their reaction to the Ethiopian war itself. The PSI was relatively forthright in its opposition to Italian aggression, but, as Tasca stated in a letter to Nenni, the Socialists had to avoid a "the worse things get, the better it is" position. Only in the context of the League and the Socialist International could the Socialists feel comfortable in backing sanctions against Italy.[24]

The Communists were even more sensitive to the popularity of the Ethiopian adventure within Italy. They were hesitant to take a public position that might seem antinational. At the Brussels congress, Ruggiero Grieco referred to the decent, but misguided Fascists as "brothers in blackshirts." Then at the meeting of the Central Committee of the PCI in October 1935, Giuseppe Dozza made it clear that with no immediate prospects for revolution in sight the only strategy was to reach out to the Catholics and Fascists who might have been alienated by the policies of the regime. Grieco went even further: "The Popular Front is not possible in Italy unless one takes into account the crucial base which is in the Fascist mass organizations; and we will be the leaders of the Popular Front if we know how to fuse, as Ercoli says, the antifascist opposition with the opposition within fascism."[25] Any hint of an opening to the Fascist "opposition" met with a firm rejection from the Socialists, who insisted that the Brussels congress was simply a manifestation of the Unity of Action pact and not the beginning of an Italian popular front.[26]

To Faravelli's annoyance Tasca kept out of the negotiations with the Communists and limited his contributions to foreign policy. Even Faravelli's hysterical warnings that Nenni was looking to Moscow for financial support failed to shake Tasca. The latter's correspondence with Nenni during this period reveals no major conflicts between the two men. Tasca seemed content to let friction mount between the PSI and PCI without actively intervening to promote it.[27] In frustration, Faravelli turned to the CSI as a counterweight to Unity of Action with the Communists. The militants within Italy needed no encouragement to reject the "brothers in blackshirts" slogan both because it confused the moral line between fascism and the opposition and because the Communists seemed willing to compromise too easily with the bourgeoisie. The CSI's solution was to work for a concrete accord on a future program for postfascist Italy with the Communists. Until such an accord was set, the PSI ought to keep full autonomy within Italy. To some extent the CSI drew closer to Tasca. Neither he nor the socialists within Italy regarded Unity of Action as a danger to be rejected under all circumstances. But, unlike Tasca, the CSI raised no fundamental objection to the alliance and protested only the willingness of the PCI to abandon principles in order to court the bourgeoisie.[28]

THE BREAKDOWN OF UNITY OF ACTION

The new year, 1936, opened with the relations between the PSI and PCI at a low ebb. In a letter to Tasca on 1 January, Nenni complained about the Communists' failure to honor the terms of the pact; the *Nuovo Avanti* accused them of selling out the socialist program to win bourgeois support. Almost simultaneously, Togliatti was writing to Dozza to urge a much firmer line with the PSI over extending the United Front to Italy.[29]

Perhaps the depth of Nenni's anger is indicated by the fact that he turned to Tasca to draft the PSI's response to the Communists. Not unexpectedly, Tasca placed the entire blame for problems on the PCI.[30] The PCI was similarly unwilling to compromise. The Communists pressed the Socialists in two areas where they were least secure: their refusal to extend cooperation with the Communists to Italy and their fear of allowing too much cooperation with the Communists within the Italian community in France. Playing on the obvious divisions within the PSI, the Communists indicated that they could negotiate better with regional leaders than with the national Direzione of the PSI.[31] Again Tasca was charged with the task of responding to the Communists. Nenni even wrote to him on 7 February 1936, that he need not hurry, since the Communists waited a month before answering the Socialists' first letter.[32]

Charges and countercharges flew between the two parties through-out the spring and into the summer of 1936. More than ever, the Socialists worried about the Communist tactic of moving ahead with the creation of front organizations that they controlled before inviting the Socialists to join. This happened in the case of "Fronte Unico," a satellite organization of the PCI that began to solicit individual memberships from Socialists. In response, the Direzione of the PSI forbade its members to join associa-tions controlled by rival parties. The *Nuovo Avanti* insisted that the PSI was interested only in a "united front from above" and not in the disper-sion of its forces by unauthorized initiatives aimed at the base of the party.[33]

Tension between the PSI and PCI was evident at the April meeting of the Unity of Action Committee when Nenni protested against Communist attacks on his party. Emilio Sereni, who had recently escaped from Italy, responded that he met many socialists at home who were far more favor-able to Unity of Action than reports from the CSI would indicate. Giuseppe Di Vittorio summed up the differences aptly: the Socialists seemed to view Unity of Action as a generic political orientation, whereas the Communists considered it as a concrete program of action with constantly expanding horizons.[34]

The first half of 1936 marked a low point in the relationship between the PSI and PCI. Negotiations for renewing the Unity of Action pact or en-larging it to include GL stalled completely amidst much bickering. Most sectors of the PSI, including Tasca, pressed for tangible indications from the Communists that they were seriously interested in Unity of Action.[35] At the same time the Socialists were aware of the attraction of Popular Front experiences that were underway in France and Spain. Moreover, the elec-toral defeat of the Parti Ouvrier Belge in spring 1936 indicated to the Ital-ians that there were real limitations to the neoreformist strategy offered by De Man and others. Uncertain of their future and torn by incompatible al-ternatives, the PSI seemed adrift on the eve of the events in Spain that were to change the whole context of cooperation on the Left.[36]

A Foreign Policy for a Dying Europe

During the years leading up to the Spanish Civil War Tasca was increasingly caught up in the intricacies of foreign policy. He started writing a regular column on foreign affairs for *Le Populaire* in February 1934. His prominent role as commentator on international relations for the SFIO's daily paper made it urgent that he regularize his status in France. To avoid attacks from the Right, Tasca formally applied for and was granted French citizenship on 7 August 1936.

A few months after beginning work at *Le Populaire*, Tasca assumed a similar function for the *Nuovo Avanti*. From 1937 to 1939 he wrote about foreign affairs for the Radical weekly *Lumière* and in 1938 and 1939 contributed still another regular column to the Popular Front papers, *Oran Républicain* and *Alger Républicain*. Finally, in 1940 he joined a number of anti-Munich French socialists to publish the weekly *Agir*, which was dedicated to mobilizing opinion on the Left in favor of greater resistance to Germany.

CONFLICT OVER FOREIGN POLICY WITHIN THE SFIO

When Tasca began to write for *Le Populaire*, the French Socialist party was about to enter a debate over foreign policy that would carry it to total paralysis. The political director of *Le Populaire* was Léon Blum. In charge of the foreign desk was Oreste Rosenfeld, Blum's friend and associate editor. Neither man worked from a dogmatic position in foreign policy. Blum, especially, coupled pragmatism with a passionate desire for peace and a firm belief in collective security. Like the majority of socialists, he believed that war and capitalism were intertwined but broke with many in the SFIO by distinguishing the bourgeois democracies from the rising Fascist powers. Moreover, Blum was willing to accept traditional foreign policy initiatives, such as the Franco-Soviet alliance of 1935, if they could be seen as reinforcing collective security.[1]

Up to 1935 there was a consensus on foreign policy within the SFIO, not because all factions held the same views, but because the issues that arose did not yet test the party in a divisive way. Even the Nazi victory of 1933 did not immediately force rethinking of fundamental positions. At the Thirtieth Congress in July 1933, apart from the Neosocialists, only two speakers, Salomon Grumbach and Georges Weill, dealt with the Nazis as a serious threat to peace. The majority, including Blum, rallied behind the Faure-Bracke motion against any alteration in the policy against participation in bourgeois governments under pressure from foreign or domestic crisis. The threat from Hitler tended to reinforce the pacifism within the SFIO.[2]

The political balance within the French Socialist party was held together by a fragile understanding between Léon Blum and Paul Faure. Faure was a pacifist in foreign policy who had bitter memories of the cooperation offered to the government by the French socialists during the early years of World War I. He was equally firm in his hostility to the Bolshevik Revolution and to the French Communist party. At the Congress of Tours in December 1920 Faure had been on the losing side as the victorious Communists took control of the party newspaper and political organization. Faure welded the SFIO apparatus back together after Tours and had a strong emotional attachment to it. In Faure's eyes, party unity was paramount; when the Neosocialists threatened this unity in 1933 with their call for participation in the Daladier government, Faure fought them. Unity of Action was an even more insidious threat, because, like Tasca, Faure believed that the primary aim of the Communist party was the destruction of their Socialist rivals. Thus, a combination of pacifism and anticommunism made Faure suspicious of the alliance between France and the USSR, collective security through the League of Nations, and support for national defense. On Faure's left were the revolutionary defeatists led by the charismatic Marceau Pivert. This faction comprised a heterogeneous mixture of ex-Communists, Trotskyists, and Left socialists who were united on an antireformist, antiparliamentary, and antiwar program. The revolutionary left wing of the SFIO was hostile to meeting the Fascist danger through conventional alliances or through collective security. Moreover a substantial part was also fiercely anticommunist. It would, however, remain within the general party consensus until late 1936 and early 1937, when differences over domestic and foreign policy led Marceau Pivert to break with Blum.

Between 1934 and 1936 the bond holding the various currents within the SFIO began to dissolve. Unity of Action with the Communists was an important step in undermining the consensus because it increased fears of anticommunists on both left and right in the party that the PCF would use the pact to maneuver the Socialists into supporting a war in defense of the USSR. The outbreak of hostilities between Italy and Ethiopia in 1935 showed the question of sanctions and support of the League of Nations in a new light. Blum tended to support the League, but the party's Left and center did not. Similarly, the signing of the Franco-Soviet treaty and the PCF's shift in favor of national defense expenditures increased the suspicions of the Faurists against the Communists.

Blum was trapped between his desire to react to Fascist aggression and the knowledge that any break with party tradition would lead to a revolt by the revolutionary Left and the pacifist center. Some support for Blum existed on the far Left from Jean Zyromski and his followers. Zyromski, a former ally of Marceau Pivert and a leader in the Paris federation, reacted to the rise of Hitler by severing relations with his former friends and advocating Unity of Action with the PCF, the alliance with the USSR, and the formation of a Popular Front. In 1935 he joined with the Russian Menshevik Theodor Dan, the Austrian Otto Bauer, and Amedée Dunois to publish a pamphlet, *L'Internationale et la Guerre*, that urged the socialists to consider supporting national defense in the name of antifascism.

Given the often incompatible points of view, the SFIO most easily defined its policy in negative terms: opposition to the Versailles system, to national defense, and to traditional power politics. Apart from a few mavericks like Zyromski, it was difficult to find many on the party's left who would draft a positive response to a concrete problem. They simply refused to distinguish between Hitler's and other forms of bourgeois government.[3]

TASCA'S ANTIFASCIST FOREIGN POLICY

Tasca began to write for *Le Populaire* as a supporter of Blum's flexible policies. In his articles he sought to educate the readers about the complexities of international politics. The articles often dealt with the underlying connections between foreign and domestic policies, such as that between the rightist policy of Colonel Beck and Poland's rapprochement with Hitler after 1934 or destruction of the Austrian Left by the clerical conservative government of Dollfuss, which removed one of the strongest internal obstacles to Anschluss with Germany.[4]

The Italian Fascist regime was a frequent target. Tasca argued that the failure of corporative economic policy to solve Italy's economic crisis increased the internal pressure on the regime and the danger of war. The whole purpose of the Fascist-controlled economy was war preparation.

Therefore, concessions to Mussolini would not necessarily ease the danger of conflict: "There is everywhere a close and direct relationship between the rise of fascism within countries and the rise of international conflict."[5] Tasca never considered Mussolini to be other than an unprincipled opportunist. Yet Tasca, like Blum, was willing to support a short-term agreement with Italy if it seemed to advance the cause of peace. Consequently, his reaction was skeptical but not absolutely hostile to Laval's overtures to Mussolini in 1935. Tasca noted, however, that Mussolini came away with suspiciously little from his January meeting with Laval. Far too little had been offered to entice Mussolini into a status quo bloc for Central Europe. In the *Nuovo Avanti*, Tasca drew the correct conclusion that a bargain might have been struck for Ethiopia and almost immediately thereafter introduced this theme in his column for *Le Populaire*.[6] Similarly, Tasca called the April 1935 Stresa conference between England, France, and Italy a defeat for the League and for collective security and guessed that Mussolini had been given a free hand in Ethiopia.[7]

Tasca correctly perceived that a fundamental defect in any anti-German block was England's refusal to commit itself. His worst suspicions about British wavering were confirmed with the announcement of the Anglo-German Naval Accord in June, which marked the end of the Stresa Front. Temporarily at least, the failure of traditional diplomacy convinced Tasca that Unity of Action was still necessary because only the united pressure from the Socialist and Communist workers could impress on the governments the general desire for peace.[8]

When Mussolini attacked Ethiopia, the tone of Tasca's articles was uncompromising. He portrayed it as an assault against Europe, the League, and the entire structure of the peace. British and French efforts to compromise with Italy, reflected in the Hoare Laval proposals, were a complete concession to aggression. When the plan collapsed, Tasca felt that the French and British governments had wrecked the League and had lost Italy nevertheless: "Nice work, no," he commented bitterly.[9]

EDUCATING THE LEFT ON FOREIGN POLICY

Tasca was convinced that the European Socialist parties had never given adequate attention to foreign policy. In early 1935 he tried to interest the British Labour party in the publication of a Europe-wide foreign policy bulletin for the Socialist movement: "First the leaders and then the membership must realize that peace and the interests of the working masses in all countries cannot be defended without 'putting one's hands in the European mud.'"[10] The entire strategy of the socialist movement had to be revised in the light of the international situation. Even when Tasca was writing for *Monde*, his sole justification for Unity of Action was that it was a tool to defend the peace. In the Socialist press between 1934 and 1938 he continued to press this case. Thus, although Tasca supported Unity of Action for different reasons than did Nenni, he was no less sincere than the party secretary in 1935 and 1936. His preoccupation with foreign policy also explains why Tasca was less responsive to Faravelli's urgings for a stronger stand against Nenni's policies.

Tasca also joined Blum and Nenni in supporting the Franco-Soviet pact. They all viewed the treaty as an essential weapon to counter Hitler, even if they had some doubts about the national defense ramifications of the pact. An editorial in the *Nuovo Avanti*, which bore the imprint of Tasca, argued forcefully that the USSR worked for peace and collective security. The only limit placed on this blanket approval was a warning that the Socialists might not support a declaration of war, even if the USSR were involved.[11]

Tasca's midyear assessment for 1936 in the *Nuovo Avanti* described the total deterioration of the European order: the collapse of sanctions against Italy, the rupture of Anglo-French cooperation, the crisis of the League, and the newfound freedom for Fascist Italy and Germany. In view of this totally passive balance, Tasca seemed closer to Nenni and Saragat, who urged a policy of clear resistance to the Fascist regimes. But a new split within the PSI became evident when Modigliani reiterated the traditional socialist position against support for bourgeois wars. This debate merged with that over Unity of Action. Saragat and, to a lesser extent, Tasca favored the alliance with the Communists and support for the USSR. Modigliani brought forward the party's pacifist heritage, now buttressed by the suspicion that Unity of Action served only the interests of the Soviet state.[12]

THE MOSCOW PURGE TRIALS

Yet another issue arose to complicate the debate over Unity of Action. From August to October 1936 the *Nuovo Avanti* covered the Soviet purge trials of Zinoviev and Kamenev with mounting incredulity. The Socialists attacked the seemingly forced confessions, the immediate death sentences, and the strange conclusion that Stalin was the only old Bolshevik who did not betray the revolution.[13] On 5 September Tasca linked the trials with Soviet foreign policy and the Unity of Action pact: The USSR could hardly convince the world that it was working for peace if it terrorized its own people. He could not understand "how they could condemn to death sixteen militants for only *planning* terrorist acts." How could the Communists wage a battle for the right of exile when they pressured the Norwegian government to expel Leon Trotsky? Why, he asked, was any Communist who was not a Stalinist automatically an agent provocateur: "I do not have to say that we have no sympathy for Trotskyism and even less for the Trotskyists; but that does not stop us from repeating that you do not liquidate a movement, not with sixteen, not with thirty-two, executions."[14]

THE SPANISH CIVIL WAR

These and other articles were, in effect, a declaration of war on the Communists and would have carried relations to a new low if the entire political scene had not been altered by the outbreak of the Spanish Civil War. Spain had been on the brink of open political warfare since the victory of the Popular Front in the elections of February 1936. But the military revolt against the Spanish Republic, which began on 17 July 1936, had a devastating impact on the French and Italian Left. The Spanish experience offered a graphic example of how much more dynamic and resourceful the Communists were than the Socialists. Aided by the USSR, the Communists advanced from a minor party in the Popular Front coalition, when they won only sixteen seats, to a major force in the unions and in the army. But it was not so much the policies of the Spanish Communist party as the wholesale importation of Stalinist methods of political repression into Spain that particularly alarmed many Socialists. The consequences of Spanish internal politics inevitably spilled over into France, where the split between those who favored and those who opposed Unity of Action within the socialist movement deepened. This, in turn, contributed to the disintegration of the SFIO as a political force in the waning days of the Third Republic. Perhaps most painful of all, Spain confronted the Socialists with political choices that were extraordinarily difficult. The French Socialists saw no alternative but to support the alliance between Communists and Socialists in Spain and had little option but to continue the policy of official French neutrality between the contending factions in Spain, if they wanted their own Popular Front government to survive. Yet nonintervention was one of the most unpopular policies of the Blum government and continued to sap the vitality of the French government, while gaining Blum no support on the center and right of the political spectrum.[15]

Léon Blum's Popular Front government, which had been formed in May, expected opposition from conservatives and Catholics to whatever stand it took in favor of Republican Spain. Fearing such pressures and pushed by England and a sizable segment of both the French Radical and Socialist parties, the French government opted for nonintervention between the legitimate Republican government of Spain and the military rebels at the beginning of August. The unequivocal support for the Spanish Republic by the French Communist party, which was in the Popular Front coalition although outside the government, led Paul Faure and his supporters to accuse the Communists of betrayal. As the war in Spain continued, the pacifism and anticommunism of the Faurists became one. Yet, even those who supported aid for Spain but sided with Blum through loyalty about nonintervention found the war to be a long ordeal in which their political sympathies were completely at odds with government policies.

The Spanish Civil War demonstrated the inapplicability of the lessons of the Great War to the political world of the 1930s. For almost fifteen years pacifism had been a dogma. The struggle against Franco's forces in Spain revealed that antifascism and pacifism might conflict. Many on the extreme Left had no idea of how to provide effective aid to the Spanish Republicans without involving the government. As a result, some were forced closer to the militant antifascism of Zyromski. Yet the war also had the effect of increasing bitterness toward the Soviet Union because of clear evidence of the persecution in Spain of the Partido Obrero de Unificación Marxista (POUM) and the Trotskyists by Stalin's agents. Moreover, the development of the United Front in Spain was hardly reassuring. In March 1936 the youth organizations of the Spanish Socialist and Communist parties agreed to merge on the basis of a Communist proposal.[16]

The first reaction of Le Populaire to the war was extremely cautious. Tasca, who sought to resolve the problem of aiding the Spanish Republic without destroying the Popular Front, stressed that the victory of the Popular Front in the Spanish elections in February 1936 and in France shortly thereafter had greatly enhanced the value of the Franco-Soviet pact. He felt that within Spain the anarchists might cause problems but saw no serious issues arising to trouble relations between the Spanish Socialist and Communist parties.[17]

RENEWED FRICTION BETWEEN THE PSI AND PCI
The news from Spain did not improve relations between the PSI and the PCI. Both parties actively mobilized to offer aid to the Spanish Republicans. Nenni visited Spain as part of a delegation of the Socialist International and came back more than ever convinced of the necessity for a United Front as the nucleus of resistance to fascism. But his desire to make the Socialist-Communist alliance the focal point of both parties' activities continued to conflict with the Communists' multifront strategy. Nenni's position was further complicated by his being in the minority within the deeply divided Socialist International. The Communist International had proposed a joint meeting to plan common action with the Socialists; it was held on 14 October but had little impact. In a letter to Nenni, Grieco criticized the PSI's inability to do more to produce an international United Front.[18]

THE UNITED FRONT WITHIN ITALY
The Communists also continued to push for their policy of persuading the Centro Interno Socialista (CSI) to accepting the Communist strategy of working within the Fascist unions. Nenni wrote to Tasca on 16 October for

advice about responding to the Communist proposals. He was especially concerned that the PCI seemed to consider the Fascist unions as true worker organizations. He also called "grotesque" another suggestion of the PCI that the somewhat radical Fascist program of 1919 might be used as the basis for propaganda in Italy.[19]

No copy of Tasca's response exists, but Nenni's letter to the PCI on 20 October was a blanket rejection of the Communist proposals. A week later Nenni raised another delicate issue; throughout the summer the PCI had singled out Modigliani for special attack because of his open and oft-stated opposition to both Unity of Action and the Franco-Soviet alliance. Although Nenni did not agree with Modigliani, the tone of the exchange forced him to defend the right of any socialist to criticize the policies of the PCF or the USSR. The exchange of letters emphasized the differences between the two parties on a number of issues. The Socialists rejected the Communist position that Spain was more important than Ethiopia. Nenni advocated the maintenance of sanctions against Italy and refused to curb party criticism of the Moscow purge trials. The two parties had come to an impasse on the question of strategy within Italy when the PSI announced that it would not be associated in any way with any appeal to "honest Fascists." Finally, the Socialists were angry about the increasingly hostile attitude taken by the PCI toward the Blum government. Sensitivity increased because the Socialists themselves were unhappy with nonintervention in Spain.[20]

GROWING DISCONTENT OVER SPAIN

As 1936 drew to a close, the differences between Socialists and Communists seemed to increase; yet the Spanish war was the overriding reality that kept them together. In a letter to Faravelli in early December, Tasca summarized the problem for the PSI. He urged the party to continue its unpalatable policy of working with the Communists and the equally unappetizing support for nonintervention. He made the same point in an editorial in the *Nuovo Avanti* on 12 December that attacked the French Communists for causing difficulties for the Blum government: "By continuing on this tack, not only will they eventually force the government to resign, but they will undermine among its own voters the authority which is vital for effective exercise of power."[21]

Tasca's writing about Spain reflected the perplexity and fear that plagued the Socialists as they contemplated the future. In *Le Populaire* on 21 December he described the fusion of the Catalan Socialist and Communist parties and the association of the unified party with the Comintern. This merger led to the ouster of the Trotskyist POUM from the government of Catalonia. That these events were simultaneous with the Moscow trials of August 1936 through January 1937 that convicted Zinoviev,

Kamenev, and Radek as Trotskyist agents only increased the tension. Nevertheless, Tasca reluctantly accepted the merger of the Catalan parties and the ouster of the POUM on the ground that the needs of the common struggle ought to prevail over advantages to any single party. His political judgment made him side with the Communists who preferred to defer revolutionary change until after the civil war. Yet, despite his scant sympathy for Trotsky and the anarchists, Tasca understood the dangers in their suppression. Like the entire Socialist movement, Tasca was forced to choose among unattractive alternatives.[22]

Another, potentially more dangerous, issue arose from Tasca's analysis of the consequences of the Spanish war on the SFIO. In a letter to Nenni he described the way that Communist exploitation of the unpopularity of nonintervention worked against sympathy for the Republican cause among many French Socialists "because it provoked on all levels of the Socialist party a self-defense mechanism which threatens the Spanish cause. By tying the question of aid for the Spanish Republic and the offensive against the government, especially against Blum, they [the French Communists] have created a terrible, but inevitable, situation, for which they share direct responsibility." Tasca felt that the Communists ought to limit their pressure on the government to the strict necessities of the war in Spain rather than launch a general attack: "By trying to kill two birds with the same stone, they are playing into the hands of their enemies." More ominous was the Communist effort to gain control of the CGT, which,

> if it succeeds, will totally alter the political situation in France and will begin to liquidate at the same time the Popular Front and Socialist-Communist Unity of Action. Moreover a blast of anticommunism will be unleashed which will sweep part of the SFIO and the old union leadership. That will certainly lead to a profoundly reactionary situation.

Tasca correctly foresaw the crisis that would drive many socialists to defeatism and ultimately to Vichy. The efforts to escape from the pressures of national and international events would split both the French and the Italian Socialist parties. Spain, which might have served as a link to bind the United Front, gradually became a principal cause for rupture. Moreover, the rupture would not be healed but would prolong itself into the war and postwar periods and would cripple the socialists as a political force in both France and Italy.[23]

The Renewal of Unity of Action

Tasca had not taken a leading role in the debates over Spain and had adopted a loyal, if critical, stand on cooperation with the PCI. Pressures on him to oppose Unity of Action increased as it became clear in 1937 that the pact would either have to be renewed or lapse. The anticommunism of the minority within the PSI became more intense as time passed, but they had no alternative to offer to the party. Moreover, the debate was complicated by the spectacular purge trials in Moscow, the breakdown of the Popular Front in France, and increasing evidence of tension between factions in Republican Spain of which the Catalan uprising in May was the most important sign.

Tasca's personal life was greatly altered during this period as well. After a series of sentimental attachments in the early 1930s, he established a lasting relationship with Liliane Chaumette, the ex-wife of the writer Ramón Fernández. Chaumette's background was quite different from Tasca's, probably increasing her attraction to him. She had been a student of Paul Desjardins and had met Tasca through their common interest in Pontigny. According to Charles-André Julien, Chaumette filled Tasca's longing for refinement, a passion that he had largely restricted to his notebooks. Mme. Chaumette's interest in religious problems, the strong idealist formation that she carried from Pontigny, and a kind of contempt for the material world of passions in favor of a rather cold spiritualism strongly influenced Tasca as he entered the final stages of his break with Marxism.[1]

Tasca's relationship with Liliane Chaumette compensated in part for the frenetic pace of his political activities. In 1937 he was a member of the

Direzione of the PSI and a regular contributor to the *Nuovo Avanti, Le Populaire, Lumière,* and *Oran Républicain,* a new paper sponsored by the Popular Front in Algeria. He was codirector of the CSI and engaged in the final stages of his *Rise of Italian Fascism.* Finally, around this time, Tasca, who had become a French citizen in August 1936, joined the French radio to direct the Italian-language broadcasts. Within the SFIO he was more than ever associated with the foreign policy of Léon Blum and of the antifascist wing of French socialism. Thus, despite his neo-revisionism and hostility to the Communist party, Tasca supported the concept of the United Front and took a relatively favorable attitude toward the USSR in his writings for *Le Populaire* and *Oran Républicain.*[2]

PROBLEMS WITHIN THE SFIO

The SFIO was experiencing increasing stress in 1937. Blum attempted to hold the party together by emphasizing collective security and the unity of the democracies, but he avoided a full-scale debate within the party on national defense. His allies, Salomon Grumbach and Louis Lévy, led the battle, along with Jean Zyromski on the Left and Marx Dormoy, Jean Monnet, and André Philip of the Blumist center-Right. Increasingly overt in his opposition to the Communists and in his insistence on absolute pacifism was the powerful leader of the SFIO's administrative apparatus, Paul Faure. Faure was joined by a heterodox group of recruits from Right and Left, syndicalists, and old militant pacifists, such as J.-B. Séverac, René Belin, Charles Spinasse, and Louis L'Hévéder.[3]

Within the SFIO Tasca's hostility to the USSR and to the French Communist party made him a logical ally of Faure, but his political ties were all on the other side in 1937. Moreover, he favored a firm response to Fascist aggression and had never been a doctrinaire pacifist. From 1936 to 1940 Tasca sought the correct combination of political, diplomatic, and military power with which to resist the Fascist powers. His hostility to the USSR did not push him toward a policy of abdication but led him to substitute Roosevelt's America for the Soviets in the antifascist front.[4]

THE MOSCOW TRIALS RESUME

Throughout 1937 Tasca was drawn into a more public position against the USSR. In January 1937 a new series of Moscow purge trials in which Trotsky served as the chief target became a pretext for a Comintern Europe-wide campaign against Trotskyist organizations. The Socialists were obliged to acknowledge the trials despite their alliance with the Communists, but they found accepting the events in the Moscow courtroom increasingly difficult. For their part, the Communists complicated matters by making acceptance of the trials a test of cooperation in Spain.[5]

The first indication of trouble came not from the trials themselves but from André Gide's celebrated *Retour de l'Urss*, in which the author, who had previously been lionized by the Soviets, bitterly criticized Soviet life. The book created a sensation when it was published in November 1936. It received a relatively favorable review in the *Nuovo Avanti*, but Saragat, who might have been expected to be sympathetic to Gide, attacked both the timing and the content as detrimental to the antifascist cause.[6]

Saragat's sensitivity underlined the problem that the Socialists faced in their treatment of the Moscow trials. On 30 January the *Nuovo Avanti* balanced a notice that the trials were occurring with Trotsky's denials of counterrevolutionary activity. Tasca wrote a relatively factual article for *Le Populaire* on 23 January that related that in their trial Zinoviev and Kamenev had implicated Radek, Piatakov, Tomsky, Bukharin, and Rykov. He limited himself to biographical information about the major defendants.[7] Only Giuseppe Faravelli threw caution to the winds with a bitter article against the trial as a Stalinist perversion and linked the trials to the systematic persecution of the Trotskyist POUM in Spain. The *Nuovo Avanti* coupled this article with a warning to the Communists to stop using joint meetings for Spain to make propaganda for the Moscow trials.[8]

THE PCI AND THE MOSCOW TRIALS

The PCI had attempted to preempt such criticism. The *Stato operaio* openly accused Radek and Piatakov of working with Trotsky on orders from the Fascists. One of the channels of such influence was said to be the Socialist International and the PSI, which refused to purge Trotskyists from its midst and even included their supporters in its leadership.[9] Dozza went even further: "Certain articles by antifascists and certain others which were dictated by the Propaganda Ministry in Rome resemble each other like two drops of water." Dozza singled out Lombardi (Faravelli) and in retaliation broke off all relations with him as liaison with the CSI.[10]

The Socialists could hardly afford to remain silent before such a frontal assault. On 6 March Tasca wrote to Nenni that the party had to express public solidarity with Theodor Dan, the Russian Menshevik whose name arose in conjunction with the trials. He asked Nenni to issue the protest in the name of the entire Direzione; otherwise, he would raise the issue for discussion at the next meeting.[11]

Faravelli informed Tasca that the CSI totally supported the party's refusal to break relations with the Trotskyists. Yet, even Faravelli was uncertain about the correct way to react; he had absolutely no sympathy for the Trotskyists and felt that the charges against the POUM might have had some basis even if those against the Soviet opposition seemed false. Similar confusion was evident in the reaction of Oddino Morgari, a longtime socialist leader who had been invited to Moscow by the Soviet trade union movement and had been sending back glowing reports to the *Nuovo Avanti*. Morgari's public position belied a growing disquiet, but he feared the use that the Fascists might make of criticism of the USSR. When Morgari accepted the possibility that the charges against the old Bolsheviks might be true, the *Nuovo Avanti* dissented and warned the Communists that they would be making a mistake to turn the issue of the trials into a test of Unity of Action.[12]

THE PCI AND THE SPLIT WITHIN THE PSI

The Communists exploited the differences between Nenni and Saragat and a perceived emerging Tasca-Modigliani-Faravelli opposition. Both Modigliani and Faravelli had received heavy criticism, and Montagnana added Tasca to the list by pointing out that at the next congress of the PSI "the report on the action of the party in Italy will be entrusted to a renegade from our party, known from his writings as a fierce opponent of Unity of Action and as an advocate of anticommunist alliances."[13]

In fact, Tasca was not totally committed to Faravelli and Modigliani at that time, and the substantive differences between Tasca and Nenni over the alliance with the Communists in Spain and France were still manageable. However, Ruggiero Grieco tried to accentuate them by arguing that Tasca's loyalty to the Blum government put him out of step with the PSI. Tasca denied that he differed with his party over Spain and accused the Communists of trying to set the leaders of the PSI against one another.[14]

THE UNIONE POPOLARE ITALIANA AND
LA VOCE DEGLI ITALIANI

An issue arose that would eventually create friction between Tasca and Nenni, however. Since 1933 the Communists had been promoting the Fronte Unico, an organization controlled by the PCI that appealed to members of all parties (the united front from below). The Socialists insisted that cooperation occur primarily between parties and asserted that United Front organizations based on individual memberships merely represented an effort to raid the Socialist mass following. The Communists decided to disregard the PSI's objections and moved ahead with plans to transform the Fronte Unico by calling it the *Unione Popolare Italiana* (UPI) and opening it to all Italians of good will. In February 1937 the PCI proposed the creation of a new daily newspaper that would be the organ of a Communist-sponsored organization of antifascist Italians. In April at the inaugural Congress of Lyons, plans for the *Voce degli italiani*, the new daily, were announced by Romano Cocchi, the secretary general of the UPI and a member of the PCI's Central Committee. If the mere existence of the UPI were not sufficient, Alessandro Bocconi, a dissident member of the PSI who had been expelled from the Direzione for lack of discipline on the Fronte Unico issue, was prominently featured in the leadership of the UPI.[15]

Nenni's relatively mild response provoked both Faravelli and Modigliani, who felt that continued weakness only invited the Communists to interfere in the internal affairs of the PSI and objected particularly to the Communist attack on Tasca's role at the next congress.[16] In an ill-timed gesture, Pietro Nenni, writing under the pseudonym *Pietro Emiliani*, launched a proposal to revise and strengthen the Unity of Action pact. He also expressed optimism that the problems with the PCI relating to the Unione Popolare might be resolved. Nenni's conciliatory stand further outraged Modigliani, who accused the party secretary of trying to change policy on cooperation with the Communists.[17]

GRAMSCI'S DEATH

During most of 1937 Tasca was strangely absent from the political battles of the Italian Left. He did, however, publish two important articles to commemorate Gramsci's death on 27 April 1937, which revealed the political danger he posed to the Communist party. Except Togliatti, Gramsci's close collaborators were either in prison or in opposition. Tasca, with his prestige as an old militant and his rich archive, threatened the PCI's monopoly of the Gramsci legacy. He gave a concrete example of how troublesome he could be when he revealed Gramsci's letter of October 1926 in which the leader of the PCI expressed his concern about the struggles within the Soviet party and other documents about conflicts in 1923 and 1924 between Togliatti and Gramsci about the former's continued support for Bordiga. Ruggiero Grieco accused Tasca of defaming Gramsci and of publishing stolen correspondence, a charge that Tasca vehemently denied. He retorted somewhat disingenuously that these publications were merely designed to augment the historical record. That they cast Togliatti in an unfavorable light was purely coincidental![18]

Yet Tasca still moved cautiously in attacking the Communists. He refused to allow the death of the anarchist Camillo Berneri at the hands of the Stalinist agents during the May uprising in Barcelona to enter the polemic with the PCI. Tasca wrote a relatively cautious obituary for the *Nuovo Avanti* and rejected all appeals to do battle with Nenni over the treatment of the anarchists in Spain. Throughout early 1937 Tasca supported cooperation between Socialists and Communists in both France and Spain. He agreed that Nenni was too willing to make sacrifices in the name of Unity of Action, but he refused to take the leadership of the anticommunist minority.[19]

THE SOCIALIST PARTY CONGRESS

Only at the party congress on 26–28 June 1937, did Tasca begin to emerge as an alternative to Nenni. The discussions at the congress revolved around the contrasting positions of the two men. Nenni argued that there was ample ground for resolving the points of conflict with the PCI. He felt that the Socialists ought to discuss all issues with the Communists, including that of the UPI. He also emphasized that the international situation made ending Unity of Action impossible. The Socialist-Communist alliance had to be the basis of all other policies because, unlike in France, there was no possibility of a true Popular Front inside or outside Italy.[20]

Tasca spoke for all those who had doubts about Unity of Action, but he had not as yet an alternative policy to replace the alliance with the PCI, which remained popular among most socialist militants. He argued that the change from social fascism to unity of action represented no fundamental ideological revision by the Communists but was dictated more by the needs of Soviet foreign policy. Yet Tasca partially undercut his own argument by stating that he agreed with current Soviet policy. The crux of his argument was that Unity of Action need not be the sole means of waging the struggle against fascism. The PSI had to reach out on its right as well as on its left to create a broad antifascist front. On the international level such an alliance would include London and Paris, where the Communists were not dominant, as well as Moscow.[21] Tasca also attacked Nenni for caring too little about principles. The secretary's predisposition to action was a disadvantage in dealing with the Communists. Unity of Action was possible only when the Socialists had a clear idea of their own goals. Nenni tended, perhaps wisely, to postpone detailed discussion about programs for a postfascist Italy.[22]

Most of the speakers who followed Nenni and Tasca realized that there was no alternative to Unity of Action. Saragat, especially, took the position that the crumbling international order left little recourse but proletarian solidarity. In the end the congress gave Nenni an ample mandate to negotiate a new pact with the PCI. The new party directorate reflected the outcome of the congress. Its members tended to favor Nenni, although Saragat and Rugginenti had been close to Tasca in the past.[23]

After the congress Tasca was again pressured by Chiaromonte and Silone to continue his leadership of the anti-Nenni opposition. Tasca had been working to draw Silone into the PSI, but without much success because of Silone's antipathy to Nenni's style of leadership: "Nenni embodies all that was negative about Serrati—a certain demagoguery, a certain superficiality, a certain habit of playing dumb when serious questions are under discussion. . . . Nenni is not the entire leadership of the party but he is the director of the paper."[24] Tasca's inability to enlist Silone or other close friends with whom he could work into the party might account for his unwillingness to yield to those inside and outside the PSI who wanted him to confront Nenni. Some of this irritation was evident in a letter to Chiaromonte in which he complained of those who

> stand by the window clapping their hands if I write an "interesting," "reasonable," "courageous" article, as if to say: you are all right, but Nenni, but the Socialist party, but Blum, but France, but the devil. . . . Silone writes to assure me that he is in total agreement, but no sooner than I suggest to him to take a certain initiative, he tells me that some speech of Saragat is unbearable, that some article of Nenni etc. etc.

Chiaromonte, like the others, responded that it was not a question of doing nothing. He was more than willing to work with Tasca but not with the PSI or the SFIO, whose policies held no appeal whatsoever.[25]

Nenni, for whom the congress represented a victory, was determined not to allow the reopening of the debates that had earlier soured relations with the Communists. He attacked those who wished to use the death of Berneri to question the role played by the Communists in Spain and, writing in the Communist-controlled *Voce degli italiani*, he openly doubted the loyalty of the anarchists in Barcelona. In the *Nuovo Avanti* Nenni insisted that any attempt to criticize the USSR for its conduct of the purge trials was criminal in light of the aid that the Communists gave in Spain.[26]

If Tasca seemed to mute his criticism of Nenni, he was much less tolerant toward Saragat, with whom he had had good relations. Giuseppe Saragat, who would head the post–World War II Social Democratic party and would eventually serve as president of the Republic, began his career as a member of the reformist Partito Socialista Unitario in 1922. He went into exile in Austria in 1926, where he fell under the influence of Otto Bauer's version of Austro-Marxism. By the early 1930s Saragat seemed to be a firm ally of the right wing of the party, but the rise of Nazism changed all that. He swallowed his reservations about an alliance with the PCI, backed Nenni wholeheartedly on the question of Unity of Action, and made it clear that the weakness of the democracies left little choice but to give full support to the USSR: ". . . under present circumstances one thing is certain: the future of French democracy, of the French proletariat, is tied to the life or death accord with the Russian state."[27] Ungenerously, Tasca regarded Saragat's shift to Nenni as a betrayal and attributed his wholehearted support for the alliance with the USSR to a feeling of guilt about failing to volunteer for the war in Spain: "He remained with an 'inferiority complex' which he more or less compensates for by enthusing about those who did go and thus about the Communists and the USSR." Not only was this assertion untrue, but Saragat, like Nenni and unlike Tasca, clearly was willing to sacrifice almost anything to the primary goal of defeating Hitler and Mussolini.[28]

UNITY OF ACTION RENEWED AND APPRAISED

Negotiations for a new Unity of Action pact began immediately after the end of the Socialist congress and were concluded by 25 July 1937. The pact represented some advance over that of 1934. Its aim was the establishment of an Italian democratic republic based on the workers and the peasants. The pact advocated the unification of all parties and organizations in an Italian Popular Front, and the Socialists accepted the formation of the UPI as a first step in that direction. Divergences between the two parties over the means of waging the battle within Italy were overcome by the ambiguous formula urging exploitation of all the legal possibilities offered by the regime. Support for the Spanish Republic, for collective security, and for the defense of the USSR were included. Furthermore, the two parties agreed to strive for organic unity and for greater cooperation between the respective Internationals. Both parties maintained their organizational and ideological independence, limited only by the commitment to work in a disciplined manner to further Unity of Action on all levels.[29]

Although the terms of the Unity of Action pact were sufficiently vague to satisfy all sides, the pact itself continued to be a burden on the Socialist party. The PSI was constantly forced into a reactive position by the PCI. Although this might have happened even without the pact, the fact remains that the Socialists were simply too slow and too ideologically divided to maintain their equality with the PCI. This disadvantage was worsened by Nenni's belief that the PSI was too weak to act alone. Thus, for as long as the pact lasted (from 1934 to 1956, with the exception of the rupture at the time of the Stalin-Hitler pact), the PSI lost ground to the Communists. It should be pointed out, however, that the Socialists fared little better after they broke the alliance with the Communists and moved to the right during the late 1950s. It was likely that the historic position that the PSI occupied between outright social democracy and revolutionary socialism had been undermined and that the PCI had become the great party of the Italian Left.

Despite the leadership's desire to avoid continued polemics with the PCI, the minority within the Socialist party was determined to limit as far as possible the consequences of the new pact. Simultaneously the majority called for disciplinary action against the minority. The *Nuovo Avanti* reassured the opposition that there was no question of overt discipline but warned that continued polemics weakened the Socialist party.[30] When

Rugginenti wrote to Tasca to ask his advice about publishing the renewed debate, Tasca felt that it should be a collective decision of the Direzione. He voiced his own fears that a loose interpretation of Article 11 of the pact, which pledged that each party would not disrupt the functioning of the alliance, might allow the Communists to interfere in the PSI's internal debates, especially with regard to the Trotskyists. The possibility of a conflict with the minority depended on Nenni's attitude. If the party secretary stayed within the limits imposed by the congress, all would be well: "As far as it depends on us, we must save Unity of Action. . . . On the other hand, you know how much I believe in the need for safeguarding the political, ideological, and organizational autonomy of the Socialist movement in all those areas which are outside of unity of action."[31]

INTERNATIONAL POLITICS AND THE UNITED FRONT

Tasca also made it clear to Nenni that the main justification for the pact was the international situation: "I think that we will be increasingly forced in the future to shift the axis of our 'alliance' with the USSR (and therefore with Stalin) to the level of foreign policy because, there, above all, active mutual interests—dominant interests—exist." His only reservation, a major one, concerned Soviet policy in Spain: "I would certainly not have spoken of 'Moscow's policy in Madrid' because that might give the impression that we approved of that entire policy, including the methods which you yourself judge to risk compromising victory."[32]

Despite their disagreements, the three key figures in the PSI—Nenni, Tasca, and Saragat—still shared a common vision of the international situation that provided the basis for their cooperation within the party. All three leaders believed that Europe was moving toward war. None accepted Modigliani's dogmatic pacifism, and each sought to bring the party to confront reality. As Saragat stated: "I also believe that we are on the brink of another war. I don't see how Mussolini can or will back down. On the other side, France has arrived at the extreme limit of its concessions. For us it is a question of preparing the party for the terrible situation which is unfolding."[33]

Tasca's analysis of the international situation also seemed to point in the direction of urgent action to support the resistance of the democracies against fascism. In a background paper for a report by Nenni to the Socialist International in March 1937, he outlined his views on the Fascist danger. He described the Fascist powers as following a coherent and coordinated foreign policy in Spain, Eastern Europe, and the Balkans. The Spanish war was a test both of collective security and of the will of Britain and France to resist aggression. Throughout the year Tasca continued to insist that there was little room for an accommodation with the Axis states.

Clearly he interpreted Hitler's *Mein Kampf* literally, especially in regard to the admonition to separate France from its potential allies. As Tasca saw it, by the end of 1937 France was already surrounded by hostile powers. England had lost ground in the Mediterranean, and the USSR was cut off from an active role in the European balance. The only comforting news came from the United States, where Tasca predicted with amazing accuracy the future course of American policy: "Personally we think that, despite all the 'neutrality acts,' the United States cannot remain absent from the future war, precisely because it will not just be European but worldwide. But the road which will lead to intervention will pass this time by way of the Pacific and not the Atlantic." [34]

TASCA'S GROWING HOSTILITY TO THE USSR

A disquieting note in Tasca's writing at the end of 1937 was his increasing hostility to the USSR. He stressed the danger to the Soviet state from Germany but then systematically undercut this argument by condemning the Soviet regime as completely contrary to the spirit of socialism. Thus, although the USSR was on the right side in its foreign policy, its domestic policies posed a serious obstacle to support from the European Left. Tasca broke with the majority of Italian socialists on this point. Most agreed with Nenni that the USSR should be supported because its internal system had a certain symbolic value as a concrete realization of socialism. [35]

Tasca's evolution during the late 1930s followed a pattern more common in the French than in the Italian Socialist party. He called on socialists to abandon the concept of the dictatorship of the proletariat in favor of a simple appeal for democracy. Returning again to a recurrent theme in his writing since the early 1930s, Tasca argued that the battle for the allegiance of the petite bourgeoisie demanded much more flexibility than was offered by outmoded concepts such as the dictatorship of the proletariat. The transition from capitalism to socialism involved a much longer time than Marx had proposed:

> In such case the dictatorship of the proletariat will prolong itself for an indeterminate period, losing the character of a transitional, emergency regime. That implies serious inconveniences, above all the risk that an instrument, used for such a long time, begins to substitute itself for the end and destroys it. [36]

Throughout 1937 Tasca remained in a precarious balance. Although he continued to support the Unity of Action pact and the Popular Front in France, he moved to separate support for Soviet foreign policy from the alliance with the Communists. He had not yet drawn the full consequences from such a disjunction. The Communists' attacks on him were also having an effect on a personal level. A diary notation in late December 1937 expressed all the mounting frustration: "To carry out a policy independent of the Communists with the aid of the Communists: 'squaring the circle'?" He still put this idea in the form of a question. The coming year would eliminate all remaining doubts.[37]

PART 3
THE COLD WARRIOR,
1938–1960

11

The Decline of
Unity of Action

The new year, 1938, was a turning point for Tasca. By the end of the year, his rupture with Nenni would be consummated, and he would come to oppose openly the alliance with the Communists. Politically and ideologically he moved to the right, abandoning any vestiges of Marxism and reading back into the entire Marxist tradition his disenchantment with the Bolshevik Revolution and with Stalinist Russia.

The year began on a note of triumph with the publication of *The Rise of Fascism*. This book, more than any other achievement, assured Tasca a place among historians of modern Italy. Not only was it a confirmation of his considerable gifts as a historian, but it was an important contribution to the debate over the future of the European Left on the eve of another war. Tasca provided a neoreformist version of the way fascism might have been defeated and offered a strategy for the late 1930s.

Tasca had three objectives in writing it. First, he sought to analyze the process by which Mussolini took power. Second, he offered a critique of socialism's own revolutionary heritage. *The Rise of Fascism* singled out the Maximalists as primarily responsible for the failure of the PSI between 1918 and 1922. Finally, Tasca charted a future course for French and Italian socialism. His neoreformist critique questioned the applicability of the Bolshevik experience to other societies. The book was a direct challenge to the Communists, as well as to Nenni, who was the foremost representative of the Maximalist tradition in the PSI.

The thesis of *The Rise of Fascism* was that Mussolini attained power as much through the errors of his opponents as through his own abilities. The failure of the Left to provide an outlet for the revolutionary aspirations of Italian society opened the door to fascism. The crucial error occurred when the PSI opted for a frontal assault on the liberal state without the power to carry it through to a victorious revolution. The rejection of any democratic or parliamentary strategy meant that the Socialist party was able to use its strength in parliament only for obstruction and its support in the country for futile attacks on the local level. In short, the Maximalists sought to apply the Bolshevik model to Italy under totally inappropriate conditions.[1]

On the Left there had never been adequate leadership willing to work within the limitations imposed by Italian society: "Above all, what is missing in Italian society is that long evolution, that accumulation of experiences, that predictability of reactions, of habits which made democratic development in England and France possible."[2] The real struggle should have been to create the basis for a modern democracy after 1918. This had been the aim of the PSI's reformists, who proposed their ideas in the party program of 1917 only to see it abandoned a year later in the enthusiasm for revolution.[3]

Some of Tasca's most perceptive analysis was devoted to the social conflicts that led to the rise of fascism in the Po Valley. In this bastion of socialism, potential divisions existed between tenants and small landowners and the landless day laborers and poorer sharecroppers who were organized ino the Socialist peasant leagues. Tasca felt that the demands for collectivization advanced by the Socialists were unrealistic without a parliamentary strategy to ensure adequate financing for land reform. The ambitions of the Socialist cooperatives squeezed the small merchants and farmers. When the Fascist reaction developed, there was room to play off one group against another. Fascism was able to find a rural mass base among the agricultural petite bourgeoisie, which had been alienated by the PSI.[4]

But the Socialists were no more prepared to confront the challenge of reaction than they had been to meet that of revolution. Once again the Maximalists were at fault: "Thus, Italian maximalism is a maximalism of amorphous and chaotic crowds with neither unity of spirit nor outlook."[5] Nor were the Communists any better. Tasca had always criticized the split that took place at Livorno in 1921 as too far to the left. In *The Rise of Fascism* he carried this analysis further by arguing that the new Communist party helped paralyze the socialists by increasing their fears about appearing sufficiently revolutionary. Under Bordiga the PCI played a completely negative role in the development of the crisis leading to fascism:

> In practice they fought against the fascists no more nor less than the others but their stand represented a precious contribution to fascism. For them [the Communists] everything was fascism: the state, the bourgeoisie, democracy,

the socialists. Therefore they had to fight on all fronts. . . . In reality, the Communists only fought seriously and systematically against the socialists.[6]

Neither the Socialists nor the Communists understood the changes that occurred during World War I. The Left was unable to appeal to the veterans or to those who had been socially and psychologically uprooted by the conflict. The war had mobilized large numbers of Italians and sharpened class conflict but left the sociopolitical equilibrium in relative balance. Fascism emerged as an alliance of various elements of the middle class that were offended by socialist militancy. The key to its dynamism was the ability of the industrialists and agrarians to harness the energy of the lower middle classes to their program of capitalist restoration. But fascism was clearly a reactionary movement, even if it rested on a mass base "because its entry [into political life] shifted irrevocably the axis of social and political forces."[7]

Although Tasca appreciated Mussolini's political skills, he gave no hint of admiration. His distaste for the Duce dated from the betrayal of 1914. Tasca contrasted the moral rigor of Giacomo Matteotti with the essential dishonesty of Mussolini, who had never been more than an adventurer in search of more power.[8]

Fascism's only achievement was the militarization of society: "But to become a military nation, [Italy] has ceased to be a nation. The Italian people are an army, not a nation."[9] The concentration of economic power in the hands of the state was designed for war rather than for the collective good. Despite its rhetoric, the regime was in no way anticapitalist; it merely sought to stabilize the system through war. Autarchy and extreme nationalism could not paper over the economic contradictions caused by insufficient consumer demand, overproduction, an inefficient state apparatus, and an ever-worsening financial situation.[10]

From the mid-1920s onward, Tasca had argued that the proletarian base of Italy was so small that an alliance with the lower middle class had to be formed. In a long analysis, written in the 1920s, Tasca noted that the economic policy of the Fascist regime deliberately aimed to slow the rate of growth of the proletariat. In those years Tasca argued that the Italian Communist party would have to adopt a flexible policy that would offer the largest base for alliances with the "middle classes" during an intermediate phase between the fall of fascism and the triumph of the revolution.[11] Tasca lost the debate within the PCI, but he never changed his views on the need to win the support of an important part of the lower middle class to the antifascist struggle. His outline for an antifascist alliance remained controversial, however. He contended that it would be extremely dangerous to force a choice between fascism and bolshevism. Such a choice might force a total identification of fascism with the dominant classes and the state bureaucracy, as occurred between 1919 and 1922. Instead, the struggle had to be conceived as a battle to break up the bourgeois bloc that sustained fascism.[12]

Like the Belgian Henri De Man, Tasca sought an ethical basis, outside Marxism, for his socialism that would appeal to nonproletarians. As he expressed it in his diary:

> The notion of equality among men is the basis of all justice and that concept is not operative, does not involve man completely unless it becomes the capacity to feel the existence, the needs, the dignity of any other man (even our enemy) as our own existence, our own needs and dignity. 'Love others as you would love yourself' is the real, concrete principle underlying justice.

In *The Rise of Fascism* socialism became the effort to subject necessity to human will and to make human values predominate over the economic considerations.[13]

The reaction to Tasca's book varied according to the reviewer's political preference. The most perceptive comment was by "Subalpino" (Umberto Calosso) in *Giustizia e Libertà*, touching on Tasca's political evolution completely away from Marxism in practically all his political analysis. The Austrian Socialist Otto Bauer emphasized that the failures of the PSI were not the whole story. The German and Austrian Socialist parties took positions that were substantially different from that of the PSI, yet with the same results. Thus, Bauer contended, the causes of fascism arose from conditions that might exist independently of the tactics pursued by the socialists. Nothing should excuse the errors, "but it is no less dangerous to try to explain as tactical errors what can only be explained by the development of the class struggle in capitalist society and that no tactic can avoid."[14] If the reformists saw in Tasca's study a vindication of their past and present policies, Nenni gave the book a lukewarm reception and questioned both the excessive blame placed on the Maximalists and the need for a complete change in policy.[15]

THE FUTURE OF THE POPULAR FRONT

The Rise of Fascism became part of the debate over the options open to the socialist movement in 1938. Three questions dominated the debates on the Left at the beginning of the year. There was the continuing polemic over the value of Unity of Action and the Popular Front, a debate further complicated by the ongoing purge trials in the Soviet Union. Finally, looming ever more ominously was the bitter debate over the policy the socialists should adopt in the case of war among the European powers.[16]

Tensions between Socialists and Communists in France and Spain inevitably had an impact on the Italian Left. The PCI stressed the need for continuation of the Popular Front wherever it existed and urged its extension to Italy. The Italian Socialists viewed the decline of the French Popular Front as due in large part to the deteriorating relationship between the PCF and SFIO. The *Nuovo Avanti* blamed the Communists for trying to take advantage both of participation in the coalition and of opposition. Yet most socialists still agreed that there was little alternative to continued cooperation with the Communists.[17]

THE TRIAL OF BUKHARIN

Complicating everything was the furor over the new round of purge trials in the USSR, which threatened to become the catalyst for an anticommunist backlash within the socialist movement. The trials of February and March 1938 touched Tasca more directly than any of the others because they involved Bukharin and Rykov. He made no attempt to hide his disgust: "The indictment with its mixture of the smallest details and crazed hypotheses truly brings to mind certain documents which are well familiar to psychoanalysts." Tasca pointed out the obvious lies such as the accusation that the Menshevik Theodor Dan had worked with Nazi intelligence, that Trotsky accepted subsidies from the German military, and that Magdeleine Paz, Tasca's former colleague at *Monde*, received money to conduct Trotskyist agitation. The reaction of the Communists only worsened the situation. Giuseppe Berti charged the *Nuovo Avanti* of engaging in anti-Soviet activity in violation of its promise to support and defend the USSR. Tasca retorted that the Socialists would abandon neither their right to criticize Soviet conduct nor their support for the overall aims of Soviet foreign policy.[18]

As we have already seen, Tasca's refusal to base support for the USSR on its being the only socialist state undercut a fundamental premise of the Unity of Action pact. Publicly he had not yet arrived at the point of equating Lenin with Stalin; privately, Tasca was much more pessimistic about the evolution of the USSR. He felt that the outcome of the revolutionary process in Russia was simply to have produced another national state. Moreover, the USSR and the Fascist dictatorships seemed to be converging: "Thus, the USSR on the one hand, Germany and Italy on the other might evolve in opposite directions and the two regimes might end by finding themselves, in a certain sense, on the same level while harking back to different ideologies." He noted that Germany and Italy tended to accentuate their "anticapitalism" in preparation for war. Autarchy and extreme nationalism combined to counterbalance the drive for profit and to replace it with the will for power. Similarly, the USSR seemed to emphasize nationalism and autarchy in its economic planning. Tasca argued that the Fascist regimes were becoming less capitalist and the Soviet state more nationalist. In their political practice they shared the mystique of the leader, single-party dictatorship, and controlled mobilization of the masses. Nonetheless, Tasca believed, an alliance between the two systems was impossible: ". . . precisely because they are so much alike the two regimes are irreconcilably opposed; they have in the play, the clash of world powers, a contrary star and are destined to fight each other to the death." By 1938 it almost seemed that his argument for a conflict between the two regimes was less persuasive than his case for their potential alliance.[19]

THE COLLAPSE OF AUSTRIA AND THE DANGER OF WAR

Tasca watched the collapse of Austria in March 1938 with growing desperation and a sense of complete impotence:

> For three nights I have almost not closed an eye. The rush of events, their seriousness, create a suffocating atmosphere of catastrophe: the occupation of Austria, the government crisis in France, the agony of Republican Spain, the Moscow trials, . . . I take the shock waves of these events as though on raw flesh, with an unbearable feeling of helplessness.[20]

Tasca warned that Hitler had managed to abolish the distinction between foreign and domestic policy in dealing with both the Austrian and Czech Germans, and he blamed the weakness of England, Italy, and the Vatican for allowing Austria to fall. The consequences for the remainder of the French alliance system in Eastern Europe were catastrophic now that the Czechs were virtually defenseless. British appeasement only increased Germany's appetite for aggrandizement and encouraged Mussolini to believe that the Nazis held the winning cards. Tasca called for firmness, even if it meant war: "We will answer, as for us, without pleasure but without hesitation, yes."[21]

The prospect of war in Eastern Europe sparked an open debate within the PSI. On 12 March the Direzione of the party called on all countries to block Fascist aggresson by any means. Oddino Morgari declared that war was almost certainly necessary to deter the Fascist dictators, and Saragat called for resistance at all cost and with all means, including the alliance with the Communists and the USSR: "Unity of Action against fascism and against war cannot be considered as a thesis which one can take or leave, but rather as a position which incorporates the very essence of antifascism without which antifascism ceases to be."[22]

The counterargument was made by Modigliani, who reiterated the classic pacifist position as though he were still living in the days of Zimmerwald, and by Ravazzoli, who refused to distinguish among wars fought by the various imperialist states. Modigliani even accused Saragat of offering no alternative but the alliance with Stalin and the Communists. How, he wondered, could liberty be defended by the forces of antiliberty?

Modigliani's views were widely shared in the French and Italian socialist movements by those who believed that support for Unity of Action and for the USSR was dragging the proletariat toward another war in the interests of the Russian national state. These fears began to work an ideological transformation that linked elements of the Socialist Right and extreme Left on a common program of pacifism and anticommunism. Saragat correctly pointed out the important role of neoreformism in the shift. Those like De Man and the Neosocialists, who rejected the Marxist international perspective and adopted an exclusively national framework, would eventually have to emphasize class solidarity because the theory of the class struggle led to an alliance with the Communists and to support for the Soviet Union.[23]

NEOREFORMISM, INTERCLASS ALLIANCES, AND ANTIFASCISM

The neoreformists had consistently argued that socialism needed a doctrine that justified including the middle class and those workers who were not attracted by traditional proletarian propaganda. In 1938 the CSI published a long attack by Bruno Maffi on such a reversal of alliances and on neoreformist doctrines of "planisme." Tasca, who wrote the introduction to Maffi's pamphlet, revealed for the first time the influence of De Man on his break with Marxism even if he did not have much enthusiasm for the actual realization of De Man's ideas by the Belgian socialists. Tasca questioned Maffi's contention that the socialists would attract part of the lower middle class by remaining true to a policy of orthodox Marxism: "Today we can no longer take for granted the 'working class' as though it offered a solid and accepted starting point. In reality, confronting the problems of this historical period, we must begin from the beginning and win back to the struggle for the new society both the working class and the middle classes."[24]

Tasca argued that the nature of capitalism had been altered by World War I and the economic crisis of 1929. Centralization of economic power in large corporations and in the state bureaucracy had created instruments that could be used either for the exclusive advantage of the capitalists or by society to control the excesses of the capitalist system. Europe confronted choices among various forms of controlled economies. It was a question of how to plan and for what ends, of finding the correct balance of state participation, private capital, and worker control. In short, the socialist parties would have to operate within the framework of a mixed economy.[25] Despite his clear tendency toward neoreformism, foreign policy separated Tasca from Modigliani. He was too closely tied to the Blum faction in the SFIO to become the Paul Faure of the PSI. Still, Tasca's positions offered ample justification for those who wanted to shift alliances both domestically and internationally and who thought purely in terms of a national strategy for the socialist movement.

Despite Nenni's efforts to keep the PSI on a course of cooperation with the PCI, problems that made the United Front more difficult arose. Nenni, Rugginenti, and Saragat were even forced to stop their collaboration with *La voce degli italiani* temporarily in early 1938 as a result of policy differences with the Communists.[26] Spain continued to be a source of friction as well as of solidarity. A critical report on relations between the Communists and other parties in Spain was received by the Direzione in March 1938. Randolfo Pacciardi, the Republican leader of the Garibaldi Brigade, returned from the Spanish war after a bitter altercation over what he viewed as a Communist attempt to dominate the International Brigades. He then proceeded to use his energies to create an antifascist front that would exclude the Communists.[27]

EFFORTS TO BROADEN UNITY OF ACTION

The possibility of broadening the alliance with the PCI to include other parties now appealed to those within the PSI who had not been completely happy with Unity of Action. They used *Problemi della Rivoluzione italiana*, a review published off and on since 1931, to propagate their views. The editor of the magazine was Francesco Volterra, who, with Antonio Chiodini, had passed from the Republicans to the PSI while keeping close ties to other antifascist formations such as Giustizia e Libertà. In 1938 Tasca wanted *Problemi della Rivoluzione italiana* to fill the same function as the defunct *Politica socialista* in serving as a rallying point for those Socialists who wanted to act independently of the Communists. Consequently, Tasca urged Volterra to resist any pressure from Nenni to allow unrestricted access to the review.[28]

The most likely partner in any move to broaden Unity of Action remained Giustizia e Libertà. In June 1938, under the influence of Emilio Lussu, who emerged as a key figure in the movement after the murder of Carlo Rosselli on 9 June 1937, GL published a new and clearly socialist ideological charter and again appealed to the Socialists and Communists to restructure the Unity of Action alliance. GL called on Tasca to act on his doubts about the United Front unequivocally supporting the broader pact. Although not accepting the offer, Tasca indicated his willingness to accept an alternative alliance when the time was right: "We must 'ally' with Russia in foreign policy but without abandoning the specific content of our movement and we must be ready to abandon the alliance at the point where differences over ends lead directly to differences in practical conduct."[29]

MUNICH AND TASCA'S RESIGNATION FROM
LE POPULAIRE

Debates within both the French and Italian socialist parties were momentarily interrupted in September 1938 by the Czech crisis. When they resumed after the Munich conference, coexistence of the various factions within the PSI and SFIO was practically impossible. Within the French socialist party, Faure made it clear that he preferred the maintenance of peace to the salvation of Czechoslovakia. In contrast, resolute antifascists such as Pierre Brossolette and Marx Dormoy clearly advocated resistance at whatever cost. Blum, who had tried to bridge the hostile camps, was torn between his desire to resist aggression and relief that war over Czechoslovakia had been avoided. Tasca noted in his diary that, when a representative of the Czech socialists visited *Le Populaire* to sound out opinion on the French reaction if the Czechs stood their ground, the results were less than positive: "It seems to me that the answers of Blum were not very encouraging." [30]

Tasca's resignation from *Le Populaire* occurred during the Munich crisis. However, no evidence indicates that his position differed from that of Blum. Although Tasca had never been a member of the inner circle around Blum, he could not have held his position from 1934 onward if he did not enjoy the confidence of the Socialist leader. But there were signs by 1938 that Tasca was increasingly unhappy at not being promoted to head the foreign desk when Oreste Rosenfeld became editor in chief. In early May Tasca complained of his complete isolation at *Le Populaire*. Blum, however, reassured him that there were no substantial differences over policy. At least Tasca came away convinced that Blum agreed that the Popular Front was dead and that a purely Marxist front from Thorez to Blum would drive the Radical party into the hands of the Right: "On none of the major questions which justify the autonomous existence of a party are we in agreement with the Communists—neither on the very concept of socialism, nor on the means to achieve it, nor on the nature of the state and its relationship with the masses, nor on the place of the individual in society." [31] A few months later, however, Tasca complained that his multiple obligations left him little time for larger projects. During September and October he wrote to Max Ascoli and Gaetano Salvemini about the possibility of finding a teaching position in America. [32]

On 5 October Tasca informed Rosenfeld that he would leave *Le Populaire* for health reasons, but a few weeks later he admitted that the decision had been maturing for some time. Tasca's position at the paper was temporarily taken by Pierre Brossolette, who also opposed appeasement. Both men would collaborate on the anti-Munich periodical *Agir* in 1939. [33]

The Czech crisis exploded while Tasca was on his annual vacation from *Le Populaire*, but his articles in the *Nuovo Avanti* and *Oran Républicain* reflect no break with the position of the SFIO. On 19 and 20 September he warned of the terrible consequences of a German victory, yet, like many French observers, Tasca momentarily forgot his predictions of disaster in the euphoria following the settlement at Munich. But, even in his most optimistic moments, he noted that Munich only gained time. In one of his last articles for *Le Populaire* he predicted that Poland and Hungary would not be able to resist German pressures.[34]

TASCA'S BREAK WITH NENNI

In the first weeks after Munich there were no apparent differences between Tasca and Nenni over the possibility of war. Throughout the Munich crisis Nenni had engaged in a long debate with the Communists over the Moscow trials, and on 1 October he made a full-scale indictment of the Soviet regime and of the authoritarian practice to which Bolshevik principles seemed to lead.[35] But the overwhelming disaster that befell Czechoslovakia pushed all other issues into the background. The old division between proponents and adversaries of Unity of Action was now becoming a struggle between the Nenni-Saragat group, which favored both Unity of Action and an aggressive policy of resistance to fascism, and a faction headed by Tasca, Faravelli, Modigliani, and Ravazzoli, who were united in opposition to Unity of Action, but divided on the issue of war.[36]

On 12 October Nenni made a last effort to separate Tasca from the opposition. He sent Tasca a draft motion on the tactics of the PSI that strongly backed Unity of Action as the basis for all other alliances. Nenni suggested that they work together to improve sections of the draft dealing wth the Socialist party's commitment to democracy and its continuing differences with the PCI.[37]

Tasca, however, had already decided to make his break. It came in two articles, "Prospettive sulla situazione interna ed internazionale," published in the *Nuovo Avanti* on 29 October and 4 November. Although elements of Tasca's new position had already been evident, the articles came as a surprise to friend and foe alike. He argued that Munich marked the end of the French system of alliances, of the Popular Front, and of the Franco-Soviet alliance as a central focus of French foreign policy. Tasca did not deny that the interests of the USSR coincided with the maintenance of peace, but the interests of the proletariat had shifted after Munich. No longer could the working class afford an exclusive alliance with the USSR. The antifascist front had to be broadened both domestically and internationally beyond the Popular and United fronts. Instead, the largest bloc of states had to be organized on a program of peace and economic cooperation.

To realize such a bloc, the Socialists would have to press for broad internal alignments involving democrats of all varieties, Catholics, and nonfascist conservatives. The balance within the alliance would shift from left to right. In France the SFIO would have to end the Unity of Action pact and work for the formation of a French national bloc. Tasca urged the Communists to recognize that their participation in any prominent way would be an obstacle to success. Similarly the USSR would have to play a subsidiary role in the formation of an international bloc. Furthermore, the Soviet state would have to integrate its economy more fully with those of the other European States.[38]

Turning to Italy, Tasca argued that the Fascist regime sought escape from an unstable equilibrium in frenetic preparations for war. Because it neglected both the development of an external market and internal consumption, fascism was vulnerable to pressures from the masses for a better standard of living. The maintenance of peace accentuated tensions on the regime. Therefore, in a curious way, Tasca squared the circle by arguing that a policy of peace was the most effective way to fight fascism. He urged the PSI to end its pact with the Communists and to withdraw from the UPI. He concluded by calling for the convocation of the Consiglio Nazionale and a party congress to ratify the new policy.[39]

Predictably, the reaction of the PCI to these articles was outrage. Within the PSI Pietro Nenni lost no time in attacking the fragile basis of Tasca's argument. Nenni accepted the ideal of a large antifascist front, but he noted that even Tasca seemed uncertain that such an alliance was possible. In light of this he wondered why Unity of Action was so bad; it did not preclude other alliances but ensured the proletariat against the disunity on the Left that had caused so many past defeats.[40]

Even Tasca's allies understood the power of Nenni's rejoinder. As one member of the minority stated:

> The weak point of our position can be found in my opinion in the fact that to the Italian Socialists, reduced to desperation by so many years of struggle, defeat, and disillusionment, the Communists and their friends in our party are in a position to point to Russia, not only as one of the forces, but the only force which tomorrow will be able to face up to the struggle against the Fascist powers.

Francesco Volterra and Alberto Jacometti wondered why, precisely at the moment when the Left had been abandoned by the bourgeoisie at Munich, Tasca chose to shift alliances in a way that would never be understood by the base of the party.[41]

Tasca responded in an article, "Prima e dopo Monaco," in which he noted that at the time of the 1937 congress the PSI tried to balance between Unity of Action and autonomy, but that after Munich this course was no longer possible. He tried to turn the tables on his critics by noting that the Socialists all over Europe were forced to shift from denunciations of the Versailles Treaty to its defense by rearmament and military alliances but without preparing the masses. Thus, during the Czech crisis they found that pacifism passed to the other side of the barricades. The Right moved in step with the popular mood of hostility to war. Tasca called on the Left to rethink its entire political position in order to regain the initiative.[42] But his position rested on a growing contempt for the USSR that was mixed with the certainty that Stalin had no other options but to ally with the West on any terms. Politically, he came dangerously close to lumping the Fascist powers and the Soviet Union as symbols of the evil against which the democracies had to struggle.[43] Moreover, Tasca failed to convince the party that the alternatives that he offered were valid: Saragat wrote to him on 19 November that he had drawn exactly the wrong conclusions from the defeat at Munich.[44]

The crisis came to a head at the meeting of the Consiglio Nazionale on 3 and 4 December 1938. Nenni moved that the struggle against fascism, based on unity of action, remain party policy. Tasca continued to insist that, because the USSR and Nazi Germany could never ally, a successful shift in alliances was possible. Nenni's motion passed overwhelmingly. Within the Direzione Boschi, Nenni, Saragat, and Taroni voted for it, Ravazzoli opposed, and Tasca abstained. Of the nonvoting members, Faravelli opposed and Buozzi abstained. The results from the federations showed Nenni's strength in the party. The federations of Sud-Est, Est, and North Africa voted unanimously for Nenni's motion. Only the Swiss federation opposed, and the Paris federation was marginally in favor.[45]

The meeting of the Consiglio Nazionale made Tasca the leader of the minority and chief enemy of the Communists, but he was far from rallying the party behind him. At the end of the year he noted in his diary:

> A sad, terrible year in which suffering and disasters have piled up without any compensation, without reducing in any way the price which humanity must very soon pay for having failed itself and betrayed its own destiny. I think of the future war with horror because nothing reassures me that the bestial forces which it will unleash will not cast both the winners and losers in the same abyss.[46]

The Rupture of Unity of Action

Tasca's positions after Munich were based on his understanding of the crisis in French foreign policy and of the problems facing the SFIO. At the Congress of Montrouge in December 1938 the two wings of the party practically deadlocked. Blum's motion favoring firmness in the face of Fascist aggression won, with 4,332 votes to 2,837 for Faure's reaffirmation of traditional pacifism, but there were over 1,000 abstentions.

Although Tasca did not write for *Le Populaire* after October 1938, his relations with the French Socialists were as close as ever. He belonged to a group of French Socialists, which included Georges Monnet, Pierre Brossolette, Georges Izard, Pierre Viénot, Leo Lagrange, and Daniel Mayer, who attempted to push Blum into a more open stand against appeasement.[1] In February 1939 Monnet began to publish the review *Agir* to advance their views. He made it clear that his target was the "peace at any price" foreign policies of Bonnet and Daladier and of the Faurists within the SFIO. To combat Germany *Agir* advocated an alliance of the Western democracies with the USSR. But many in the *Agir* group were also hostile to Marxism and were involved in the formulation of a new, European-oriented, technocratic socialism that would appeal to all classes as a modern alternative to capitalism and communism.[2] Tasca fit in well with this group. He shared with Brossolette and Monnet a long-range ambition to bring the United States into the European balance and their immediate fears that Germany had slipped out of control after the Munich conference. The *Agir* group looked to England rather than to the USSR as the cornerstone of French foreign policy, but they were concerned that England begin to develop its ties with the USSR. Tasca felt that the obvious counter to the Nazi move into Prague in March 1939 was the Anglo-Soviet entente. He was convinced that Hitler preferred reaching some understanding with Poland in order to attack in the West and urged the English to avoid giving firm guarantees to the Poles that would only make them more intransigent in their dealings with the USSR.[3]

Tasca was aware of some of the early indications of the Nazi-Soviet pact but did not realize their importance. During May and June he criticized Britain for allowing the negotiations with the USSR to drag on too long. The dismissal of Litvinov; Stalin's speech to the party congress in March, which put the Western democracies on the same level as Nazi Germany; and his address on foreign policy of 28 April, which contained no reference to Germany made Tasca speculate on the possible meaning, but he dismissed out of hand any notion that the USSR might reverse alliances.[4]

In *Agir* Tasca argued that the alliance between Socialists and Communists was the only way of winning mass support in the struggle against Fascism. The Socialists needed the backing of the Communist following: "All the same it is absurd to say 'go to the Communist masses' but fight their leaders." The socialists simply could not afford to struggle against both the Fascists and the Communists at the same time. However, Unity of Action, as practiced from 1934 to 1938, worked to the exclusive benefit of the Communists. He suggested a strategy of alliance that would put the Communists on the defensive by stressing ideological differences, especially "in the relationship between democracy and socialism, a concept which is at the heart of all doctrinal, tactical, and organizational questions that define the specific content of the two parties. The Russian experience, which one can in no way leave aside, proves that you cannot create democracy with dictatorship."[5] But Tasca expressed the consensus of the *Agir* group when he argued in favor of subordinating hostility to communism to the battle against fascism.[6]

TASCA BETWEEN THE SFIO AND PSI

An understanding of Tasca's position within the SFIO is essential to an evaluation of his role in the PSI. Within the SFIO Tasca was part of the majority. His support of a strong line against fascism, a firm policy in dealing with the Communist allies, and a call for revision of ideology was accepted by many in the center and right of the SFIO. These same positions placed Tasca within a minority in the PSI, out of step even with the dogmatic pacifism of Modigliani. What bound Modigliani, Tasca, and Faravelli together was a determination to break with the PCI. In an undated letter written to his two Italian colleagues, Tasca argued that the socialists should forge a new alliance with the Republicans and Giustizia e Libertà. If the Communists objected, then the PSI would have to draw the necessary conclusions: "Therefore we have decided to act for the revocation of the action pact with the Communists so that the alliance among all antifascist parties may become possible and efficacious."[7]

The Communists understood Tasca's aims and continued to attack him, but this strategy played into the hands of the anti-Nenni group. Faravelli wrote to Tasca, Modigliani, Buozzi, and Ravazzoli on 6 January that Nenni's failure to defend Tasca might offer a vehicle for rallying support for their faction. Like the Communists, Faravelli leapt at any chance to widen the split between Tasca and Nenni. He urged Tasca to meet with Modigliani, Ravazzoli, and him to draft a common thesis on the issue of war and Unity of Action to present to the Consiglio Nazionale or to a future party congress. Faravelli also suggested that leaders of the minority cease their collaboration with the *Nuovo Avanti*, as Tasca already had in January.[8] On 18 February the minority-controlled Marseilles section and the Federation of the Sud-Est and Centro passed a resolution attacking unity of action. Both raised the issue of Spain, from which disquieting reports of the persecution of socialists by communists had been filtering back for some time.[9]

Nenni countered by arguing that a broader antifascist alliance was neither more necessary than the pact with the communists nor incompatible with it. Privately, he wrote to Tasca to ask him to reconsider his refusal to write for the *Nuovo Avanti*: "I tried to call you but you were not in. Your refusal to collaborate on *Avanti* is not a coincidence but a political act. . . . An allusion of Buozzi leads me to believe that you consider yourself—how to say it—offended that I allowed certain slurs against you by Grieco to stand uncorrected." Nenni recalled that he had been attacked by the Communists in the past and urged Tasca not to give such attacks undue weight: "In any case, if I made a mistake, our relationship is sufficiently friendly and loyal so that you would immediately tell me about it." Tasca's response was anything but promising: "For now each of us will follow his own way without meaning or implying a personal conflict."[10]

To the last Nenni tried to win Tasca's support. He warned Tasca that his alliance with the pacifist elements was illogical and dangerous in light of Tasca's own positions:

> You are mistaken. Look around in the French party and to some extent in our own and you will realize that the danger is the same that made us lose twenty years ago: a refusal to fight, to not meet obstacles. . . . I have the impression that even you have been a bit won over by the inclination to oppose for opposition's sake. The truth is quite simple . . . it is that all of your worries are shared by me, while all your conclusions are at odds with the thesis of Modigliani and of Santini. Certainly our respective biographies, as you correctly say, are different. You are a professor, I an agitator. And an agitator can only realize his potential if he has at his side one or several professors. . . .[11]

NEOREFORMISM AND APPEASEMENT

Nenni was correct that there were differences between Tasca and Modigliani or Faravelli. All three could agree on anticommunism and feared that war might lead to revolution, which would mean the triumph of the communists. As Faravelli stated, "The revolution is inseparable from the GPU."[12] But Tasca did not share Modigliani's pacifism, and the latter reciprocated by doubting that Tasca's proposed United States of Europe was a realistic alternative. The common ground of the minority was purely negative: its hostility to communism.[13] The minority lost by a wide margin at the meeting of the PSI's Consiglio Nazionale on 18 and 19 March: Tasca's motion, which reflected the views expressed in his recent articles, was defeated by a vote of 317 to 69.[14]

Yet the meeting of the Consiglio Nazionale did force Nenni to reemphasize his commitment to negotiations for a broad antifascist front. Conversations with the PCI began on 22 March and were followed soon after by discussions with GL. It soon became apparent that the Socialists and Communists disagreed about the extent of any antifascist pact. The Communists preferred an agreement limited only to the attitude to be taken in the event of war. Furthermore they wanted the UPI to sponsor the recruitment of a corps of volunteers to fight within the French army in the event of war. Giustizia e Libertà pressed both the PSI and PCI for a completely new pact to supersede Unity of Action. Knowing that it had considerable support within the PSI, GL continued to call for the dissolution of Unity of Action as the precondition for any broader alliance. Lussu proposed the formation of a single leadership committee, a common newspaper, and the absorption of both the UPI and the *Voce degli Italiani* into the new structure. The Communists reacted by postponing the negotiations with GL and strengthening their ties with the Socialists, even to the extent of making concessions about integrating them into the leadership of the UPI.[15] Curiously, the position of the communists and that of Tasca on some issues was quite close. Like Tasca, the Communists tended to avoid any talk of revolution in the interests of winning the allegiance of the majority of Italians. However different their ultimate aims, both judged the program of GL too aggressive for the existing circumstances in Italy.[16]

RELATIONS BETWEEN TASCA AND NENNI

Nenni's effort to draw Tasca back into the fold met with some success after the failure of the minority during the meeting of the Consiglio Nazionale. He seemed to believe that his differences with Tasca might be overcome with good will:

> You know that I haven't the slightest intention of aggravating or deepening our differences. In a small party like ours we cannot afford the luxury of sys-

tematic internal battles, and I remain convinced that we must instead search for a way of eliminating, completely or in part, our disagreements. . . . Your absence from the paper might eventually take on the character of a complete rupture. And this is not possible.[17]

Tasca resumed his collaboration with the *Nuovo Avanti* in March. The occupation of Prague shook his confidence that war was not imminent, and he returned to the paper shortly after the meeting of the Consiglio Nazionale with several articles in which he traced the development of Fascist foreign policy from Versailles to Anschluss to demonstrate that the Italian government had abandoned any true defense of Italian national interests.[18]

Tasca's return to active participation in the leadership did not indicate that he had reached an understanding with Nenni. Nenni remained faithful to his belief that the PSI and PCI had much more to gain by cooperating than by taking separate roads. Even the recriminations between Socialists and Communists after the collapse of the Spanish Republic did not discourage him about the prospects for Unity of Action. The enemy was not communism, but defeatism:

> Our duty is to expose and unmask all the excuses of the party of capitulation: pseudopacifism, pseudohumanitarianism, anticommunism. Anticommunism is the minimum common denominator or, if you prefer, the geometrical point of convergence of an international conspiracy which is not always and everywhere intentionally philofascist, but is always and inexorably in its results.[19]

NENNI AND TASCA: TOWARD A FINAL RUPTURE

By midyear the crisis within the PSI had reached the point of rupture. Modigliani and Nenni could no longer even agree on a common policy to present to the Socialist International. Nenni fought the effort of the English to reduce the power of the exiled socialist parties, which tended to be more radical than the legal parties such as Labour and the SFIO. Modigliani supported the caution of the British and had no particular objection to restructuring representation within the Internationale Ouvrière Socialiste (IOS). On 4 April Modigliani announced that he had resigned as representative to the IOS. Nenni tried unsuccessfully to heal the rift by appointing a committee of Tasca, Buozzi, and Saragat to persuade Modigliani to change his mind. Ravazzoli also submitted his resignation from the party leadership.[20]

By June and July, the minority seemed to be moving toward a split within the party. Faravelli sought to rally the potential leadership of the anti-Nenni forces into a well-organized, permanent faction that would include Tasca, Volterra, Olindo Gorni, Alberto Jacometti, Giovanni Fara-boldi, Ravazzoli, and Modigliani.[21] This socialist minority, headed by Tasca and supported by the leaders of GL, sought to restructure both Unity of Action and the UPI. On the other side were Nenni's majority and the PCI, who refused to dissolve Unity of Action into the broader alliance. The most that was accomplished in the months before the outbreak of the war was an agreement in principle of the PCI, the PSI, GL, and the Republicans to establish a broad antifascist front. Nothing conclusive about the relationship between the projected front and the UPI, which was the other mass organization of antifascist Italians, had been decided. In an effort to resolve the impasse within the PSI, the Direzione decided on 7 July to hold a congress in November to set basic strategy for the Socialist party. It was a congress that would never take place.[22]

THE NAZI-SOVIET PACT AND THE OUSTER OF NENNI

During the summer of 1939 Tasca was involved on several fronts. He had assumed a leadership role in the movement against Nenni within the PSI. In the French socialist party he was active on the weekly *Agir* until that paper ceased publication at the beginning of the war. In addition to his journalism and work for the French radio, he served as secretary for a meeting, set for the summer of 1939 at Pontigny, that was to have brought together the two wings of the SFIO to discuss the relationship between democracy and socialism. Although the conference never took place because of the war, it represented a last effort by the Blum forces to pull the party together.[23]

The news of the Nazi-Soviet pact of 23 August was a bombshell. The first reactions of the PSI were shock, confusion, and anger. Tasca's draft of a manifesto on 24 or 25 August 1939, referred to the "shameful betrayal of that cause for which we fought for so many years." He accused the USSR of passing into the enemy camp. On 25 August the Direzione, in the absence of Nenni, condemned the Nazi-Soviet pact and declared Unity of Action dead. When Nenni returned on 27 August he asked the Direzione to reconsider its denunciation of Unity of Action and to appeal to the Communists to continue in the old policy. Tasca, supported by the majority, opposed any compromise with the PCI. Nenni and Saragat were designated to meet with the Communist representatives to inform them of the decisions of the Direzione. Saragat was also delegated to meet with GL and the Republican party.[24]

On 28 August the Direzione met again. Nenni reported that the PCI representatives reiterated their party's support for the Nazi-Soviet pact.[25] Despite this lack of success, Nenni appealed to the socialists to do nothing to widen the gap with the PCI. Again Tasca led the opposition. When

Saragat reported that GL and the Republicans were favorable to the formation of an antifascist alliance without the Communists, Nenni argued in vain that such a move would reverse the policies of the past five years and would necessitate his resignation from the secretaryship and from the *Nuovo Avanti*. Tasca urged the party to move as quickly as possible to conclude the pact with the other parties, even if that meant Nenni's departure. He proposed a provisional secretariat of Buozzi, Morgari, and Saragat. The latter attempted to compromise by urging the party to wait a day.

When the Direzione met again, Nenni submitted his resignation but protested that the Direzione could not make such a drastic policy reversal without convoking the Consiglio Nazionale or a congress. Saragat and Morgari then moved that the Direzione call a meeting of the Consiglio Nazionale for 1 September. The crisis of the Direzione was not over; on 30 August the Direzione met once again to deal with a letter from Tasca, who announced that he would not participate in any further meetings of the leadership until the Consiglio Nazionale set policy.[26]

The frustration against Nenni that had been building among the minority finally exploded into a determination to oust the secretary and to end the alliance with the PCI in one move. The Nazi-Soviet accord provided the pretext for action. Nenni had opposed it as firmly as the others, but he refused to draw the conclusion that a denunciation of the pact automatically demanded a complete redirection of policy. The new party majority wanted both abandonment of the pact with the Communists and withdrawal from the UPI. This was the course urged on Tasca by Giovanni Faraboldi, the leader of the Toulouse socialist federation. But the aims of the anti-Nenni faction were even more sweeping. A series of resolutions from the Paris section, which the anticommunists controlled, advocated a purge of all those who refused to back the break with the Communists and urged the party to drive the Communists out of the UPI.[27] The antifascist alliance became the new battle cry of the anti-Nenni group. Tasca had already communicated with Emilio Lussu, who was as harsh as Tasca in demanding a total rupture with the PCI and UPI.[28]

For the first time, Tasca, rather than Nenni, emerged victorious from a meeting of the Consiglio Nazionale. Although the PSI did not sanction the immediate and unconditional stipulation of the antifascist alliance, it ratified the break with the Communists and called for continued negotiations with the other parties. As a first step in that direction, the PSI joined with the Italian League for the Rights of Man, GL, and the Republicans in an Italian National Committee. On 7 September the *Nuovo Avanti* published Nenni's last article as director. Morgari, Saragat, and Tasca jointly assumed the secretariat and control of the party paper. The new leaders decided to remain within the UPI but to force that organization to condemn the PCI's position.[29]

TASCA'S RETURN TO *LE POPULAIRE*

The outbreak of war also caused a significant change in Tasca's position within the SFIO. Throughout the spring and summer, conflict between the Blum and Faure factions persisted. As at Montrouge in December 1938, the Congress of Nantes on 27–30 May 1939, saw contrasting motions proposed by the two wings of the SFIO. Despite the growing international crisis, Faure refused to abandon traditional socialist positions. Blum and his supporters (Bracke, Lebas, Dormoy, Auriol, Viénot, Brossolette, and Rosenfeld) supported both the continued alliance with the Communists and a firm stand against Fascist aggression.[30]

The announcement of the Nazi-Soviet pact surprised Blum and his supporters. The leader of the SFIO referred to it as "almost unbelievable" and wondered whether it was a sign of weakness of the Soviets. Blum's strategy was to rally the Communist masses in France against the stand of their party and to encourage dissension within the PCF. Consequently, he was unenthusiastic about harsh measures such as the suppression of *L'Humanité* in August, the dissolution of the PCF the following month, and the expulsion of the Communists from parliament in early 1940.[31]

Almost immediately after the signing of the Nazi-Soviet pact, Oreste Rosenfeld informed Tasca that Blum desired his return to *Le Populaire*. Tasca's new column, entitled "La Situation" and signed *XX* instead of *André Leroux*, was devoted to a close analysis of the motives and aims of Soviet foreign policy and generally received Blum's full support. In fact, these articles, which were more prominently featured in *Le Populaire* than were Tasca's old columns, led to criticism from the right-wing paper *Gringoire* about allowing an Italian to fill such a prominent post.[32] Two themes appeared in Tasca's writings between August 1939 and the outbreak of war in the West. There were the obligatory attacks on Nazi Germany and the USSR. Tasca was especially critical of the Soviet Union, which he described as following the expansionist policies of the Czars, moving either East or West until forced by opposition to swing in the opposite direction. It was, he predicted, the long-term conflict between German and Russian imperialism that would undermine the pact.[33]

The second theme was more surprising and revealed the extent of the difference between Tasca and the other Italian exiles. After the August pact Tasca began to consider Italian fascism as a secondary evil that might even be tolerated temporarily if it would help to defeat Germany and the USSR. Tasca began to appeal to Italian self-interest. Mussolini's famous opportunism now became a factor that might extract Italy from the alliance with Germany. Tasca was willing to pay a far higher price for this outcome than any other Italian exile, however. Above all, he was eager to prevent Italy from joining the war against France:

we must conceive of, foresee [Italy's] evolution within the framework of fascism, of a fascism which returned to its beginnings, freed from the German model which rediscovered its concerns for individual liberty, initiative, resistance to state worship which characterized it in 1919. From this point of view the "fascism of the first hour" had a sense of the crisis of values of the postwar, an awareness which was lost in the subsequent triumph of hypernationalism and hyperstatism.[34]

Tasca stressed the common interest of both Italy and the Western democracies in Finland and in Balkan independence. His articles attempted to convey a sense that time was working against England and France in their effort to keep Italy out of the war. For a few weeks Tasca was joined by Blum, who wrote that the Socialists never excluded good relations with the Italian government and that the Duce had been in a better position when he played the European balance of power. These editorials, which hinted at a new Stresa Front, cited Tasca as an authority. But, by May, both Tasca and Blum seemed to have abandoned all hope that Italy might break from the Axis alliance.[35]

THE USSR AND THE FAILURE OF MARXISM

Agreement between Tasca and Blum extended to other issues: increased hostility to the USSR with respect to Finland, an effort to persuade Japan not to side with Nazi Germany, and the determination to thwart any peace conference that would ratify the German victories resulting from the pact with the USSR.[36] But a close reading of Tasca's articles on foreign policy in 1939 and 1940 reveal that he drew far more sweeping conclusions about the nature of Bolshevism than did Blum. The Soviet system revealed itself to Tasca as greatly inferior to bourgeois democracy:

> One of the most characteristic aspects of the evolution toward democracy is represented by the fact that the intermediate "class" that is situated between the nation and political power is drawn from all social categories, becomes more and more numerous, and keeps a direct contact with the people, thus avoiding turning itself into a closed and autonomous class.

Tasca contrasted France, with its large and talented petite and middle bourgeoisie, with the USSR, whose bureaucracy comprised servile sons of workers and peasants.[37]

Tasca seemed to conclude that the USSR was the case upon which the whole development of Marxism stood or fell. Since his student days Tasca sought to understand the reciprocal interaction between consciousness and the environment, or, to put it another way, the effort of consciousness to gain mastery over the material world in order to achieve human liberty. He was drawn to Marxism because it offered a satisfactory and coherent explanation of the process by which humankind overcame the obstacles posed by the material world. These obstacles, created by capitalist production, could not be overcome on the individual level but could only be surmounted by the entire working class. When Tasca was expelled from the Communist movement in 1929, he was still well within the Marxist tradition. He believed that the oppression of each individual could only be overcome on the collective level. Then, following the footsteps of De Man, although not drawing the same conclusions in every case, Tasca stressed Marx's "humanisme réal," which was the progressive identification of the aspirations of the proletariat with the general good of all humanity.[38]

Over time, Tasca began to question whether the determinism imposed by capitalism was the chief obstacle to human liberty. The problem of human freedom transcended any particular economic system, to involve the subjection of man to all political and economic institutions that were beyond individual accountability. Marxism offered no defense against the vast, impersonal forces unleashed by the Bolshevik Revolution.

The Soviet revolution was the product of Marxist doctrine, Leninist revolutionary theory, and Stalinst practice. Tasca rejected Trotsky's argument that the Stalinist regime was a deviation from an essentially correct vision of socialism. The entire Soviet experiment was an error and so was the Marxist tradition on which it was based: "In our opinion, all statization of property and of the economy . . . leads to the formation of an apparatus which, by its structure and size, leaves no place for liberty and individual initiative. . . ."[39] Tasca came to believe that there were two types of revolutions: the libertarian and the bureaucratic. All depended on the role assigned to the state: "The state . . . must assure the predominance of the general interest, set the general directives, but afterward, allow the institutions and economic persons to play their role. . . ."[40]

Of greater importance were the ends that socialism set for society and the conception of humanity that lay at the basis of the system. For Blanqui and Lenin, "the road to socialism begins 'with' the seizure of power; but, if it is true that socialism is consciousness and understanding of human existence, it must begin 'before.'" Socialism was no longer automatically superior to capitalism. Its value depended on the nature of the revolution against capitalism, distinguished not in its productive goals but rather in the determination to avoid the subordination of the human to the economic."[41]

For years Tasca believed that the proletariat was the carrier of universal values and that the struggle for its emancipation was at one with the struggle for the liberation of all humanity. When Tasca rejected Marx in the late 1930s, he did much more than shift the basis of his socialist convictions. Although he had yet to draw all the conclusions from the shift, he had altered his entire ethical system.[42] In turning away from Marx, he considered religion as a possible source of transcendent values: "in reality, there are two conceptions: the pagan and Christian; and socialism is related to the latter, precisely because it introduces into economics and thus into life, the notion of limits and of subordination." Tasca's renewed interest in Christianity did not include a formal return to the Catholic Church. Instead, he sought a guarantee of human value that stood outside the process of history:

> Today humanity is menaced above all by a lack of limits. Therefore socialism (which is a doctrine of liberation, of unshackling) is no longer sufficient to make progress possible, nor to guarantee it: the present historic duty is summed up in the formula "socialism plus Christianity." In saying this, I do not preach a new socialism or a new religion. I note the interdependence, the confluence of two great historical movements.[43]

TASCA AND THE POLITICS OF THE PSI

Because Tasca's own ideological crisis coincided with the shift in his interests from Italian affairs, the Italian Communist party was barely mentioned in his writing from 1939 to the early 1950s, whereas the betrayal of Stalin and of the French party were the subject of several books and articles. Such a change was hardly compatible with his new leadership role in the PSI. Tasca's partners in the secretariat, Saragat and Morgari, certainly shared Tasca's strong feelings on the subject of Soviet policy, but they had no desire to use it as a weapon to work a complete change in the ideology and policies of the PSI. They stood somewhere between Tasca's determination to forge ahead toward a new socialism and Nenni's loyalty to tradition.[44]

Nenni was unrepentant in his refusal to condemn Soviet policy before the pact with Germany; nor did he abandon his support for those within the PSI who refused to break all relations with the PCI. Tasca, backed by Faravelli and Modigliani, wanted a declaration of war on the Communists and their supporters within the PSI. Modigliani, in particular, called for a much more thorough purge of the party than had been taken by the Direzione up to that point and the resignation of Nenni from all posts of responsibility. In words that recalled earlier splits, Modigliani demanded clarification: "Let's clean house: the Socialists with the Socialists, the Communists with the Communists." He left absolutely no doubt where he thought Nenni belonged.[45]

Tasca and Nenni continued their struggle for the soul of the PSI into December 1939, when they presented dramatically opposing analyses of the international situation to the Direzione. Nenni balanced his attack on the Nazi-Soviet pact with strong condemnation of the British and the

French for their past conduct and their present unwillingness to wage a true antifascist war. He rejected any wholesale condemnation of Unity of Action or of the USSR.[46] The position of the majority, written by Tasca and Saragat, was a scathing denunciation of the Soviet Union for the pact with Germany and for the war against Finland and of the communist parties in general: "a militia at the service of the Russian state, held together both by fanaticism and corruption." The report advocated a complete break with the communists and with those who refused to denounce the USSR. Buozzi, Faravelli, Morgari, and Saragat voted with Tasca to make his position official policy. Buozzi and Faravelli were added to the Direzione to replace Santini. The new party executive banned all contacts between socialists and "Stalinists."[47]

Despite the triumph of the new anti-Nenni majority, there was little progress toward an alliance of all noncommunist Left parties. Tasca was still less than eager to merge the PSI into a larger antifascist organization; to do so would mean diluting his control over the newly won party apparatus and over the *Avanti*. Tasca was unwilling to do that until he achieved his ambition of forging a new Italian Socialist movement that would be forever free of communist influence.[48]

TOWARD A NEW ANTICOMMUNIST SOCIALISM

Ironically, when Tasca became the leader of the PSI, the party fit only marginally into his plans. He was much closer to those French socialists who sought to elaborate a non-Marxist, antistatist socialism within the European context. The leaders of such a movement were Jean Monnet, Pierre Viénot, and others of the *Agir* group who wanted to rethink socialism in a technocratic and international context. This relaunching of socialism was to be the theme of the meeting set for summer 1939 at Pontigny. When that meeting was cancelled because of the outbreak of the war, plans were laid for *Europe Libre*, a theoretical review to plan for the new order that would emerge from the struggle against Germany. Tasca placed great hopes in the publication of the new journal. He wrote to the historian Ernest Labrousse: "The review must become a sort of 'diary' for all of us, the bridge between our internal life and the people with whom we can and must work." Potential collaborators were to include Clement Attlee, Hugh Dalton, Blum, Bracke, Solomon Grumbach, Viénot, Modigliani, and Hilferding, among others.[49]

From his new European perspective, Tasca believed that the entire heritage of Italian socialism as represented by Nenni was outdated and harmful, and he was determined to reshape it. Ideologically and politically, Tasca found himself in total opposition to Nenni by the end of the 1930s. The latter remained primarily an antifascist who never placed hostility to the USSR over his desire to topple the Fascist government in Italy. Moreover, he kept faith with the classic tradition of Italian socialism, which refused to accept a radical and unbridgeable split between the Italian Socialist and Communist parties.[50]

For Tasca, the crisis of the war was an opportunity to place the PSI on a new basis. There could be no return to Unity of Action: "There is nothing in common between our anticommunism and that of the reactionaries. . . . We are anticommunists only to the degree that we are socialists and democrats. . . ." Even as antifascist martyrs, the Communists were unworthy of consideration: " 'Communist courage' is today a counterrevolutionary factor precisely because it is detached from conscience. It lives off the suppression of every conscience and substitutes for it a servile and fanatical discipline." It should be noted, however, that others in the Direzione, notably Saragat, did not use this tone of moral excommunication.[51]

Despite its victory, the new leadership of the PSI did not feel entirely confident of its support in the base of the party, where Nenni enjoyed great popularity. At the meeting of the Direzione on 2 February Tasca attacked Nenni for failing the renounce his past policies and for condoning the Communist repression against the opposition in Spain. In a letter to the Direzione, he made it clear that he wanted Nenni expelled from the party: "You know my opinion of the moral and political (more moral than political) incompatibility of men like Pietro Nenni with membership in a socialist organization. I inform you that I have decided to resolve the problem, in so far as it concerns me, by resigning from the Direction of the party. . . ." As for his own future, he announced that he was going to devote himself to the international struggle against Stalinism, and he hinted at the plans for the new journal that his French friends intended to publish.[52]

It is unclear which of the two motivations—the party's failure to expel Nenni, or Tasca's desire to work on the international level against communism—was more important in leading to his resignation. Faravelli insisted that his friend stay the course. He wrote that Saragat was seeking a compromise with Nenni and that the new majority might not continue to triumph without Tasca. Faravelli hoped to use the March meeting of the Direzione to complete the purge of Nenni's supporters by expelling Boschi and appointing Modigliani and Jacometti as the new representatives of the Socialist International. Nenni, possibly backed by Saragat, sought to appeal to a Consiglio Generale of the party against the decisions of the Direzione.[53]

The leadership did decide to convoke a meeting of the Consiglio Generale for 27–28 April to ratify the work of the Direzione and to settle the question whether those who refused to support the new policies could continue to hold positions of responsibility in the party. Although he had resigned, Tasca was designated to give the principal political report to the meeting. At the end of a bitter debate that opposed Nenni and Tasca, the decisions of the new majority were ratified. Nenni and his followers were ousted from all positions of power. On a motion of Modigliani, the PSI decided to withdraw from the UPI. His victory assured, Tasca accepted election to the new Direzione of the party.[54] At that point events overwhelmed both the Italian and French Socialists. On 9 April the Germans attacked in Denmark and Norway. A few weeks later the front was opened in the west through Holland and Belgium and into France. Out of this crisis came the decisions that would destroy Tasca's political career.

13

Tasca's Vichy Gamble

Tasca's decision made between June and August 1940 to remain in France and to continue working with the new government altered his life, ended the possibility of a political career, and sullied his record as a socialist leader. His defection was never forgiven. Friendships, such as those with Modigliani and Saragat, were broken and never renewed. This decision was explicable in a French rather than in an Italian context, however. Tasca's actions after 10 June resembled those of other government bureaucrats. He received orders to abandon Paris for Tours and then for Bordeaux, where he arrived to witness the final French collapse. At that point Tasca faced a choice. His good friend, Pierre Viénot, who had been the deputy at the foreign ministry in Blum's 1936 government, found him a place on a ship bound for London. Everything indicated that he should leave. The Italian-language broadcasts had ended with the armistice. The other employees at the radio, along with the bureaucrats at the Ministry of Information, retreated with the government from Paris to Tours to Bordeaux and, finally, to Vichy in the chaotic days after the defeat. In fact, the entire service of the Ministry of Information was to be reorganized by the new regime with no guarantees for the holdovers with an antifascist background. As a socialist militant and a recently naturalized citizen, Tasca's prospects were certainly not bright in the new political order.[1]

Why then did he stay? We have already seen that Tasca responded to the events of the 1930s differently from most Italian exiles. Although both Tasca and Nenni were well integrated into French life, Tasca became French. He was a member of the SFIO and wrote for its newspaper. His associations made him respond quite differently to events such as the failure of the Popular Front and the crisis of the French socialist party. He had friends and associates on both sides of the fundamental division within the SFIO. Although he was close to Blum and to the *Agir* group, his anti-communism drew him to the Faurists. Once the collapse came, old political positions were thrown up for grabs. Despair at the failure of democracy and virulent anticommunism became the dominant considerations. Tasca's actions in June and July 1940 resembled those of many, if not the majority of, French socialists. Morale in the party buckled with the collapse of France. Only thirty-six socialists voted against full powers to Pétain and ninety voted in favor, although only a few of those came from Blum's group. Sixty-four followers of Paul Faure voted for Pétain. Moreover, a sizable minority decided to work actively with the Vichy regime, although Faure himself played little role. A convergence of revisionism, pacifism, and a belief that the failure of democracy meant the triumph of authoritarian regimes throughout Europe carried the day with many socialists, including Tasca. As he stated in trying to explain the split from his Italian comrades: "I see the origin of it in the experience which I had undergone for many reasons and with such an intensity as to isolate me from them, to lead me to a different vision of the present and of the future."[2]

Tasca's personal and family situation also weighed heavily in the balance. According to Charles-André Julien, Tasca feared the disruption of his life for a third time. He had lost his wife and two of his children despite a desperate attempt at reconciliation in the early 1930s. Then, relatively late in life, he developed a close relationship with Liliane Chaumette, but now this tie was threatened by war and further exile. In June 1940 Tasca faced the prospect of leaving France and abandoning the life that he had carefully constructed since 1930.[3]

A CRISIS OF FAITH

In July 1940 Tasca believed that Pétain represented the best solution under the circumstances. He felt a deep disillusionment with the experiences of socialism during the 1930s. In a statement composed to facilitate his reintegration into the civil service in October 1940, Tasca stated that the Popular Front was "a complete failure in all areas." It started badly, with the strike wave of May and June 1936 but was condemned to total failure by the presence of Communists in the alliance.[4] By 1939 the situation within France led him to the conclusion "that it was henceforth necessary to abandon political parties as an instrument of political leadership and of spiritual inspiration. . . ." Instead of traditional political action, Tasca recalled that his friends thought in terms of elite movements that would assume the task of national renewal. The defeat in 1940 demanded radical surgery:

I felt that it was absolutely not a question of a simple military defeat, but of the collapse of a regime, of a society in which practically every resource was overturned and corrupted. . . . I felt that the absolute precondition for an escape from this apocalypse was an immediate and brutal rupture with the past at the price of any sacrifice, a break which would make possible a new beginning. . . . To change the personnel, alter the institutions, transform political culture. Such a miracle was possible only if a broadly based movement formed and attracted the vital forces of the nation. The Socialists, who had a large part of the responsibility for the debacle, had their duty set out for them: to help in the creation of this movement. . . .[5]

Although Tasca later attempted to create the impression that his actions were dictated by a momentary loss of hope, it is clear that his intellectual reorientation was quite profound:

I believe that my absolute certainty about the mission to be accomplished has not been without influence on the attitude of my friends. Thus I have been able to contribute to the overwhelming vote of the socialist deputies who on July 10 understood that they had to embark on a new road and entrust the destiny of France in the worthiest of hands—those of Marshal Pétain.[6]

Although it was clearly in his interest in October 1940 to stress his contributions to the "New Order," such statements cast doubt on his later protestations of minimum involvement. In 1945 Tasca admitted that he had been too deeply affected by the need to break with the past and by hopes for the Révolution Nationale that turned out to be totally unrealistic.[7]

TASCA AND THE "NEW ORDER"

Despite his favorable attitude, Tasca was far from assured of his position in the first months. The citizenship granted him on 7 August 1936 was revoked on 1 November 1940. The Italian Political Police reported to the Ministry of the Interior that Tasca might be vulnerable and prepared to ask for his arrest.[8] At that point he turned for help to Professor Henri Moysset, who, with René Belin, a former deputy secretary general of the Socialist labor confederation and now Minister of Labor, intervened to obtain the restoration of Tasca's citizenship. Moysset, in addition to being a specialist on the work of the socialist writer Pierre Joseph Proudhon, was an expert on Eastern Europe and on naval questions and had been quite important as a high official during the Third Republic. He was a French representative to the London Naval Conference of 1930 and at the Geneva Disarmament Conference of 1932. Moysset had been a professor at the Centre des Hautes Etudes Navales and was a friend of both Pétain and Admiral

Darlan. In short, he was a conservative nationalist who rallied to Vichy with the hope of saving France from total occupation. He served as minister of state under successive Vichy governments, reaching his greatest influence under Darlan, until April 1942 and had a role in drafting the Labor Charter.[9]

Moysset, who had overall supervision of the Secretariat of Information in the new government, took Tasca on as an adviser after he prepared a long report in September 1940 on the causes of the fall of France and on the future prospects of the new regime. This report revealed Tasca's basic sympathy with the "patriotic" faction at Vichy and offered a series of policy options to the new authorities. To establish its legitimacy, Tasca suggested, the government had to tap the anticollaborationist feelings of wounded national pride. The danger was that the Germans might make Vichy seem too much a temporary shadow regime. Thus, the "New Order" would have to create for itself an image that was well distinguished from nazism, fascism, or bolshevism. It was essential for the salvation of France that the National Revolution succeed. Pétain's New Order would have to depend on all the resources of the state. He urged that the new regime avoid a vast purge of the state bureaucracy. The new rulers should look to the future rather than to the past and do all they could to bring in the Socialists who were willing to collaborate.[10]

Tasca also suggested what the fusion of the national and the social might entail under Vichy. Marxism and capitalism, he believed, had been superseded by events in the 1930s. Both were based on a common error that harmony would arise out of conflict: the free play of markets under capitalism and the notion of the unregulated class struggle for Marxists. In its search for a substitute ideology, Tasca suggested that Vichy might tap a strong national tradition of socialist thought that developed from Proudhon, the hero of revisionists and "national" socialists. But the linkage of the social with the national would be inadequate without another element, the Christian: "Socialism died because it did not know how to become the second Christian revolution which affirmed and rescued from the grip of rampant materialism the very human values which Christianity affirmed and saved within pagan society."[11] As for the relationship between the new France and Germany, Tasca argued: "Collaboration with Germany is a necessity: one must hope, since it is necessary, that it may be possible."[12] There is no reason to believe that Tasca was not sincere during these first months about interpreting the National Revolution as a new beginning. He obviously was willing to collaborate with the new regime in two ways: continued service within the Vichy bureaucracy and a column for the weekly paper *Effort*, the publication of the "national" socialists who opted for the regime.

REINTEGRATION IN THE CIVIL SERVICE

Tasca was always somewhat vague about his activities under Vichy. He mentioned in his postwar articles that he worked as director of the Research Bureau of the Ministry of Information and made it seem that this collaboration was dictated by the desire to gather information about German troop movements for the Belgian resistance.[13] His work for the government was, however, much more extensive and implied, as we shall see, a high degree of commitment in important areas.

Tasca worked from 1941 onward in the Ministry of Information's Service du Contrôle de l'Opinion Publique. This service was part of a reorganized propaganda apparatus under Vichy. Throughout most of the interwar period, France had had a somewhat disorganized information and propaganda structure over which the Foreign Ministry, the Ministry of Posts, the Interior Ministry, and the presidency of the council shared power. In August 1939 the government created the Commissariat Général à L'Information and appointed the playwright Jean Giraudoux to fill the post. He was succeeded in March 1940 by the ex-secretary of the PCF, now a socialist, L. O. Frossard, who headed a new Ministry of Information until the defeat in June 1940. The new structure attempted to centralize the various functions that had been dispersed. The ministry was dissolved, however, in June 1940. There followed in the rest of 1940 a dizzying succession of new titles and officials as the Vichy regime sought to organize its own propaganda machine. Finally, in early 1941, Paul Marion took over the role as chief propagandist with the title "Secrétaire Général adjoint à la vice présidence du Conseil chargé de l'Information." Marion had aspirations to model the Vichy propaganda ministry after that of Goebbels. Fortunately, he was a poor and inefficient administrator, who lost the support of his principal backers in the government, Darlan and Moysset, in early 1942 and was eased out when Laval returned to power in April. Under Marion the propaganda ministry was divided into two sections. The first dealt with the radio, press, and cinema, and the second, the Service de Propagande, occupied itself with the formation of cadres, the development of propaganda themes, censorship, and postal controls. The Service de Propagande worked through the Délégués à la Propagande, who were drawn from the militants of the National Revolution and from its local representatives. It also had sections for specialized propagandists and ran a training school, the École Nationale des Cadres Civiques.[14]

Directly under the Secretary General was a Bureau d'Études (Research Bureau), where Tasca was employed as director. Tasca entered the Bureau as a friend of Marion and was charged with "carrying out historical and sociological research on the conditions necessary for French recovery." Tasca's office worked closely with the Service de Propagande and with a special bureau, the Service de Propagande Anticommuniste, that was created in January 1942. A key responsibility that attracted Tasca was the role of the Research Bureau and the Service de Propagande Anticommuniste in monitoring the Communist political activities. Tasca's position gave him access to documentation on the Communist party, and a part of this material in his archives bears the official stamp of the police or the Deuxième Bureau.[15] In addition to his responsibilities at the Ministry of Information Tasca might have been involved in one other project for the regime. Through his contacts with Moysset and René Belin, it is possible that Tasca had some role in the drafting of the Labor Charter, but the evidence on this point is inconclusive.[16]

From 1941 to 1944 Tasca also lectured at the École des Cadres Civiques of the Sécrétariat Général à la Propagande. This school was established at Mayet de Montagne, near Vichy, to prepare leadership cadres among labor leaders, teachers, and bureaucrats. Marion, the ex-communist, intended it to be something like the Lenin school in Moscow. Perhaps because of that, it became a rallying point for some ex-communist and ex-socialist collaborators such as Tasca and Eugène Gaillard, a former administrator of Le Populaire who passed to Vichy.

The regime apparently assigned the school special importance. Laval, Marion, and Moysset all spoke there at one time or another.[17] Tasca's official title when he lectured was Directeur du Bureau d'Études of the Secrétariat Général. His courses dealt with Marxism, communism, the USSR, and the social content of the National Revolution. They are extremely important in determining Tasca's true views during the war, precisely because they reveal a strong continuity with his prewar writing.

Tasca worked loyally and actively with Vichy to the extent that it served as a barrier against communism. His collaboration was sincere even after he lost his illusions about the National Revolution. Tasca believed in the anticommunist mission of Vichy to the end. In fact, anticommunism was the link between his work with Vichy and his activities with the Resistance. In both cases, Tasca worked against all resistance movements that he saw, rightly or wrongly, as communist-controlled. He took his work at Vichy with great seriousness as a way of destroying Marxism and communism within France.[18]

One of Tasca's lectures, "Révolution Nationale et Révolution Économique," given in August 1942, clearly reveals this continuity with the past. He argued that the defeat of France was due in large part to the inability of the French to respond to the challenges of the modern world brought on by new technology and the appearance of new rivals on the world scene. Other countries used various methods such as the Five Year Plan in the

USSR or Fordism in the USA. Italy and Germany sought middle-class revolutionary solutions. Now, in France, the National Revolution had the responsibility of freeing society from the domination of the economic.[19]

In a series of lectures, delivered in mid-1943, Tasca traced out the National Revolution's "Third Way" between the liberal guardian state and the totalitarian system that was the sole judge of the rights of the individual. His analysis began from the premise that liberal and parliamentary democracy had never been able to come to grips with the new problems created after World War I:

> Personally, I believe that it is mistaken in its very premise. The political factor is the highest form of national collective consciousness that we find in each citizen. I do not believe that we find it to the same degree, at the present point of historical evolution, among all the citizens, and no guarantee at all is offered by the fiction of 'one man one vote' which, by a simple arithmetical calculation of a majority, gives the best choice of men to represent the collectivity and of programs which these men are to enact.

Therefore, universal suffrage would have to be modified to take into account the natural inequalities of the citizens.[20] Political participation would be linked to social function: "Naturally, the masses themselves cannot enjoy all aspects of political life because they are not ready. . . . The strength of the State is in direct relationship to the number and the quality of its elites, but one should not pose the problem of elites in contrast to the problem of the masses."[21] Just as the masses had little importance in modern democratic politics, they were a negative factor in the revolution as well. Contrary to Marx's beliefs, revolutionary movements were not the result of a rising from below, but came from above. Only the middle class was a truly active historical force.[22]

But revolution was the last consideration in the minds of his audience. Thus, Tasca emphasized the virtues of social stability and class harmony. No longer was revolution necessary. Those who sought change should work for a moral transformation of the already existing political class: "In the formation of a new consciousness, of an enlightened consciousness of the middle classes we find the best guarantee for their useful leadership role. History shows the way, but for this road to be taken demands will, consciousness, and organization."[23]

Tasca's immediate target at the École des Cadres was the French Communist party. As late as May 1944 he urged his audience to reject the belief that the victory of the French Communist party was inevitable. Tasca became a passionate defender of the bourgeoisie, which was the strongest bulwark against the triumph of communism, but, even with a strong French middle class, the struggle against communism would not be easy and might even be quite violent: "In France where, despite everything, a numerically important and fundamentally anticommunist middle class persists, the struggle for power might evolve through a civil war which, from the beginning would be extremely bloody."[24]

MARXISM AND MORALITY

Tasca's lectures at the École des Cadres revealed the extent of his evolution away from previously held theories of materialism and environmentalism that had been the original basis for his Marxism. But his new position was as much antiliberal as anti-Marxist. Already before 1940 he argued that Marxism shared many of the defects of liberalism. The latter was at the root of determinism in Marx and the source of the fallacy that the general interest would be served by class conflict. Both ideologies were seen as "extraverse"; that is, they sought the solution to the problem of liberty by manipulating the environment. The search for such external solutions inevitably became mechanistic, whereas, in fact, the real quest for freedom lay in developing Tasca's "twenty-fourth hour." The struggle for survival imprisoned individuals twenty-three hours a day; only for brief moments could they escape to become truly human: "We are ourselves, truly human, only at moments, by leaps, through abrupt decisions, by a rupture." But the Marxists failed to understand this point and reduced all the hours and days of human existence to a single unity of measure. Tasca no longer considered consciousness as the link between the individual and the mass, but rather the characteristic that distinguished the exceptional individual from the ordinary run of humanity. Moments of conscious choice resembled the illumination that faith brought to the Christian: "From this perspective we can better appreciate the Christian notion of the redemption of an entire wasted life by the sudden illumination of an act of faith." In both cases spiritual salvation came from inside, rather than outside.[25]

Precisely because it subjected the individual to the domination of outside forces, Marxism was inevitably totalitarian: "We can say that the first of the totalitarian doctrines of the modern era is Marxism and its idea of the dictatorship of the proletariat. . . . No other totalitarian system has pushed the notion of state power and the idea of social engineering as far as Marxism does on the basis of the dictatorship of the proletariat."[26]

There was no guarantee that the interests of the state, even under socialism, would coincide with those of the proletariat, nor that the interests of the proletariat were congruent with those of humanity. The central issue of modern political philosophy was the protection of the individual against the mass. But secular morality seemed ill equipped to accomplish this task: "But what separates us from Marx is not that he placed productive forces above the test of justice or of the individual and collective conscience, but rather that it is impossible to draw from his system, as it is conceived, a lasting, concrete, and satisfying vision of man which is able to serve as a motivation of change."[27]

EFFORT AND THE "NATIONAL" SOCIALISTS

The École des Cadres Civiques was less important as a rallying point for the ex-socialists who passed to Vichy than were the many newspapers and periodicals that attempted to relaunch a version of socialism within the New Order. Déat's L'Oeuvre was flanked in Paris by the antisemitic L'Atelier and Charles Spinasse's Le Rouge et le Bleu. Spinasse, a long-time socialist who had been a member of Blum's Popular Front government, was also connected with L'Effort, which appeared in Lyons. Tasca collaborated only on Effort, which was somewhat less compromised than was Le Rouge et le Bleu, but both periodicals offered loyal support to the National Revolution. He began to write a column on foreign affairs in August 1940 but stopped temporarily in November because of political differences. Later he contended that he resumed writing for the paper in April 1941 only as a way of staying in Vichy so that he could continue his work for the Resistance. He also denied that his collaboration was significant: "I never wrote articles on international or foreign policy for the paper. . . . Therefore there is no basis for the totally fabricated assertion that I had charge of the foreign policy column." He merely offered "simple informative commentaries on events in various countries, excluding France."[28]

These statements were manifestly untrue. Tasca did stop writing for Effort in November 1940. However, the articles signed "R" from April to June 1941 are very likely by Tasca. It was also possible that those signed "Interim" from February through March were also written by him because his archives contain copies of the originals with notations and stamps of the censor. Thus, his collaboration might have been interrupted only from November to the end of January 1941. Moreover Tasca's articles were not simply marginalia, but were a continuation of his writing for Le Populaire with an occasional excursus into ideology.[29] If he wrote little that was overtly favorable to the Axis, the context in which he wrote was often very compromising as Effort became more openly favorable to Nazi Germany and increasingly Fascist in character.

Effort grouped a number of ex-socialists and pacifists, such as Étienne Gaillard, a former administrator of Le Populaire, a Socialist deputy Paul Rives, François Chasseigne, an ex-communist (one of many!) who served as Paul Marion's Directeur de la Propagande, and Jean Arnol. Effort was divided between those, like Spinasse, who looked on collaboration as a necessity but wished to find a basis for socialism within the French tradition of Proudhon or Saint Simon, and those, like Paul Rives, who were gradually drawn into an overt pro-Nazi position. The politics of *Effort* were set by Paul Rives, who already before the defeat had worked on an extreme right-wing news agency. He now called for a long-needed break with the past: "We have cleaned house, if not with a light heart, at least without regret." Charles Spinasse argued that the fall of the Third Republic was a blessing in disguise: "What died in France was a regime which was profoundly corrupted by an electoral system which atomized and levelled humanity . . . it is an economic system which ended in misery and unemployment. . . . But neither democracy nor socialism went down with our former life."[30] Rives and Spinasse made it clear that French socialism had to break with the past to create a new nationalist and anticommunist ideology in which class struggle would be replaced by hierarchy and discipline.[31] But there were those who went much further. Victor Marguerite, openly collaborationist, called on the socialists to accept the German victory, and Marcel Déat demanded the development of a new socialism modeled on Fascist or Nazi principles. Somewhat less openly, Spinasse agreed that France might find its place in a Nazi-dominated Europe. Rives urged a "loyal and honorable" collaboration on the French. All of these articles were written before Tasca suspended his column in November 1940. During the period of rupture the tone became neither more nor less openly favorable to the Nazis. In fact, after Tasca returned, Rives emerged as the dominant figure on *Effort* and gave it a clearly pro-Nazi tone.[32]

TASCA'S COLLABORATION ON *EFFORT*

Tasca's articles from the August–November period dealt with the foreign policy options of the various European powers. He was certain that nothing the other powers, including the USSR, could do would alter the fact of the German victory. The Nazis would attempt to defeat England and then settle with the United States of America.[33] Tasca's attitude did not change after his return in February or April 1941. He contributed to the mood of resignation and defeat that gripped France, although his columns were often quite acute and informative.

When war between the USSR and Germany began, Tasca predicted confidently that Soviet resistance would be insufficient, although he never advocated a Nazi victory as did Rives and Peschadour.[34] When the United States entered the war at the end of 1941, Tasca became notably more cautious and predicted a long and costly war that would be decided as much by the quantity and quality of the personnel that each side could muster as by the material resources.[35]

By mid-1942 Tasca began to wind down his collaboration with *Effort*, although there was no indication that he had lost his faith that the Germans would win. His last articles in August 1942 on the fighting capacity of the Soviet army pointed out that the Russians had failed to understand the nature of modern warfare. They adopted techniques of mass production, but in place of quality, they substituted quantity, which would never be sufficient.[36]

Tasca broke with *Effort* because Rives finally went too far in the direction of the Nazis. By 1942 the split within the two camps of Socialist collaborators reached the point of rupture. Led by Déat, Victor Marguerite, Rives, and Arnol advocated a reversal of alliances and a clear alignment of France on the side of Nazi Germany. Already in early 1942 Tasca learned from Rives that Laval wanted a federation of all socialist collaborationist groups. He was informed in September that *Le Rouge et Le Bleu* had been suspended, and Spinasse removed from any responsibility for both papers after a break with Déat. Tasca, who had favored Spinasse's more limited vision of cooperation with Vichy and Germany more than the views of Rives and Gaillard, decided not to return from his vacation.[37]

TASCA AND VICHY: THE AMBIGUITIES OF COLLABORATION

Tasca's extensive wartime diaries offer confirmation that Tasca viewed Vichy as a real, but lost opportunity for change. He believed that its leaders erred in using their power for revenge rather than for national unity but that Marshal Pétain did not personally favor the policy of repression. Tasca was persuaded by the presence of former deputies such as Frossard and Laval that the fanatics would not take charge.[38] After the fall of Laval's government at the end of 1940, Tasca viewed the Flandin interlude with some suspicion. He was no less worried about the designation of Admiral Darlan in February 1941. Tasca felt that Darlan and his advisers, Lucien Romier and Moysset, were neither rigidly hostile to England nor pro-German, but their vision of France's imperial mission might lead them to a compromise with Germany on the Continent. On the whole, Tasca's vantage point inside the regime and the information that he received from key figures such as Paul Marion only seemed to increase his alienation from the National Revolution.[39] By late 1942 and early 1943, Tasca wrote that many officials in the Foreign Ministry were seeking to jump ship to save their "tender consciences" and their careers at the same time. Frossard reported to him from Paris that all the Germans, except the convinced Nazis, considered the war already lost. By February 1943 Tasca's diary notations, formerly full of scorn for the Soviet army, now traced the superiority of the Russians over the Germans and predicted the end of the war by the end of 1944.[40]

THE FIRST COLD WARRIOR

In 1943 Tasca began to envision the United States as a counterweight to Soviet influence. He felt that much more planning had to be devoted to the postwar political order: "We must think of the peace and of Europe as Lenin thought about revolution. From this moment we must draw up plans, making them as realistic as possible. . . . These plans, more than preparing for the peace, will prepare the men who will take on that task. That is the essential thing." [41]

Tasca envisaged for himself a role in the postwar construction of France. During the war he had been working on several studies on the postwar outlook for France and for Europe and had sent his ideas to Pierre Viénot in London. At the beginning of April 1943 he had a long conversation on the need for a Third Force between the Communists, who had control of the democratic movement, and Giraud, who was surrounded by reactionaries. The Vichy regime, even in its waning days, might offer a bridgehead to the future if those in the administration who were interested in the maintenance of order could find a sympathetic ear among those on the other side who were interested in the same issues. In a France divided between the Communists and the Anglo-Saxons, Third Force elements, if placed in important ministries, might be able to create an alliance of anticommunist Gaullists, radicals, socialists, and syndicalists.[42] Clearly, the primary enemy, as it had been since the beginning of the war, was the Communist party. The problem of the collaborationists was already receding into the background: "We can imagine collaboration dictated exclusively by love of France. This sentiment played no decisive role in the attitude of the French Communists in August and September 1939, nor did it afterward." The problem again was the low level of political understanding of the masses who accepted communist propaganda: "The mentality of the majority of men remains 'primitive,' that is to say immune to the power of true logic." [43]

TASCA AND THE RESISTANCE

Tasca was both an observer of and a participant in the Vichy experiment. His collaboration was real, if limited, to the extent that he first considered Vichy a bulwark against collapse and then as a defense against communism. But, as he also justly pointed out, his support for Vichy was not his sole activity during the war. In February 1941 Tasca began to work with the Belgian Resistance. The diplomat P. Cavyn contacted Tasca with a letter of presentation from Jef Rens, an old socialist acquaintance of Tasca. Beginning in early 1941 and continuing throughout the war, Tasca submitted weekly reports to Cavyn. According to Cavyn, Tasca risked his life several times in the process of passing information. In addition to what he gave to the Belgians, Tasca also passed information on to Pierre Viénot in London. As he played his double game, Tasca received help from a number of individuals, most notably the diplomat Jacques Fouques Duparc, who had been in charge of supervising the Italian-language broadcasts when Tasca headed that service before the defeat in June 1940. Through the good offices of Fouques-Duparc, Tasca was able to help Faravelli, Giovanni Faraboldi, and Mario Levi when they were arrested by the Vichy police and threatened with deportation to Italy. Tasca also intervened to help Pietro Nenni and claimed that he indirectly aided the "Libérer et Fédérer" group of which Silvio Trentin, a leader of GL who would be killed during the Resistance, was a part.[44]

There is no reason to doubt Tasca's work with the Resistance, but it does not entirely resolve the problems created by his collaboration. Perhaps the most severe indictment of Tasca was made by Silvio Trentin's son Bruno in a letter to Salvemini of 14 October 1952. Although Trentin, a noted Communist, might have had partisan motives, the issues remain valid. Trentin argued that Tasca should have seen the reality behind Vichy and thus that his initial collaboration was naive at best and criminal at worst. Moreover Tasca's conversion to Vichy had such a demoralizing effect at the time that it negated any possible good. Nor did Trentin find the "double game" excuse convincing, because it was used by collaborators of all kinds. Finally, Trentin accused Tasca of working with the "official" Belgian and English resistance to thwart any popular movement from below.[45]

There was much truth to these accusations, and the Vichy years cast a shadow over Tasca's later life. By 1940 he had evolved to the point that he had little in common with the main body of socialist opinion. He had lost faith not only in Marxism but in the whole process of parliamentary democracy. Thus, when the defeat came, Tasca was psychologically prepared to accept many of the remedies proposed by Vichy. But he never advocated the victory of Germany. When his confidence in Vichy rapidly waned, he continued to support those activities of Vichy that seemed to be specifically directed against the communists. Anticommunism became the link between Tasca at Vichy and Tasca the member of the resistance. The moral ambiguity of his position escaped Tasca then and later. It cost him a political career both in France and in Italy.

Although it is difficult to justify Tasca's position from the point of view of Italian antifascism, the ambiguities of his actions did reflect the basic confusion of many French. From the French perspective, Tasca's great fault was that his motivations contradicted the myth of a France that heroically resisted the Germans and of a Communist party that inspired the

Resistance. Tasca was embarrassing to the Socialists as a symbol of the party's failure of will in June and July 1940. He was embarrassing to the Resistance because of his fierce anticommunism, even though he played a role in the struggle against Nazism. Tasca could never understand the rejection that he experienced after the war. Only when anticommunism became the official ideology of the West were the doors opened once again. But it was a high price to pay. In this sense Tasca was not only a precursor of the cold war, but also a victim of the negative conception of politics that marred so much of the period after 1945.

14

Cold War Politics

The war ended for Tasca, as did his political career, on 3 September 1944, when he was arrested by the new French provisional government. Some weeks before, he had noted in his diary: "Over four years endured, suspended over the abyss, between a past which disgusted me, a sordid, hardly bearable, present, and an uncertain future."[1] Tasca realized that the future would be difficult, but he believed that the problems would arise more from his rupture with his socialist past than from a general ostracism because of his actions during the Vichy period. He greatly underestimated the hostility that his collaboration engendered in both the French and Italian Left. To Tasca Vichy was a kind of tragic hiatus on both a personal and political level that he hoped to put behind him as soon as possible. He resumed his former relationship with Madame Chaumette and married her soon after the war, although he apparently did not inform her immediately of his wartime relationship with Alice Naturel and of his new daughter.[2]

Tasca expected that other contacts would be as easily revived. He counted heavily on Pierre and Andrée Viénot to reestablish himself after the war, but the death of Pierre, who knew of his Resistance activity, and the hostility of Andrée, who did not, ended his hopes in that direction. The deaths of Pierre Brossolette; of his brother-in-law Renato Martorelli, murdered by the Fascists in August 1944; and of his old friend Enrico Tulli added to his sense of isolation.[3]

ARREST AND IMPRISONMENT

The postwar era began badly for Tasca. On 2 September, a detachment of Communist-led partisans attempted to arrest him. Tasca believed that they intended to execute him immediately for his work against the party. The next day, when he complained to the police, he was officially detained and taken to Clermont Ferrand for interrogation. Luckily he was able to give the address of his contacts in the Resistance to Alice Naturel, who passed the information on to Charles-André Julien, Liliane Chaumette, André Philip, and Valeria Tasca in Paris. Tasca believed that the evidence about his work in the Resistance would be sufficient to gain his release. He appealed directly to Foreign Minister Georges Bidault, Robert Lacoste, the Minister of Production, and André Philip without apparent effect. Continued imprisonment made Tasca increasingly desperate and embittered. Only on 22 September was he able to tell his side of the story to the Regional Commissioner of the Republic in Toulouse, who collected the information from Cavyn and others that finally led to Tasca's release. Even then, he regained his freedom only in mid-October, almost a month and a half after his arrest. The judicial proceedings were not finished until early 1947, although he received an award from the Belgian government for his services.[4]

FROM SECULAR TO RELIGIOUS HUMANISM

This period in prison deepened Tasca's alienation from the Liberation regime and from the Left in general and led him to enlarge on his earlier critique of Marxism. He had long since given up hope in a social democratic experiment based on Marxist principles. In his eyes Marxism had subjected the individual conscience to abstract historical laws. Communist practice made the party the final arbiter of truth. Tasca sought the roots of this subordination of conscience to historical necessity in the rationalist eighteenth-century thought on which Marxism was based. Enlightenment thought, which reached its extreme in Rousseau, undermined individual liberty by subjecting it exclusively to the dictates of society. Thus, the democratic and Jacobin tradition of French revolutionary thought offered little defense against the impersonal forces represented by the single party at the service of an all-powerful state.[5]

Not even the famous French Revolutionary triad, "liberty, equality and fraternity," was spared from Tasca's attack. Liberty was essentially the capacity for choice. In the Christian tradition liberty was the cause of both man's fall and his salvation. It could not be a natural right in the sense that such capacity existed from birth. Tasca considered liberty to be the end of a process, not its starting point, something gained as the human personality developed. All individuals were equal in the sense that they had the potential to be free, but the realization of this capacity depended on the growth of reason and of consciousness. Although the development of human potential depended in part on external conditions, its essence was in its internal moral dimension: "Liberty must be defined as the power (the possibility) of each man to know what is good and to act accordingly." The choice was at once an exercise in free will and a moral imperative. It implied a higher system of values that could not be found in history or society but were grounded in a transcendent concept of good and evil.[6]

As for equality, individuals were not born equal any more than they were born free. Like liberty, equality was the result of experience. It was the discovery that the measure for each individual was the common humanity shared with all other individuals. Once individuals gained this realization of the fundamental identity of each individual with all of humanity, equality became an absolute moral norm to which humanity must adhere.[7]

But equality, like liberty, had no sense if not expressed in a common notion of what was good. One must arrive at a basic conception of the 'good' to link liberty and equality in a lasting unity: "From awareness of community to consciousness of the good: community equals the good and the good is valid for all. Now there is no doubt that men have the same idea of what is represented by the good from the minute when they feel their community of nature and of destiny."[8]

In the French Revolutionary trinity only liberty and equality had been raised to cult status, whereas, in reality, fraternity was all-important. Without fraternity both liberty and equality would have no content. But fraternity could only have its basis in a religious conception that offered a guarantee for the value of each individual: "To rechristianize Europe and the world is to affirm ever more strongly, in the way which we have tried to do, liberty and equality, but in reference to fraternity. Without the latter we fall into the arbitrariness of anarchy or in the dictatorship of bolshevism."[9]

Tasca's long search for values whose validity could be grounded outside the historical process led him to the concept of God: "To end by saying 'all men are brothers,' we must take a long route, one which goes from God to man and then ascends back to Him, one which goes from generalized thinking about man to love." Ends and means had to be united in a religiously based conception of humanity as the supreme value:

> I arrive at the discovery and at the highest illumination which is that my liberty, my dignity, my essence are tied to those of other men, my brothers, and that there is no possibility of happiness, of consciousness, of salvation except in the common good. The moral law, let us repeat, is revelation and commandment: what the Old Testament tells of the giving of the law and of the pact which binds man and God, and the very form taken by this law as commandments symbolize the true nature of the moral law.[10]

The great danger that confronted the modern individual was no longer the oppression that resulted from capitalist exploitation but the threat of totalitarianism, which resulted from the subordination of the individual to an increasingly powerful and centralized state. The danger to liberty transcended political systems and was even greater under certain forms of socialism.[11] He now conceived of socialism as merely a generic sense of social solidarity and as the desire to create in every individual the potential for self-liberation through mastery of economic necessity.[12]

THE REJECTION OF LIBERATION FRANCE

Tasca's positions left him almost totally isolated in Liberation France, a situation for which he was initially unprepared. It seemed to Tasca in the months following the Liberation that his experience had been wasted: "The true misfortune is not the lack of money, loneliness, the injustice endured; it is the inability to do the good that urgently must be done . . . to feel useless, that is the true misfortune." He wrote to a friend that he prepared himself to contribute to the rebirth of France, yet, after his return to Paris, he met a wall of hostility: "I violated the laws of the clan and that is what the jungle pardons the least. . . ."[13]

No political party commanded his adherence. Although he was quite sympathetic to a religious view of social problems, he viewed the Catholic parties primarily as a bastion against communism.[14] Alienation from the Resistance also reinforced Tasca's sympathy for the conservative nationalists of Vichy. He felt that many of the Pétainists condemned after the war had been motivated by sincere patriotism. He attempted to help Paul Marion at his trial and remained strongly attached to Henri Moysset, with whom he worked closely under Vichy.[15] Not unexpectedly, Tasca liked Francois Mauriac's appeal for mercy in the purges after the war: "Mauriac takes the role of spiritual guide, and one understands better in reading him the campaign which he has led for charity in the purges."[16]

Tasca's relations with the French Socialists during these years were marked by hostility on both sides. Well after the war a letter, misdirected to him at *Le Populaire*, was returned with "he betrayed" scrawled on the front. Tasca learned of Blum's remark "What a pity. If Rossi had held out a few days longer, he would play a major role today in Italy" and responded with outrage: "I 'held out' for four years and for quite different ambitions than to become a deputy or minister in the French or Italian Constituent Assembly." If the socialists viewed him as a traitor, he felt that the SFIO was unjust and hypocritical toward Vichy and allowed itself to become a prisoner of the Communist party. The decline of the party was the fault of Blum, who, although personally admirable, had never been a political leader.[17]

In 1945 Tasca gravitated to the Mouvement National Révolutionnaire, which advocated the reconstruction of society on a communitarian basis, European unity as an alternative to domination by the USSR or the United States of America, and anticommunism. Tasca began writing for its review, *La République Moderne*, under the name *Jean Servant*. His contribution was to sketch out a theory of the state that would have a corporative political structure in which communities of labor would be represented in a territorial and functional parliament.[18] Briefly, in late 1946 and 1947 Tasca believed that De Gaulle was the only force standing between France and communism, but, despite the urgings of noted Gaullists such as Louis Vallon and André Malraux, he refused to join the Rassemblement du Peuple Français.[19]

MILITANT ANTICOMMUNISM

Without a party or the possibility of an active political career, Tasca came to see his role as leading the intellectual battle against Communism. He realized the dangers that this position implied:

> Apart from my desire not to become a "technician of anticommunism" and to avoid the professional deformation which so often results from it, you know as well as I that the struggle against the Communist party is only to a quite limited degree a technical struggle and that its effectiveness depends primarily on the general policies which shape this struggle. . . .[20]

Tasca realized that his only weapons were the books he could write. Beginning in 1948 with *La Physiologie du Parti Communiste Français*, Tasca began to publish a series of works on French communism and on Soviet foreign policy. *La Physiologie du Parti Communiste Français* was followed by *Deux ans d'alliance Germano-Soviétique* and *Les Communistes Français pendant la Drôle de Guerre* and by numerous articles on specific aspects of Soviet policy such as the Khrushchev report of 1956. In these carefully documented books, Tasca sought to make two points: that the USSR, motivated exclusively by national interest, betrayed the Left by signing the alliance with Hitler, and that the French Communist party was merely a faithful executor of Soviet directives. In *La Physiologie du Parti Communiste Français* and in *Les Communistes Français pendant la Drôle de Guerre*, Tasca portrayed the PCF in its worst moment as it urged defeat on France and cooperated with the German authorities. His point was that the French Communists acted between 1939 and 1941 in much the same way as did Vichyites such as Charles Maurras and had little claim to monopolize the heritage of the Resistance. The logic of Tasca's argument was that the PCF had never really been a French party at all and was not a suitable participant in French political life. In fact, in *La Physiologie du Parti Communiste Français*, Tasca came close to asking for its suppression and urged a full-scale political and ideological war against it: "The Communist party is not an internationalist party, but a foreign nationalist party because it has its own patriotism—Soviet patriotism."[21]

As one of the first historians to deal with the Nazi-Soviet pact and with the role of the French Communist party between 1939 and 1941, Tasca was extremely dangerous to the Communists. He was able to accumulate an enormous amount of material from his Vichy years that revealed the nature of Communist propaganda during the 1939–1941 period. He was able to cite and reproduce documents and manifestos that were extremely compromising, even if one did not agree with the general message contained in Tasca's books. Thus, it was only a matter of time before the PCF counterattacked with an article in *La France Nouvelle* by Roger Maria, a Communist journalist and Resistance veteran. Maria accused Tasca among other things of having been a spy for the Nazis and of having built an entire career on betrayal.[22] The libel suit that Tasca brought against Maria symbolized Tasca's break with his past. Pietro Nenni and the French Socialists Gilles Martinet (Buozzi's son-in-law) and André Blumel testified for Maria. The diplomats Cavyn and Fouques-Duparc and the historian Gaetano Salvemini supported Tasca in his successful action.[23]

TASCA AND *IL MONDO*

This case revealed the extent of Tasca's difficulty in renewing ties with his old friends on the Left. Initially, even Giuseppe Faravelli had been convinced that Tasca had betrayed the cause, but Tasca was able to persuade his friend that he had never collaborated. When the two men met in October 1947, Tasca described his role in obtaining the release of Faraboldi, Levi, and Faravelli.[24]

In fall 1949 Tasca visited Italy for the first time since his departure for exile in 1926, and his return whetted his appetite to return to the Italian political scene. He had been writing for the reformist *Critica Sociale*, edited by Faravelli, and his volumes on the French Communist party and Soviet foreign policy had appeared in Italy. Then, in 1950, Tasca began a long and fruitful collaboration with Mario Pannunzio's *Il Mondo*, the best of the Italian political weeklies of the postwar period. *Il Mondo*, like its editor, was radical, democratic, and, above all, heretical. It was a good place for Tasca, who published his important contributions on the early years of the Italian Communist party and a series on his life in France during the war in Pannunzio's magazine. But engaging Tasca presented a delicate problem for Pannunzio, who realized the potential for controversy. Only the support of Silone and Salvemini, both having impeccable antifascist credentials, made it possible.[25]

In fact, difficulties arose in 1952. Tasca had been writing for *Il Mondo* for almost two years when Gaetano Salvemini opened a full-scale debate by responding to the accusations of betrayal made by Alberto Jacometti, one of the leaders of the interwar PSI, against Tasca in his memoir *Quando la storia macina*. Salvemini, who was convinced that Tasca's work with the Resistance was a valid reason for staying in Vichy, asserted that belief in a letter on 24 May to *Il Mondo* that led to further exchanges involving Jacometti, Salvemini, and the family of Silvio Trentin. Salvemini admitted that Tasca, like many French, had a crisis of faith in 1940 but overcame it. It was unjust and inhumane to hold this condition against Tasca, since others at the orders of Moscow had served the aims of Hitler from 1939 to summer 1941. As Salvemini wrote to Bruno, Franca, and Giorgio Trentin: "This [the role of the Communists between 1939 and 1941] truly was a double game but among the worst."[26]

TASCA AND THE AMERICANS

During this period, Tasca, who wholeheartedly favored Italy's pro-American foreign policy, acted as a kind of arbiter between Faravelli and the American supporters of Italian Social Democracy. Two old friends of Tasca who were leaders in the American International Ladies Garment Workers Union, Vanni Montana and Luigi Antonini, had helped finance the PSI since the 1930s. After 1947, when the PSI again split between reformists and maximalists, this aid was directed to the Social Democrats, but the Americans could not understand why Faravelli and others on the party's left wing could not accept the Atlantic Alliance and had scruples about working with the Italian Christian Democratic party. Tasca continually intervened with Montana, the head of the New York Local 89, to ensure that poor relations with Faravelli would not endanger support for the party. He also wrote directly to the American embassy in Rome to explain his friend's views.[27]

Although Tasca had resumed contact with Montana in 1946, it is unclear whether his ties with the Americans developed through Montana or had existed independently. In his memoirs Montana wrote that he was informed by the American State Department of Tasca's resistance activity in 1945. Thereafter Montana gave constant assistance to Tasca in obtaining books and newspapers and even passed one of Tasca's books to William J. Donovan, the head of the United States Office of Strategic Services during the war. Tasca and Montana exchanged information about the future of the Social Democratic movement in Italy and about Communists who held influential positions in various agencies such as UNESCO.[28]

Tasca also turned to Montana at the time of the legal case against *La France Nouvelle*. He asked whether Antonini and David Dubinsky might be interested in helping pay the costs of the trial. Montana was able to obtain five hundred dollars from Dubinsky and other support from the anti-communist liberal Max Ascoli and from Jay Lovestone of the American

Federation of Labor. The money was sent through Irving Brown who was the American Federation of Labor (AFL) representative in Europe. Tasca was also instructed to approach Brown directly for money from a special fund that he controlled.[29]

These contacts open the possibility that Tasca had some connection with the American Central Intelligence Agency. The Americans were actively organizing the noncommunist Left in those years, and Tasca was viewed as an expert on the communist movement and even lectured at the NATO Defense College on communism. From 1948 onward he actively, but unsuccessfully, sought a fellowship in America at the Russian Research Center at Harvard. Tasca wrote to Montana in July 1953 that he wanted to visit Washington to speak with officials in the State Department: "You know as well as I the reasons."[30] While in Washington he spoke before academic and semiofficial organizations on the dangers of communism. A few months later, in September 1953, Tasca spoke with an official at the American embassy in Paris on the possibility of a Popular Front in either France or Italy and the French problems with the Viet Minh.[31]

Tasca's relationship with the Americans did not end there. He was approached by the United States embassy to prepare an article on the relationship between the French Communist party and the USSR. When the American-sponsored review *Problems of Communism* was published, Tasca was immediately contacted to ensure his collaboration. He also participated in various organizations designed to mobilize noncommunist intellectuals, which were later found to have received CIA funding, such as the Congress for Cultural Freedom and the Amis de la Liberté.[32] Without the records of the Central Intelligence Agency, it is difficult to know what to conclude from this evidence, and Tasca's vast archives shed little light on the subject. Still, it should not be surprising that he figured in the American efforts to organize the noncommunist Left during the cold war. In no sense did Tasca betray his deepest convictions. He believed fervently that the Soviet Union had to be combatted by any means. The question of the relation of this attitude to Tasca's earlier beliefs is irrelevant because he had long since abandoned them.

ILLNESS AND DEATH

In 1956 Tasca began to be seriously affected by the central nervous system disease that was to take his life four years later. In fact, the first indications might have been evident around 1950, when Tasca noted in his diary: "Very slight trembling in the right hand or, rather, a slight difficulty in firmly grasping the pen, diminished feeling in the tips of the fingers on the same hand. From time to time, when I go to brush my teeth, I have noticed that the right cheek was less mobile and very slightly swollen. Nothing special about the lower limbs."[33]

Tasca was in these years greatly dependent on his wife. His sole income was from his writing and from his wife's earnings, and he worked under somewhat cramped and difficult conditions. After 1956 the course of his illness made him more and more isolated and dependent. By 1957 he wrote that he had been immobilized for two months. Saddest of all for one who had compiled hundreds of diaries in a clear and meticulous script, in mid-1958 he was forced to apologize to another friend for his almost illegible handwriting. These years were filled with much suffering and disappointment as countless visits to specialists produced no cure for the progressive debilitation.[34]

Shortly before his death, however, he entered into negotiations to sell his vast archive and library to the newly created Giangiacomo Feltrinelli Institute in Milan. As much as anything else he accomplished, the collection of records, diaries, and books that he guarded through exile and war remain a monument to his industry and dedication to maintaining the record of the Communist and Socialist movement from 1927 to 1940. On 3 March 1960, Tasca died in Paris.

Conclusion:
The Outsider
as Politician

Throughout the preceding pages we have sought to understand something of Angelo Tasca's long and often controversial political career and of the history of the political movements to which he belonged from 1910 to 1945. Two tragedies shaped both Tasca and the Italian Left. The triumph of fascism severed Tasca from Italy and destroyed his family. Then he was driven into exile a second time when he was expelled from the Italian Communist party on Stalin's orders in 1929. But this event had an equally dramatic impact on the PCI, which was subjected to a process of Stalinization in the early 1930s. Tasca spent the remainder of his life fighting the two great evils, fascism and Stalinism, that so altered his personal and political life.

The battles were of a different order, however. The struggle against fascism brought out the best in Tasca. His clear understanding of the nature of the Fascist movement and the strategy that he suggested to combat it established him among the leading figures of the antifascist diaspora. Tasca's other struggle in exile, the long fight against Stalin, became a civil war in which he rejected many of the ideals of his youth without ever arriving at an equally positive and coherent position. He came to merge anti-Stalinism with anticommunism and anti-Marxism. In his eyes the whole Marxist tradition was fundamentally flawed. But Tasca's Marxism had been intertwined with his faith in democracy and with his humanistic vision of socialism. The results of his repudiation of Marxism were negative and tragic because he never found a totally coherent set of ideals to replace those of his youth.

Until the mid-1930s Tasca often seemed to represent common

sense and political realism. Even against the more brilliant and original Antonio Gramsci at the time of the debates over the factory councils, Tasca emerged with a good deal of credit. Certainly his advocacy of a more open Communist party after the split at Livorno and his call for a United Front against fascism were correct positions. Perhaps his finest moment came when he opposed Stalin in Moscow in 1928.

During the 1930s, however, Tasca's political career took a different direction. Influenced by theorists such as Henri De Man, Tasca moved toward neoreformism. He assumed many of the attitudes of those French socialists who embarked on the path that would take them to Vichy. Ironically, just as Tasca moved further from his roots in the Italian Left, he engaged in a long duel with Pietro Nenni for control of the Italian Socialist party. In this struggle Nenni represented, for better or worse, continuity with the traditional values of Italian socialism.

Tasca's revision of Marx during the 1930s led him in two directions. He became increasingly concerned about the danger of uncontrolled power that arose from the modern bureaucratic state. Stalin's all-powerful party-state seemed to him the greatest evil confronting the world. Somewhat arbitrarily, he drew the conclusion that it was the inevitable consequence of Marxism. But Tasca was unable to reconcile this libertarian tendency in his thought with a second, much less positive, aspect. During the late 1930s and during the Vichy period, Tasca became increasingly elitist and antiliberal. He lost faith in parliamentary democracy and in political equality. By the outbreak of World War II, Tasca was a deeply divided man. His understanding of foreign policy and his past as an antifascist militant made him want to resist Nazi aggression by all means. But the ignominious collapse of France in 1940, which he blamed on the French Communist party, brought about a crisis of faith and led to his collaboration with Vichy, a collaboration only partially redeemed by his work in the Resistance.

Tasca's career effectively ended with World War II. Although he made some notable contributions as a historian after 1945, nothing equaled his masterful study on the development of Italian fascism published in 1938. Much of his postwar work fell in the category of cold war scholarship. Anticommunism became the dominant passion of his life, but it was unable to offer him the positive ideals that guided his career as a communist and socialist.

In evaluating Tasca's career, two extremes must be avoided. The first is to judge his entire career in light of the Vichy period, negating his great contributions to the Italian Left before 1940. The second error would be to make Tasca a hero of militant anticommunism for his battles against Stalin, since his career reveals a failure to distinguish between the valid and the corrupted in the socialist heritage.

The events that shaped Tasca's life in unexpected ways also altered the history of the Communist and Socialist movements. The Italian Communist party suffered greatly from being forced to purge Tasca, Bordiga, Leonetti, Silone, and many others. Although the party never entirely abandoned its soul to Stalin, the compromises were hard to swallow and demanded a high degree of political prostitution that marked a sad moment in the history of a great political party. Yet, just because the party was wrong, Tasca was not entirely correct as a Communist leader: Rather, it was not enough to be correct. His strategy of limiting the risks that the party would take in the struggle against Mussolini was wise, but it undercut the basic claim of the PCI that it led the struggle against the Fascists at whatever personal cost. In the end, Togliatti was more successful than Tasca might ever have been in leading the party in the direction indicated by the latter in the 1920s.

Tasca's career within the Italian Socialist party was even more problematical. Here again his chief antagonist was a man of many faults. Pietro Nenni was neither a gifted political tactician nor a notable theorist. His major contribution to the party was the dubious one of blocking the merger with the PCI in 1923, but he never really gave the party a reason for being. Nenni led the PSI into a long alliance with the Communists without really understanding that he had abandoned to the PCI any political space on the Left. His brand of maximalism was, as Tasca well understood, totally obsolete. Yet it is unfair to blame Nenni for the debacle of the PSI. Nenni understood better than did Tasca the need to focus on the antifascist struggle. Tasca always had one eye on the postfascist regime that might be created in Italy and was more interested in the Communists' potential gain from the victory against Mussolini. Nenni, to his great credit, never formulated the argument in those terms.

As it turned out, neither man had a strategy to offer to the PSI. The political opportunity for the PSI simply did not exist. That peculiar phenomenon that was Italian maximalism was a product of an Italy that perished between 1914 and 1922. Maximalism was based on a society with a high degree of class warfare but a formally liberal and constitutional political order. Maximalism was spawned by this pre-1914 society that it rejected and that tolerated it as long as it never became dangerous. That toleration all ended with the revolutionary years of 1918 through 1920.

But was Tasca's alternative, which proposed the abandonment of Marxism and the adoption of a frankly reformist strategy more solidly based? Was the creation of alliances with other social groups more valid? Certainly Tasca was correct in his rejection of all totalitarian rationalizations and in his fear of collective and centralizing solutions. Still, to be effective, he had to act through a political movement. Perhaps sensing that no such political party existed on the Italian Left, Tasca turned to France, where he was more at home with his brand of reformism. Within the French party his true allies were men such as Jean Monnet, Pierre Viénot and, even, Léon Blum. At a crucial moment, however, Tasca let anticommunism become the dominant element in his political outlook. He wavered in his faith in the democratic regime that had allowed the Communists to play such an important role and that could not protect France from defeat in 1940. It was a fatal error, but one that a large number of French socialists made in 1940.

Thus, Tasca's life, like the socialist movement itself, defies neat categories. He was neither a hero nor a villain. More than anything else he was an outsider who never quite belonged in the Communist party, in the SFIO, in the leadership of the PSI, in the National Revolution of Pétain, or in the ranks of the cold warriors. Tasca was one of the saddest figures of that generation of exiles: the one who could never return home.

Notes

INTRODUCTION

1. The best study of this generational problem is Robert Wohl, *The Generation of 1914* (Cambridge, Mass.: Harvard University Press, 1979).

CHAPTER 1

1. The Associazione Generale degli Operai (AGO) was founded in 1854 to sell staples to worker members at reasonable prices. In 1874 the railway workers set up the Cooperativa Ferroviaria, which eventually, in 1899, fused with the AGO to form the Alleanza Cooperativa di Torino (ACT). See Gino Castagno, *1854 Centenario A.C.T. (Storia di una cooperativa)* (Turin: Alleanza Cooperativa Torinese, 1954), pp. 12–29, 37–41. On the general conditions of the Turinese working class, see Stefano Musso, *Gli operai a Torino, 1900–1920* (Milan: Feltrinelli, 1980), especially pp. 108–10; Renzo Martinelli, *Il Partito comunista d'Italia, 1921–1926* (Rome: Riuniti, 1977), p. 13.

2. On the all-pervasive influence of Sorel, see Jack J. Roth, *The Cult of Violence: Sorel and the Sorelians* (Berkeley: University of California Press, 1980); also David D. Roberts, *The Syndicalist Tradition and Italian Fascism* (Chapel Hill: University of North Carolina Press, 1979).

3. See the biographical note, September–October 1940, p. 3, in Archivio Tasca, Fondazione Feltrinelli, Milan (hereafter referred to as AT), Corrispondenza, fasc. Processo contro A. Tasca. For Tasca's relationship with his mother, see Alceo Riosa, *Angelo Tasca socialista* (Venice: Marsilio Editori, 1979), p. 13.

4. See Riosa, *Tasca*, p. 15.

5. On the history of the FGSI, see Giovanni Gozzini, *Alle origini del comunismo italiano: Storia della Federazione Giovanile Socialista* (Bari: Dedalo, 1979). On Bordiga's position, see "Dopo il congresso," *L'avanguardia*, 6 Oct. 1912; "Preparazione culturale o preparazione rivoluzionaria?" *L'avanguardia*, 20 Oct. 1912.

6. Amadeo Bordiga, "Discussioni interne: 'Il punto di vista,'" *L'avanguardia*, 15 Dec. 1912. See also "Le conclusioni dei relatori," *L'avanguardia*, 15 Sept. 1912. For an evaluation of Bordiga's arguments, see Andreina De Clementi, *Amadeo Bordiga* (Turin: Einaudi, 1971), pp. 12–13; Franco Livorsi, *Amadeo Bordiga: Il pensiero e l'azione politica* (Rome: Riuniti, 1976), pp. 27–31.

7. Leonardo Paggi, *Antonio Gramsci e il moderno principe* (Rome: Riuniti, 1970), p. 105. Paolo Spriano noted the influence of the syndical world of Turin on Tasca; see his introduction to *La cultura italiana del '900 attraverso le riviste* (Turin: Einaudi, 1963), vol. 6, *L'ordine nuovo*, p. 31. Tasca recalled that his ties with Bruno Buozzi and his work with the union movement in 1912 gave him an appreciation for the traditional organizations that was not shared by others in the Turin *Ordine nuovo* group. See Tasca, "I primi dieci anni del Partito Comunista Italiano: La storia e la prestoria," *Il Mondo*, 18 Aug. 1953, p. 3.

8. On Tasca's position at the congress, see Giuseppe Berti's introduction, "Appunti e ricordi," to *I primi dieci anni di vita del Partito Comunista Italiano: Annali della Fondazione Feltrinelli 1966* (Milan: Feltrinelli, 1966), p. 35 (hereafter cited as *Annali 1966*); Pietro Silva, "I giovani socialisti," *L'unità*, 12 Oct. 1912, and the letters of Tasca and Bordiga to *L'unità* in "La posta dell'Unità," *L'unità*, 26 Oct. 1912; Tasca, "Note di un culturalista," *L'avanguardia*, 22 Dec. 1912.

9. See the interesting analysis by Edmund Jacobitti, *Revolutionary Humanism and Historicism in Modern Italy* (New Haven: Yale University Press, 1981), pp. 54–55; also Paggi, *Gramsci*, p. 104.

10. AT [Tasca], "Una critica della cultura," *Corriere universitario*, 20 Feb. 1913.

11. AT [Tasca], "La concentrazione socialista," *Corriere universitario*, 5 Apr. 1913; Tasca was also influenced by the Marxist philosopher Rodolfo Mondolfo's attempt to transcend both the reformist and revolutionary positions through historical realism. See Norberto Bobbio's introduction to R. Mondolfo, *Umanesimo di Marx: Studi filosofici 1908–1966* (Turin: Einaudi, 1968), p. xlv; see also Riosa, *Tasca*, p. 23.

12. Giuseppe Fiori, *Vita di Antonio Gramsci* (Bari: Laterza, 1966), p. 92; Berti, "Appunti e ricordi," *Annali 1966*, p. 18. See also Renzo Martinelli, "Gramsci e il Corriere universitario di Torino," *Studi Storici* 14 (1973), pp. 906–16, especially pp. 907–8.

13. Both Giuseppe Berti and Andrea Viglongo, who knew both men, have painted a sympathetic picture of the young Tasca. See *Gramsci vivo* (Milano: Feltrinelli, 1977), pp. 163–64, in which Viglongo stresses the key role Tasca played among the young Turinese intellectuals before the war. This was also emphasized in an interview with Andrea Viglongo on 9 Mar. 1981. A recent English study noted that Gramsci entered the Socialist party on Tasca's recommendation in June or July 1913; see Alastair Davidson, *Antonio Gramsci: Toward an Intellectual Biography* (London: Merlin Press, 1977), p. 63. However, absolutely no evidence supports Davidson's allegations about Tasca's honesty. (ibid., p. 62)

14. Tasca, *I primi dieci anni del PCI* (Bari: Laterza, 1971), pp. 91–92; Davidson, *Gramsci*, p. 64. On Salvemini's influence on the Turinese, see Spriano's introduction to the anthology *L'ordine nuovo*, pp. 27–29; Francesco Trocchi, *Angelo Tasca e l'Ordine Nuovo* (Milan: Jaca Book, 1973), pp. 31–32. The influence of Mussolini is apparent in the qualifications that Tasca set forth for candidates in the elections of 1913; see "Per la scelta dei candidati," *Grido del popolo*, 8 Feb. 1913. Tasca also spoke at a meeting at which particular support was voiced for Mussolini

as editor of the *Avanti!*, "La sezione socialista per il Congresso nazionale," *Grido del popolo*, 28 Mar. 1914.

15. Tasca to Salvemini, dated only 1914, copy in rough draft in AT, Corrispondenza, fasc. Salvemini.

16. See Tasca, "A proposito delle 'compagnie di disciplina,'" *Corriere universitario*, 5 May 1913; Tasca, "La guerra è la guerra," *L'avanguardia*, 20 July 1913, which attacked the Nationalists' glorification of war. Martinelli notes that Tasca's stand on this issue had some influence on Gramsci; see Martinelli, "Gramsci e il Corriere universitario," p. 912.

17. The reference to Mussolini's approach to Tasca was by Battista Santhià to Giorgio Bocca; see G. Bocca, *Palmiro Togliatti* (Bari: Laterza, 1973), p. 24. Tasca's response was to warn Mussolini not to break with the PSI. For Tasca's recollection that Gramsci submitted an article to Mussolini, see Berti, "Appunti e ricordi," *Annali 1966*, p. 43.

18. Gramsci, "Neutralità attiva ed operante," *Grido del Popolo*, 31 Oct. 1914.

19. Tasca, "I socialisti e la guerra europea: Tra la Francia e la Germania, viva l'Internazionale," *L'avanguardia*, 23 Aug. 1914; "Vita socialista," *Grido del Popolo*, 1 Aug. 1914, which mentioned Tasca as a delegate to a demonstration for peace; "La sezione socialista per la neutralità assoluta," *Grido del Popolo*, 12 Sept. 1914.

20. AT [Tasca], "Il mito della guerra," *Grido del Popolo*, 24 Oct. 1914.

21. See Bordiga, "Il socialismo di ieri dinanzi alla guerra di oggi," *L'avanguardia*, 25 Oct. 1914.

22. See Bocca, *Togliatti*, p. 25; Riosa, *Tasca*, p. 53; for Leonetti's point of view and the letter from Tasca to O. Pastore, 16 Dec. 1916, see A. Leonetti, *Da Andria contadina a Torino operaia* (Urbino: Argalia Editore, 1974), pp. 188–89.

CHAPTER 2

1. Although somewhat later, the article "Sulla via aperta," *Avanti!*, ed. Piemontese, 27 Apr. 1920, is a perfect example of this position.

2. See Giuseppi Berti, "Appunti e ricordi," *Annali 1966*, pp. 30–31.

3. Ibid., p. 66.

4. On the influences that formed the *Ordine nuovo* group, see Paggi, *Antonio Gramsci e il moderno principe*, pp. 207–10.

5. See Tasca, "I primi dieci anni del PCI: L'Ordine nuovo," *Il Mondo*, 25 Aug. 1953; Bocca, *Togliatti*, pp. 34–35; interview with Elena Tasca Dogliani, 9 Mar. 1981.

6. "Battute di preludio," *Ordine nuovo*, 1 May 1919.

7. Berti, "Appunti e ricordi," *Annali 1966*, pp. 50–51.

8. Tasca, "Cercando la verità," *Ordine nuovo*, 4 Oct. 1919; see also Tasca, "Perchè siamo comunisti," *Ordine nuovo*, 6 Sept. 1919; Berti, "Appunti e ricordi," *Annali 1966*, pp. 72–73.

9. Tasca, "Il programma massimalista," *Ordine nuovo*, 30 Aug. 1919.

10. Tasca, "Cultura e socialismo," *Ordine nuovo*, 28 June–5 July 1919.

11. Tasca, "Louis Blanc e l'organizzazione del lavoro," *Ordine nuovo*, 1 May, 31 May, and 2 Aug. 1919. Gramsci seems to have objected to the importance that Tasca ascribed to pre-Marxist socialism: see Paggi, *Antonio Gramsci e il moderno principe*, p. 201, note 13. See also Tasca's article on the Commune of Paris, in which he stressed the necessity of cultural and ideological preparation in much the same terms as he had used in the *Corriere universitario*: "Dopo la Comune," *Ordine nuovo*, 24 May 1919.

186 / Notes to Pages 25–28

12. For the various positions, see Bocca, *Togliatti*, pp. 43–44; Paolo Spriano, *Storia del Partito comunista italiano* (Turin: Einaudi, 1967), vol. 1 *Da Bordiga a Gramsci*, p. 49.

13. See Tasca, "Verso il congresso del partito: Il programma massimalista," *Avanti!*, ed. Piemontese, 7 Sept. 1919. The Serrati-Gennari "massimalista elezionista" faction won a majority in the provincial congress, but the Turinese section refused to support it. See "Il congresso provinciale socialista," *Avanti!*, ed. Piemontese, 1 Sept. 1919. Tasca urged that the party avoid becoming caught up in the debate over elections; see "Fare ognuno il proprio dovere," *Ordine nuovo*, 16 Aug. 1919.

14. "L'unità del partito," *Ordine nuovo*, 18 Oct. 1919. See also Luigi Cortesi, *Il socialismo italiano tra riforme e rivoluzione* (Bari: Laterza, 1969), p. 728; and AT, "La battaglia delle idee," *Ordine nuovo*, 4 Oct. 1919.

15. In addition to his membership on the administrative council of the ACT, Tasca represented the organization at a congress in Basle in 1921. He was also administrator of the Cassa di Risparmio of Turin from late 1920. After the war Tasca rejected a teaching position in favor of working within the ACT. See Tasca to Georges Monnet, 22 Sept. 1933, in AT, Corrispondenza, fasc. Monnet. Tasca, "Le nuove vie della cooperazione," *Avanti!*, ed. Piemontese, 17 Mar. 1920 and "Per la cooperazione sociale," *Avanti!*, ed. Piemontese, 19 Mar. 1920.

16. p.t. [Palmiro Togliatti], "L'assemblea della sezione metallurgica torinese," *Ordine nuovo*, 8 Nov. 1920; Giuseppe Maione, *Il biennio rosso: Autonomia e spontaneità operaia nel 1919–1920* (Bologna: Il Mulino, 1975), pp. 47–48. On the general conditions among workers in Turin and on the April 1920 strike, see John M. Cammett, *Antonio Gramsci and the Origins of Italian Communism* (Stanford, Calif.: Stanford University Press, 1967), pp. 96–104.

17. For the most comprehensive description of the strike, see Maione, *Il biennio rosso*, pp. 116–44.

18. See Terracini's declaration in Archivio del Movimento Operaio, *Il Consiglio Nazionale Socialista 18–22 aprile 1920* (Milan: Edizione del Gallo, 1967), 1:42–43.

19. See Tasca's declaration, ibid., p. 169; for his extended remarks, see *Consiglio Nazionale Socialista 18–22 April 1920* 2:160–63, 174–76. See also "La prima giornata del Consiglio Nazionale del PSI a Milano," *Avanti!*, ed. Piemontese, 20 Apr. 1920. For continued coverage, see the issues of 21, 22, and 23 Apr. Umberto Terracini, *Intervista sul comunismo difficile* (Bari: Laterza, 1978), pp. 16–17; Spriano, *Storia del Partito comunista Italiano*, 1:53–55.

20. "Il congresso della Camera del Lavoro di Torino e provincia," *Avanti!*, ed. Piemontese, 23 May 1920; "L'ardente dibattito sulla tattica al congresso camerale," ibid., 26 May 1920; "Il programma della nuova C.E. della Camera del lavoro," ibid., 12 June 1920. See also Maione, *Biennio rosso*, pp. 189, 193–94 (for a negative judgment on Tasca's action); Spriano, *Storia del Partito comunista italiano*, 1:58. Tasca's full report is given in *I consigli di fabbrica e la rivoluzione mondiale: Relazione letta all'Assemblea della Sezione socialista torinese* (Turin: Libreria editrice dell'Alleanza Cooperativa Torinese, 1921); see pp. 3–9 for Tasca's explanation of the background of his actions.

21. Gramsci, "Lo sviluppo della rivoluzione," *Ordine nuovo*, 13 Sept. 1919. For a detailed examination of the factory council issue, see Cammett, *Antonio Gramsci*, pp. 77–95.

22. Gramsci, "Sindacalismo e consigli," *Ordine nuovo*, 8 Nov. 1919; see

also "La conquista dello stato," ibid., 12 July 1919, and "I sindacati e la dittatura," ibid., 25 Oct. 1919.

23. Gramsci, "Il consiglio di fabbrica," *Ordine nuovo*, 5 June 1920.

24. See Berti, "Appunti e ricordi," *Annali 1966*, pp. 29–30, note 14. The role of the councils in producing a new leadership cadre was brought out by Davidson (*Gramsci*, pp. 115–18). Gramsci did emphasize, however, that the party must continue to represent the aspirations of the worker vanguard: see "Democrazia operaia," *Ordine nuovo*, 23 June 1919. For Viglongo's suggestion on the representation of unorganized workers, see "Verso nuove istituzioni," *Ordine nuovo*, 30 Aug. 1919, and Gramsci's note expressing some caution about the idea.

25. For a discussion of Tasca's arguments, see *I consigli di fabbrica e la rivoluzione mondiale* and *Il potere politico e sindacale dei consigli di fabbrica* (Turin: Tipografia dell'Allanza Cooperativa Torinese, 1920). Tasca's report to the Socialist section was given on 13 April 1920, and that to the Camera del Lavoro on 22 May 1920. Pastore's article actually began the debate on representation of unorganized workers and provoked Viglongo's response. See O.P. [Ottavio Pastore], "Il problema delle commissioni interne," *Ordine nuovo*, 16 Aug. 1919. Maione notes that the CGL was interested in the councils only if they could be controlled (*Biennio rosso*, p. 94).

26. Gramsci, "La relazione Tasca al congresso camerale di Torino," *Ordine nuovo*, 5 June 1920.

27. See Tasca, "Polemiche sul programma dell'Ordine nuovo," *Ordine nuovo*, 12 and 19 June 1920.

28. See Tasca, "Polemiche sul programma dell'Ordine nuovo," *Ordine nuovo*, 3 July 1920; and the introduction of Ernesto Ragionieri to Palmiro Togliatti, *Opere, 1917–1926* (Rome: Riuniti, 1967), 1 : lxvi–lxviii.

29. See Paolo Spriano, *L'occupazione delle fabbriche* (Turin: Einaudi, 1964), for a general picture of the crisis; see also Bocca, *Togliatti*, pp. 46–47; Tasca's recollections in his speech to the congress of the Camera del Lavoro in 1922, "Alla vigilia del congresso camerale," *Ordine nuovo*, 24 June 1922; and Tasca, "Una storia del Partito comunista italiano," *Critica sociale*, 46 (20 Jan. 1954), pp. 31–32.

30. See Spriano, *Storia del Partito comunista italiano*, 1 : 101; Davidson, *Gramsci*, p. 51; Martinelli, *Il Partito comunista d'Italia*, pp. 112–15.

31. Terracini, *Comunismo difficile*, pp. 38–39; Berti, "Ricordi e appunti," *Annali 1966*, p. 68. Togliatti noted the fascination of Bordiga for the other communists: See *La formazione del gruppo dirigente del Partito comunista italiano nel 1923–1924* (Rome: Riuniti, 1962), pp. 19–20.

32. On the Circolare group, see Martinelli, *Partito comunista d'Italia*, pp. 119–20, 149. On Bordiga's reference to Tasca, see his comments in *Consiglio nazionale*, 2:218.

33. See Bocca, *Togliatti*, p. 79; Davidson, *Gramsci*, p. 172.

34. See "La relazione della segreteria generale al congresso della Confederazione," *Ordine nuovo*, 28 Feb. 1921, for Tasca's remarks. See also p.t. [Palmiro Togliatti], "La seconda giornata del congresso confederale," *Ordine nuovo*, 1 Mar. 1921. Togliatti referred to Tasca's speech as "l'unica parola alta e seria."

35. Martinelli, *Partito comunista d'Italia*, p. 161; see also, p.t. [Palmiro Togliatti], "La prima parola seria è di un comunista," *Ordine nuovo*, 1 Mar. 1921.

36. See, for example, Tasca's activities at the congress of the CGL, *Ordine nuovo*, 7, 8, and 9 Nov. 1921, and *Il comunista*, 8 and 9 Nov. 1921.

37. Togliatti, *La formazione*, p. 25.
38. Bordiga, "La tattica dell'internazionale comunista," *Ordine nuovo*, 17 and 31 Jan. 1922; A. Graziadei, "Il fronte unico," *Ordine nuovo*, 21 Jan. 1922.
39. Jules Humbert Droz, *De Lénine à Staline: Dix ans au service de l'Internationale communiste* (Neuchatel: A. la Bacannière, 1971), pp. 58–59.
40. Spriano, *Storia del Partito comunista italiano*, 1 : 192–201; see also "I comunisti e l'Alleanza del Lavoro," *Ordine nuovo*, 7 Mar. 1922; "Il grande comizio di domani dell'Alleanza del Lavoro," *Ordine nuovo*, 10 Apr. 1922, at which Tasca spoke as the representative of Turin; Tasca, *La nascita e l'avvento del fascismo* (Bari: Laterza, 1965), 2 : 330–31; Tasca, *I primi dieci anni*, pp. 119–20.
41. See, for example, "Il discorso del compagno Tasca," *Ordine nuovo*, 6 July 1922; Tasca, "Per il congresso camerale," *Ordine nuovo*, 16 June 1922; "L'attività della Commissione esecutiva comunista dall'aprile 1921 ad oggi," *Ordine nuovo*, 18 June 1922.

CHAPTER 3

1. See Radek to the PCI, 20 Sept. 1922, in Archivio del Partito Comunista Italiano, Istituto Gramsci, Rome (hereafter cited as APCI), 1922, fasc. 81/2, pp. 25–26; Humbert Droz, *De Lénine à Staline*, p. 124.
2. "Relazione del PCdI al IV Congresso della IC," APCI, 1922, fasc. 87/2; see especially "Rapporti con il Partito socialista," pp. 49–50.
3. See "Verbale della seduta del 10–11 settembre 1922," in *Annali 1966*, pp. 128–30, and Berti's remarks, p. 133; Terracini, *Comunismo difficile*, pp. 50–52; "Riunione del CC del PCdI," 12 Oct. 1922 in APCI, 1922, fasc. 104, pp. 40–41. For the position of the Comintern, see the letter of Radek to the PCI, 20 Sept. 1922, APCI, 1922, fasc. 81/2, pp. 25–26.
4. T. Detti, *Serrati e la formazione del Partito comunista italiano* (Rome: Riuniti, 1972), pp. 214–15.
5. "Le condizioni di Mosca," *Avanti!*, 2 Jan. 1923; Togliatti, *La formazione del gruppo dirigente*, p. 45; Terracini, *Comunismo difficile*, p. 49. For details on the efforts at fusion, see also Tasca to Chiarini, 18 Mar. 1923, cited in Detti, *Serrati*, p. 253; Camilla Ravera, *Diario di trent'anni* (Rome: Riuniti, 1973), p. 142; minutes of the Fusion Commission, 10 Mar. 1923, APCI, 1923, fasc. 160, pp. 35–41.
6. See Grieco to the IC, 14 Mar. 1923, APCI, 1923, fasc. 180, p. 72; Terracini to Secretariat of the IC, 6 Mar. 1923, APCI, 1923, fasc. 180, p. 58; also Togliatti, *La formazione*, p. 51.
7. For Togliatti's attacks on the PSI, see Togliatti, "La crisi della fusione," *Il lavoratore*, 23 May 1923; "Il tesoro dell'esperienza," *Il lavoratore*, 26 Apr. 1923; "Precisiamo," *Il lavoratore*, 23 May 1923, in Togliatti, *Opere*, I, 1917–1926 (Rome: Riuniti, 1967), pp. 456–58, 463–66. See also Terracini to Presidium of the IC, 8 Mar. 1923, and Terracini to Zinoviev and the C.E. (Executive Committee) of the IC and delegate of the PCI in Moscow, 30 Mar. 1923, APCI, 1923, fasc. 180, pp. 59, 90–91. For Tasca's remarks, see Tasca to Chiarini, the delegate of the IC in Italy, 18 Mar. 1923, APCI, 1923, fasc. 180, pp. 73–76.
8. Humbert Droz, *De Lénine à Staline*, pp. 117–18.
9. See Scoccimarro's report on the Fusion Committee in *Lo stato operaio*, 10 Apr. 1924, and "La discussione all'E.A. sulla mancata fusione tra il PCdI e il PSI," *Lo stato operaio*, 17 Apr. 1924.
10. Tasca, "Relazione della minoranza comunista all'E.A. di giugno," *Lo stato operaio*, 10 Apr. 1924; also in Togliatti, *La formazione*, pp. 71–87, citation from

p. 77; see also Bocca, *Togliatti*, p. 88, and Susanna Giaccai, "Angelo Tasca nel Partito Comunista d'Italia, 1921–1924," Tesi di Laurea, Università degli Studi di Firenze, Facoltà di Magistero, 1975–1976.

11. Spriano, *Storia del PCI*, 1:283; Togliatti to Gramsci and Scoccimarro, 16 July 1923, in *La formazione*, pp. 92–95; Gramsci to Paolo Palmi [Togliatti], no date and a second undated fragment in Togliatti, *La formazione*, pp. 101–2; Detti, *Serrati*, pp. 293–94.

12. See the remarks of Serra [Tasca] to the meeting of the CE (Comitato Esecutivo) of the PCI, 5 Aug. 1923, APCI, 1923, fasc. 171/2, pp. 34–36.

13. "Riunione del CC del PCI," 9 Aug. 1923, APCI, 1923, fasc. 196, pp. 2–8; also Togliatti, *La formazione*, pp. 105–14. See Berti, "Appunti e ricordi," *Annali 1966*, p. 140. For the arrest of the leaders of the PCI, see "Il processo a Roma," *Lo stato operaio*, 1 Nov. 1923.

14. "Le sedute della Direzione del Partito," *Avanti!*, 4 Aug. 1923, announcing the expulsions of Francesco Buffoni, Mario Malatesta, Enzio Riboldi, Fabrizio Maffi, and Serrati.

15. See Togliatti's report to the International of 23 July 1923, in *Opere*, 1:797; Serra [Tasca] to the Secretariat of the ECCI (Executive Committee of the Communist International), 13 Aug. 1923, in APCI, 1923, fasc. 181, pp. 42–44; Tasca, "Dopo il Convegno confederale," *Pagine rosse*, 10 Sept. 1923, in which he traced his efforts to work out Unity of Action within the CGL.

16. AT, [Angelo Tasca] "Può sussistere in Italia un partito 'independente,'" *Lo stato operaio*, 8 Sept. 1923; on Tasca's increasingly negative views of the political capacities of the Terzini, see Valle [Tasca] to the Secretariat of the IC, 17 Sept. 1923, APCI, 1923, fasc. 181, pp. 47–49; "Appunti di un colloquio con l'on Maffi," 6 Dec. 1923, APCI, 1923, fasc. 182, pp. 22–24; Valle to the Executive Committee of the IC, 30 Nov. 1923, APCI, 1923, fasc. 182, pp. 12–14, in which he described relations with the PSI as at an impasse and criticized the Terzini's lack of initiative. See also Detti, *Serrati*, pp. 311, 318–20.

17. See Tasca, "Unità proletaria," *Lo stato operaio*, 1 Sept. 1923; idem, "Autonomia di una lettera," ibid., 15 Nov. 1923; idem, "Punti sugli i," ibid., 29 Nov. 1923. The Socialist response to his efforts was negative; see "Le contraddizioni di due tattiche," *Avanti!*, 21 Nov. 1923. On Togliatti, see Togliatti to Terracini, Oct. 1923, APCI, 1923, fasc. 178/2, pp. 106–7.

18. "Frammento verbale: III Rapporto con il PSI e con la frazione terzina," late 1923 (undated), APCI, 1923 fasc. 160/3. On the negotiations for an electoral pact, see F. Ferri, "Le elezioni truffa dell'aprile 1924 e la proposta comunista di un blocco di unità proletaria," *Rinascita*, 19 Jan. 1963, pp. 17–19, for the minutes of the Central Committee of the PCI on 22–23 Jan. 1924. Ariane Landuyt, *Le sinistre e l'Avventino* (Milan: Franco Angeli Editore, 1973), pp. 6–8, offers an analysis of these events. Pressure for a favorable response came from Tasca and Humbert Droz; see *De Lénine à Staline*, pp. 204–5.

19. Togliatti to Terracini, 15 Mar. 1924, in Togliatti, *La formazione*, pp. 231–33; for Tasca's evolving position, see Ferri, "Discussioni e contrasti sulla proposta comunista di un blocco di unità proletaria per le elezioni del 1924," *Rinascita*, 24 Jan. 1924, p. 17; Landuyt, *Le sinistre*, pp. 10, 14; Humbert Droz, *De Lénine à Staline*, pp. 210–13, also believed that Togliatti worked to sabotage Tasca's efforts and forced him to take a leading role in a failed enterprise. This hypothesis is confirmed also by the letter of Terracini to Gramsci and Togliatti, 20 Feb. 1924, urging that Tasca sign all the letters because Togliatti's signature was too suspect: *La formazione*, pp. 203–5.

20. See the meeting of the Executive Committee of the PCI, 17 Feb. 1924, APCI, 1924, fasc. 231, pp. 23–31; Bocca, *Togliatti*, p. 95; Humbert Droz, *De Lénine à Staline*, pp. 165–66.

21. Spriano, *Storia del PCI*, 1:306–13.

22. Gramsci to Urbani [Terracini], 12 Jan. 1924, and Gramsci to Scoccimarro and Togliatti, 1 Mar. 1924, in Togliatti, *La formazione*, pp. 156–57, 219–20. See also Gramsci to Negri [Scoccimarro], 5 Jan. 1924, and Gramsci to Palmi, Urbani e compagni, 9 Feb. 1924, in Togliatti, *La formazione*, pp. 151–53, 194–95.

23. Gramsci to Pietro Tresso, April 1924, in Togliatti, *La formazione*, pp. 333–36. Gramsci made it clear to Togliatti that he would like to separate Tasca from the minority. See Gramsci to Togliatti and Scoccimarro, 5 Apr. 1924, in Togliatti, *La formazione*, pp. 274–75. Humbert Droz agreed that there was little difference between Tasca and the new Center; see his report to the Comintern on 13 Apr. 1924, in *De Lénine à Staline*, pp. 218–19.

24. See the minutes of the meeting of the Executive Committee of the PCI, 24–25 Mar. 1924, APCI, 1924, fasc. 238, pp. 33–34. Also "Frammento verbale della riunione del Comitato centrale del 18 aprile 1924," in Togliatti, *La formazione*, pp. 296–326; Tasca to Rákosi, end of April 1924, in Togliatti, *La formazione*, pp. 327–30. Tasca announced his resignation in a letter of 30 Apr. to the Presidium of the Comintern, citing the impossibility of collaborating with the new Center: L. Valle [Tasca] and Bernudi [Vota] to the Presidium of the Executive Committee of the Communist International, 30 Apr. 1924, APCI, 1924, fasc. 246, p. 20.

25. For the programs of the three factions, see *Annali 1966*, pp. 186–240, and Berti's introduction, p. 135.

26. "Schema di tesi della minoranza del CC del PCI," *Annali 1966*, pp. 216–40; for further comments on Tasca's support for a transitional form of government before the complete triumph of the revolution, see Berti's introduction, pp. 158–59.

27. "Elevato dibattito d'idee per la preparazione del V congresso della III Internazionale," *L'unità*, 5 June 1924. Tasca and the labor leaders of the Right minority feared that a parallel organization would offer an excuse to the CGL to drive the Communists from the organization. Gramsci considered the CGL moribund and felt that the formation of factory cells was necessary to the bolshevization of the party. See Gramsci to Terracini, 10 Apr. 1924, in Togliatti, *La formazione*, pp. 284–87; Antonio Gramsci, "Premessa," and Angelo Tasca, "Opportunismo di destra e tattica sindacale," with a comment by Gramsci, in *Lo stato operaio*, 5 June 1924.

28. Togliatti to Scoccimarro and Gramsci, 7 July 1924, in Togliatti, *Opere*, 1:927.

29. See Humbert Droz, *De Lénine à Staline*, p. 243; Berti, "Ricordi e appunti," *Annali 1966*, pp. 159, 161, 165; "Il V congresso dell'IC," *L'unità*, 4 July 1924, and Ercoli [Togliatti], "Andare a sinistra," *L'unità*, 30 Aug. 1924, in which Togliatti hailed the IC congress as a significant shift to the left.

30. See Togliatti's report to the Comintern in Togliatti, *Opere*, vol. 2, p. 7, and Ernesto Ragionieri's introductory comments, p. cxxxvii. See also Humbert Droz to Tasca, 12 Sept. 1924, and Tasca to Humbert Droz, 22 Sept. 1924, in APCI, 1924, fasc. 246, pp. 21–24. On Tasca's law studies, see Tasca to Piero Gobetti, 21 Oct. 1924, in Archivio Gobetti, Turin, fasc. Tasca. See also the reports of the prefect of Turin to the Ministry of Interior, 12 Aug. 1924, and 13 Feb. 1925, report from the Italian Embassy, Paris, to the Head of the Police, Rome, 12 Sept. 1925, and the

reports of the Prefect of Alessandria, 19 Feb. 1926, and 22 Sept. 1926, in Archivio Centrale dello Stato, CPC 5040, fasc. 24848.

31. Tasca to Gobetti, 20 May 1925, Archivio Gobetti, fasc. Tasca.

32. Landuyt, *Le sinistre*, p. 199. On Togliatti's policies, see "Andare a sinistra," *L'unità*, 30 Aug. 1924, and his reports to the Comintern, 15 Sept. and 18 Nov. 1924, in *Opere*, vol. 1, pp. 587–90, 818, 857.

33. See the minutes of the Central Committee, 6 Feb. 1925, APCI, 1925, fasc. 296, pp. 4–7; see also the letter of Tasca, undated and not addressed in 1925, APCI, 1925, fasc. 352/2, p. 45; [Serrati?] to Tasca, 18 Dec. 1925, APCI, 1925, fasc. 352/2, p. 44, expressing agreement on the syndical question.

34. See the meeting of the Central Committee, 11–12 May 1925, APCI, 1925, fasc. 296, pp. 30–33, 40–41, 61–80. Berti indicates that this meeting was held on 6 Feb. 1926; see *Annali 1966*, pp. 246–49.

35. See Spriano, *Storia del PCI*, 1:483–85; see also the minutes of the Central Committee of 18 Apr. 1924, in *La formazione*, p. 301, for Tasca's warning.

36. On the Lyons theses, see Gastone Manacorda, *Il socialismo nella storia d'Italia: Storia documentaria dal Risorgimento alla Repubblica* (Bari: Laterza, 1970), 2:529–42; see also Spriano, *Storia del PCI*, vol. 1, chap. 29.

37. See Bruno Fortichiari, *Comunismo e revisionismo in Italia* (Turin: Tennerello Editore, 1978), pp. 151–53, 156; and the minutes of the Third Congress, APCI, fasc. 382, pp. 40–42, 44–47, for the reaction of other sections of the party to the criticisms of Bordiga and his supporters.

38. For Tasca's remarks, see APCI, 1926, fasc. 382, pp. 132–38.

39. See "III congresso del PCI: Commissione politica," 20 Jan. 1926, in *Annali 1966*, pp. 243–44; on the PCI's commitment to the *comitati d'agitazione*, see Ragionieri's comments in Togliatti, *Opere*, vol. 2, pp. lxxx–lxxxi.

40. See "Intervento al VI Esecutivo allargato dell'IC," 25 Feb. 1926, in Togliatti, *Opere*, vol. 2, 1926–1929 (Rome: Riuniti, 1971), p. 7; and, Ragionieri's comment, p. cxxxvii.

41. On the difficulties with Bordiga, see Spriano, *Storia del Partito comunista italiano* (Turin: Einaudi, 1969), vol. 2, *Gli anni della clandestinità*, chap. 1. On Togliatti's veto of an appointment for Tasca, see the letter of Togliatti to the Secretariat of the Comintern, 17 Mar. 1926, in *Annali 1966*, p. 274.

42. Tasca to Gramsci, 15 Aug. 1926, in *Annali 1966*, pp. 297; also in APCI, 1926, fasc. 425/2, pp. 91–94.

43. Tasca to the Executive Committee of the PCI, 30 Mar. 1926, APCI, 1926, fasc. 425, pp. 37–44; also in *Annali 1966*, pp. 284–90, especially p. 289 and Berti's comments, pp. 284–86.

CHAPTER 4

1. See Ravera, *Diario*, pp. 254–55, 260, 265. There is, however, no trace of this suggestion outside the memory of Ravera. She did not include it in the 16 Nov. report to Togliatti that announced Tasca's departure for France. See Micheli (Ravera) to Ercoli (Togliatti), 16 Nov. 1926 in Pietro Secchia, ed., *L'azione svolta dal Partito comunista in Italia durante il fascismo, 1926–1932: Annali della Fondazione Feltrinelli 1969* (Milan: Feltrinelli, 1970), pp. 10–11, 17.

2. See Garlandi (Grieco) to Micheli (Ravera), 21 Jan. 1927, APCI, 1927, fasc. 573, p. 50; minutes of the meeting of the Ufficio politico, 26–28 Feb. 1927, APCI, 1927, fasc. 560, p. 4; minutes of the Central Committee, 2–3 Mar. 1927,

APCI, 1927, fasc. 557/2. Because official documents of the PCI rarely used the real name of the writer, the citation uses the alias on the document with the true name in parentheses. The most common aliases were Ercoli (Togliatti), Garlandi (Grieco), Gallo (Longo), Rienzi, Verri, or Valle (Tasca), Micheli (Ravera).

3. On Bukharin's views, see Stephen F. Cohen, *Bukharin and the Bolshevik Revolution* (New York: Vintage Books, 1975), pp. 253–56; Aldo Agosti, *La Terza Internazionale: Storia documentaria, 1928–1943*, vol. 2 (Rome: Riuniti, 1976), pp. 881–85.

4. On the Varga article, see Ercoli to Rienzi (Tasca), 16 Aug. 1927, and Rienzi to Ercoli, 4 Sept. 1927, in AT, busta 3 PSI-PCI 1925–27, fasc. 1927. See also Giulio Sapelli, *L'analisi economica dei comunisti italiani durante il fascismo* (Milan: Feltrinelli, 1978), pp. 26–27; Tasca, "L'analisi leninista dell'imperialismo e l'economia italiana," *Lo stato operaio*, vol. 1 (September 1927), pp. 773–86.

5. On the Tasca-Sraffa exchange, see P. Sraffa and A. Tasca, "Polemica monetaria," *Lo stato operaio*, no. 1 (November–December 1927), pp. 1089–95; Sraffa to Tasca, 6 Sept. 1927 and Tasca to Sraffa, 2 Oct. 1927, in AT, Corrispondenza, fasc. Sraffa; Tasca, "La revalutazione della lira e la crisi dell'economia italiana," *Lo stato operaio*, no. 1 (August 1927), pp. 667–92, especially p. 673; "Proletariato, fascismo ed economia italiana," *Lo stato operaio*, no. 1 (March 1927), pp. 40–42; "La politica dei prezzi del regime fascista (A proposito del capitalismo di stato)," *Lo stato operaio*, no. 2 (1928), pp. 244–55.

6. Tasca, "La rivalutazione della lira e la crisi dell'economia italiana," *Lo stato operaio*, no. 1 (August 1927), p. 673; also "Proletariato fascismo e l'economia italiano," *Lo stato operaio*, no. 1 (March 1927), pp. 39–48; Sapelli, *L'analisi*, p. 16.

7. See Valle (Tasca) to Ufficio Politico, 10 Apr. 1927, AT, busta 3 PSI–PCI 1925–1927, fasc. 1927; also in *Annali 1966*, pp. 328–32; on Tasca's views, see Valle to Comitato Direttivo of PCI, 21 July 1926, APCI, 1926 fasc. 425/2, pp. 84–86; minutes of the Ufficio Politico, 26–28 Feb. 1927, APCI, 1927, fasc. 560, pp. 4–6; the fragment of a letter from Rienzi (Tasca), 17 Nov. 1927, urging a cautious policy and the response, Uno to Rienzi, 23 Nov. 1927, APCI, 1927, fasc. 573, pp. 103–6; minutes of the Ufficio Politico, 9 June 1927, APCI, 1927, fasc. 560, pp. 66–67.

8. See the minutes of the Central Committee of the PCI, 2–3 Mar. 1927, APCI, 1927, fasc. 557, pp. 37–38, and the letter, probably by Tasca, from the Comitato Centrale of the PCI to the Direzione of the PSI, no date or signature, APCI, 1927, fasc. 557/2, pp. 46–49.

9. See Togliatti, "Lo stato operaio," *Lo stato operaio*, no. 1 (March 1927), pp. 5–9; Tasca recalled the debates over the party program in October 1927 in Quaderno 2, entry for 1 June 1928, in *Annali 1966*, pp. 404–20.

10. Gallo (Longo) for the Segreteria della Federazione Giovanile Comunista to the Ufficio Politico, 20 Oct. 1927, in *Annali 1966*, pp. 369, 372–73, 376–79. See also Ferdinando Ormea, *Le origini dello stalinismo nel PCI* (Milan: Feltrinelli, 1978), pp. 96–97.

11. On the alliance between Tasca, Togliatti, and Grieco, see Berti's comments in *Annali 1966*, p. 362; on Togliatti's views on the transition period, see "Il VII Esecutivo allargato," *Lo stato operaio*, no. 1 (March 1927), and "Fascismo e stabilizzazione," *Internazionale communiste*, 5 Dec. 1926, both in Togliatti, *Opere*, vol. 2, pp. 160–61 and 120–22; "Documento firmato da Ercoli di risposta e di commento alla lettera dei giovani," 20 Oct. 1927, *Annali 1966*, pp. 381–400.

12. See Quaderno 2, entry June 1928, p. 341.

13. See the entry for 1 Jan. 1928, Quaderno 2, pp. 250–54, citation p. 254.

14. Ravera, *Diario*, pp. 297−98; Tasca, "Per una storia del fuoruscitismo," *Itinerie*, October 1954, pp. 231−32.

15. Ercoli, "Direttive per lo studio delle questioni russe," *Lo stato operaio*, no. 1 (April 1927), pp. 128−32. At the 9 June 1927, meeting of the Ufficio Politico Togliatti, defended the United Front tactic in China and England against Longo, although his defense was not so strong as that of Tasca. See APCI, 1927, fasc. 560, pp. 55−57; see also Berti's comment on the letter from Togliatti to Tasca, 20 Oct. 1927, *Annali 1966*, pp. 362−63.

16. "La NEP vista da un comunista," *Lo stato operaio*, 16 Aug. 1923.

17. Luigi Serra (Tasca), "La costruzione socialista nella discussione russa," *Lo stato operaio*, no. 1 (June 1927), p. 413.

18. Luigi Serra (Tasca), "La costruzione socialista nella discussione russa," *Lo stato operaio*, vol. 1, November−December 1927, p. 1023; see also the continuation in the June issue, pp. 413−14.

19. Luigi Serra, "La costruzione socialista nella discussione russa," *Lo stato operaio*, vol. 1 (November−December 1927), pp. 1036−37, for citation, p. 1029.

20. See Quaderno 1, in Giuseppe Berti, ed., *Problemi del movimento operaio: Scritti critici e storici inediti di Angelo Tasca: Annali della Fondazione Feltrinelli 1968* (Milan: Feltrinelli, 1969), pp. 64−65, 152−54, 156−60, citation, p. 153.

21. See the comments of Ragionieri, *Opere*, vol. 2, pp. cxxvi−cxxvii; see the debates at Basle, APCI, 1928, fasc. 646/2, pp. 45−56, especially pp. 53−54; fasc. 646/1, pp. 3−19, for Grieco's comments and Spriano, *Storia del PCI*, vol. 2, pp. 144−47.

22. Secchia's comments in *Annali 1969*, pp. 101−3, 118.

23. See Berti's comments, *Annali 1966*, pp. 438−39.

24. See "Intervento al IX Esecutivo allargato," 12 Feb. 1928, and "Rapporto alla Commissione italiana dell'Esecutiva dell'IC," 20 Feb. 1928, and "Osservazione sulla politica del nostro partito, *Lo stato operaio*, vol. 2 (June 1928) in *Opere*, vol. 2, pp. 330−31, 334, 357−58, 362−63, 397−400.

25. See Cohen, *Bukharin*, pp. 276−92, especially 292; Ormea, *Le origini dello stalinismo*, pp. 115−16. See also Grieco, "Contributo ad un rapporto sulla socialdemocrazia," *Lo stato operaio*, no. 2 (August−September 1928), pp. 515−17; Paolo Ravazzoli, "Socialdemocrazia e fascismo in Italia," ibid., pp. 527−34.

26. "Osservazioni di Tasca e di Thalheimer al Progetto di Programma dell'Internazionale Comunista'," *Annali 1966*, pp. 450−62, citation p. 459. See also Spriano, *Storia del PCI*, vol. 2, pp. 175−76; Ragionieri's introduction to Togliatti, *Opere*, vol. 2, pp. clxxv−clxxvi.

CHAPTER 5

1. On Tasca's recollection of Togliatti's advice, see Quaderno 6 (1928), p. 215. See also Silone, *Uscita di sicurezza* (Florence: Vallecchi, 1965), p. 103; Secchia, *Annali 1969,* pp. 128−29; Humbert Droz, *De Lénine à Staline*, p. 315.

2. Bocca, *Togliatti*, p. 163; Ormea, *Le origini*, pp. 94−95; see also Ragionieri's introduction to Togliatti, *Opere*, vol. 2, *1926−1929* (Rome: Riuniti, 1971), pp. cxci−cxcii. Ragionieri noted that both men were working on a project for a publication of Gramsci's writings even during the worst of the crisis. See Ercoli (Togliatti) to Tasca (Rienzi), 27 Dec. 1928, APCI, 1928, fasc. 673, pp. 168−71.

3. Ercoli to Rienzi, 6 Oct. 1928, in *Annali 1966*, pp. 513−15. See also Ravera, *Diario*, p. 395; Ormea, *Le origini dello stalinismo*, pp. 99−102.

4. Tasca to the secretariat of the PCI, 21 Oct. 1928, *Annali 1966*, p. 523.

5. See Tasca to the PCI, 3 or 4 Nov. 1928, in *Annali 1966*, pp. 532–34, and the declaration that Tasca read at the 2 November meeting of the Political Secretariat of the IC, ibid., pp. 535–37.

6. Tasca to the PCI, 4 Nov. 1928, *Annali 1966*, pp. 538–40; Tasca to the PCI, 26 Nov. 1928, ibid., pp. 567–70. For Tasca's efforts at mediation through the IC, see Tasca to Segreteria Politica dell'IC, 22 Nov. 1928, *Annali 1966*, p. 571.

7. Tasca to the PCI, 5 Dec. 1928, *Annali 1966*, pp. 574–77, especially p. 576.

8. Tasca to the president of the IC, 5 Dec. 1928, Quaderno 3, pp. 101–2.

9. Quaderno 3, entry for 10 Dec. 1928, p. 114.

10. Tasca to Segreteria PCI, 14 Dec. 1928, *Annali 1966*, pp. 577–83.

11. Togliatti to Tasca, 17 Dec. 1928, *Annali 1966*, pp. 588–92.

12. Tasca to the Segreteria PCI, 20 Dec. 1928, *Annali*, pp. 596–98; excerpt of speeches by Khitarov and Stalin in Quaderno 3, entry for 19 Dec. 1928, pp. 244–45; Bocca, *Togliatti*, p. 176; Humbert Droz, *De Lénine à Staline*, pp. 341, 353.

13. Tasca to Segreteria PCI, 25 Dec. 1928, *Annali 1966*, pp. 608–10.

14. Togliatti to Tasca, 27 Dec. 1928, *Annali 1966*, pp. 616–18. Bocca interprets this as an attempt to offer Tasca a way out by inviting him home for discussions. See also Bocca, *Togliatti*, pp. 178–79, and Ormea, *Le origini dello stalinismo*, pp. 103–8.

15. Tasca to Segreteria PCI, 30 Dec. 1928, *Annali 1966*, pp. 624–25.

16. "Incontro tra Bukharin, Humbert Droz e Tasca in data 15 gennaio 1929," *Annali 1966*, pp. 653–59, citation, p. 654. On Tasca's recall, see Togliatti to Tasca, 2 Jan. 1929, and the circular of Togliatti to the Central Committee, 3 Jan. 1929, *Annali 1966*, pp. 628–29, 636.

17. Tasca to Segreteria of PCI, 20 Jan. 1929, *Annali 1966*, pp. 669–70. Tasca's view of Stalinist terror was shared by the Trotskyists and other Left dissidents. From Victor-Serge, he understood the fear of losing everything and being deported that hung over the anti-Stalinist opposition; see Victor-Serge to Boris Souvarine, 7 Apr. 1929, in Quaderno 6, p. 123. Tasca helped to collect money and food for the Trotskyists and their families and carried out letters from Pierre Pascal and Andres Nin when he left Moscow in January; see *Annali 1966*, pp. 647–53.

18. See Berti's comments in *Annali 1966*, pp. 627–28. Berti also noted that Tasca never used Togliatti's letters, even when the PCI attacked him.

19. Silone, *Uscita di sicurezza*, pp. 104–5.

20. Tasca's report, *Annali 1966*, pp. 689, 693.

21. Ibid., pp. 677–78, 682–83.

22. Ibid., p. 704 for citation; see also p. 703.

23. Ibid., p. 706; also pp. 762–63, 765.

24. Cohen, *Bukharin*, pp. 274–75.

25. Tasca's report, *Annali 1966*, pp. 714–15.

26. Ibid., pp. 719–20, also 726–28.

27. Ibid., pp. 731–32.

28. Ibid., p. 730.

29. See Berti's analysis, ibid., pp. 674–75; also Ravera, *Diario*, pp. 424–26, 432.

30. See Togliatti's statement in *Annali 1966*, pp. 805–28 and *Opere*, vol. 2, pp. 669–701.

31. For citation, see Quaderno 4 (1929), pp. 96–97; see also Quaderno 6, p. 11, for excerpt of a letter from a member of PCI, 21 Feb. 1929.

32. See Ravera, *Diario*, p. 435; Bocca, *Togliatti*, pp. 186–87; Feroci to Rienzi,

18 Apr. 1929, AT, busta 6 PSI-PCI 1929/2. On Tasca's comment to Ravera, see Tasca to Micheli (Ravera), 4 May 1929, *Annali 1966*, pp. 932–33.

33. On Ravera's recollection, see *Diario*, p. 442. See also a description of the meeting of 6 June and Tasca's comment, Quaderno 7, pp. 18 and 20.

34. See the comments of Berti on the Humbert Droz–Tasca case, *Annali 1966*, p. 932. Secchia confirmed that Tasca's expulsion was in part designed to force a break with the past; see *Annali 1969*, p. 233.

35. Quaderno 8 (July 1929), p. 138. See also "Memoriale sulla deliberazione dell'UP del 6 giugno," in Quaderno 8, August 1929, pp. 9, 30.

36. Tasca to Fanny Jezierska, 12 Aug. 1929, and also 28 Aug. 1929, *Annali 1966*, pp. 960–61, 964–65. On the X Plenum, see Togliatti's speech of 8 July 1929, and the report of 19 July by the Italian commission in *Opere*, vol. 2, pp. 728–43, 778–86. See also Ormea, *Le origini dello stalinismo*, pp. 121–22; Bocca, *Togliatti*, p. 197.

37. Tasca to Fanny Jezierska, 28 Aug. 1929, *Annali 1966*, pp. 964–65.

38. See the minutes of the meeting of the UP of 28–29 Aug. 1929, *Annali 1969*, pp. 235–41, especially pp. 240–41; also Ormea, *Le origini dello stalinismo*, pp. 131–35.

39. Tasca to Togliatti, 30 Aug. 1929, *Annali 1966*, pp. 966–68; also the entry for August 1929, Quaderno 7, p. 171.

40. Tasca to the representative of the IC and Tasca to the Segreteria of the PCI, 4 Sept. 1929, Quaderno 8, p. 218. Tasca complained a few days later that the party did not respond and had not designated a comrade to handle the transition: Tasca to the Segreteria PCI, 12 Sept. 1929, Quaderno 8, p. 219. He was then informed that the party had moved to expel him; see the 14 Sept. 1929 letter to Tasca inserted into Quaderno 8 at pp. 218–19.

41. Tasca to Boris Souvarine, 16 Sept. 1929, AT, Corrispondenza, fasc. Souvarine.

CHAPTER 6

1. On the intellectual climate on the French Left which bred neoreformism, see Zeev Sternhell, *Ni droite ni gauche: L'idéologie fasciste en France* (Paris: Editions du Seuil, 1983).

2. Tasca to Fanny Jezierska, 18 Sept. 1929, *Annali 1966*, p. 969. See Tasca, "La società chiusa," *Il mondo*, 11 Mar. 1950.

3. On the initial attack against Tasca, see "Via gli opportunisti dalle file del Partito comunista d'Italia," *Vie prolétarienne*, 13 Oct. 1929. For comment from the exile press, see "Tasca espulso dal PC," *L'Avanti!*, 13 Oct. 1929; "Tasca," *L'Avanti!*, 10 Nov. 1929; "Disorientamenti comunisti," *Rinascita socialista*, 1 Nov. 1929. See also Ercoli, "Come e perchè abbiamo cacciato Angelo Tasca," *Vie prolétarienne*, 10 Nov. 1929; "Malavita politica," *Vie prolétarienne*, 22 Dec. 1929, and 12 Jan. 1930. For Tasca's response, see "Dichiarazione di Tasca alla stampa in data 18 novembre 1929," *Annali 1966*, pp. 981–83.

4. See the entry for November 1929 in Quaderno 9, pp. 118–19.

5. Tasca to Fanny Jezierska, 1 Oct. 1929, *Annali 1966*, pp. 976–77; Souvarine to Tasca, 4 and 30 Nov. 1929, AT, Corrispondenza, fasc. Souvarine.

6. Tasca to Angelica Balabanoff, 10 Dec. 1929, and Tasca to Franco Clerici, 10 Dec. 1929, *Annali 1966*, pp. 984–86.

7. See the letter from Piero Sraffa to Tasca (undated, but before his expulsion

from the PCI, AT, Corrispondenza, fasc. Sraffa), reporting on a visit to Lina; Tasca to Lina, 16 Nov. 1929, in Quaderno 9, pp. 126–27.

8. Sraffa to Tasca, 14 Jan. 1930; also Sraffa's letter of 22 Jan. 1930, AT, Corrispondenza, fasc. Sraffa. See also Tasca to Lina, 25 Apr. 1930, in Quaderno 11, pp. 59–65.

9. See Lina to Tasca, 3 Apr. 1930, Quaderno 16, in *Annali 1968*, pp. 423–27; for Tasca's diary notation, see Quaderno 16, pp. 265–77, in *Annali 1968*, p. 427.

10. Tasca to Cécile Beitzman, 11 July 1930, Quaderno 13, p. 23.

11. The possibility that Lina might have cooperated with the Italian police was raised by Charles André Julien, interview of 16 Mar. 1981, and confirmed in the report of the Ministry of Interior to the Divisione Polizia Politica, 9 Dec. 1932, Archivio Centrale dell Stato (ACS), Casellario Politico Centrale (CPC), fasc. 5040, busta 24848. Other details were provided in interviews with Valeria Tasca and Elena Dogliani, 15 Mar. 1981, and 9 Mar. 1981. See also the subsequent police report of 21 Aug. 1933, from the Prefect of Turin to the Questura in Rome noting that Lina requested help from the Fascist Segretario Federale for the children. Tasca accused the Italian consulate of working to break up his family: See Tasca to M. Zimmer, Secretariat de M. le Préfet de Police, 23 Feb. 1933, and the letter to Sig. Console generale d'Italia, 23 Feb. 1933, in Quaderno 24, pp. 24–27.

12. Tasca to Pierre and Jenny Pascal, 22 May 1930, AT, Corrispondenza, fasc. Pascal.

13. Tasca, "Per una storia politica del fuoruscitismo," *Itinerari*, October 1954, p. 234.

14. Barbusse to Bureau Politique du PCF, 25 Nov. 1930, AT, Francia, fasc. 254, *Monde*.

15. For Tasca's views on *Monde*, see insert "Quelques remarques sur 'Monde,'" April 1930, in Quaderno 10; on the PCF, see Quaderno 11 (May 1930–June 1931), entry for August 1930, pp. 64–90, especially p. 71, where he referred to the PCF as a moral and political bankrupt. For the citation on Lenin, see A. Rossi (Tasca), "Les idées et les livres: De Lénine à Trotsky," *Monde*, 10 May 1930; also "L'an 1 de la Révolution russe dans un livre di Victor Serge," *Monde*, 8 Nov. 1930.

16. Rossi, "Les idées et les livres: Sur le fascisme en Europe," *Monde*, 3 May 1930.

17. Rossi, "Les deux fascismes: De Mussolini à Hitler," *Monde*, 18 Oct. 1930.

18. See Quaderno 11, p. 123; also Fanny Jezierska to Tasca, 18 Sept. 1930, and Tasca's comment in Quaderno 11, pp. 126–28.

19. Tasca to Emmanuel Berl, 12 Dec. 1930, Quaderno 11, p. 166, in *Annali 1968*, pp. 273–76, citation p. 275. On Engels as humanist and realist, see "Lineamenti di una critica dell'Economia politica," Quaderno 9 (October 1929–March 1930), pp. 151–73, in *Annali 1968*, pp. 214–16, and Tasca's comments on "Le condizioni dell'Inghilterra," Quaderno 9, pp. 143–51, *Annali 1968*, pp. 210–13.

20. See Tasca's lessons on Engels's *Condition of the English Working Class*, Quaderno 13 (June 1931), pp. 90–226, *Annali 1968*, pp. 312–55, especially p. 355, for citation and pp. 349–50; A. Rossi, "Lettres inédites de Frederic Engels," *Monde*, 6 Dec. 1930, and Quaderno 12 (January–June 1931), *Annali 1968*, pp. 305–6.

21. See Tasca's notes on the structure of the English working class, Quaderno 16 (end 1931–January 1932), pp. 131–203, *Annali 1968*, especially p. 403. Also A. Rossi, "Anticipations," *Monde*, May 1931, and "Hegel et Marx," *Monde*, 12 Dec. 1931.

22. See the notes on Robert Owen, Quaderno 10 (March–May 1930), pp. 118–47, *Annali 1968*, pp. 250–53, especially 250–51.

23. A. Rossi, "La crise doctrinale du socialisme," *Monde*, 3 Oct. 1930. On Marxist humanism, see the notes on the "Philosophie du prolétariat," pp. 129–59, *Annali 1968*, pp. 428–35.

24. See Barbusse to Bureau Politique du PCF, 8 Nov. 1930; M. T. of *L'Humanité* to Barbusse, 14 Nov. 1930; Bureau Politique to Barbusse, 15 Nov. 1930; Barbusse to Werth, 16 Nov. 1930, stating that Paul Louis could no longer write the "Semaine Politique" column. AT, Fasc. Francia 254 Monde; see also Berti's remarks on the Kharkov congress in *Annali 1968*, p. 65.

25. E. Berl to Barbusse, 18 Dec. 1930, defending the independence of the staff; Tasca to Barbusse, 15 Nov. 1930 taking the same position; Barbusse to the Bureau Politique, 25 Nov. 1930, defending *Monde* and the response of the Bureau Politique to Barbusse, 28 Nov. 1930, AT, Francia 254 *Monde*. Tasca promised Barbusse that he would use Communists wherever possible but that Louis should stay. Tasca to Barbusse, 14 Mar. 1931, and Barbusse to Tasca, 17 Mar. 1931. For Barbusse's refusal to allow Tasca to develop the United Front theme, Barbusse to Tasca, 11 and 13 Jan. 1931. On Barbusse's failure to bring in leading Communist writers, see Barbusse to PCF, 23 Mar. 1931; Barbusse to Desphilippon, 23 Mar. 1931, noting that he offered the economic section to Berlioz of the PCF; Barbusse to Berlioz, 23 Mar. 1931, and Berlioz to Barbusse, undated. All in AT, fasc. Francia 254, *Monde*.

26. See the articles in the series "Marxisme en 1933," *Monde*, 18 Mar., 25 Mar., 1 Apr., 8 Apr., and May 1933. The series provoked a ferocious response from Giuseppe Berti in *Lo stato operaio*, "Angelo Tasca, portabandiera della democrazia borghese," May 1933, pp. 261–69.

27. "Marxisme en 1933," *Monde*, 17 June, 8 July, 5 Aug. 1933. Tasca also argued that Engels believed much earlier than the 1890s that universal suffrage was a means for forcing other changes. See "Marxisme en 1933," *Monde*, 29 Apr. and 27 May 1933.

28. On the need for alliances, see "Marxisme en 1933," *Monde*, 13 May and 12 Aug. 1933.

29. For citation, see "Questions et réponses de Monde," Quaderno 11, p. 165, in *Annali 1968*, p. 272. On Jaurès, see "Notes pour l'étude sur Jaurès," Quaderno 14 (July–December 1931), pp. 97–171, *Annali 1968*, pp. 359–74; Rossi, "Jean Jaurès, aujourd'hui," *Monde*, 1 Aug. 1931.

30. "Marxisme en 1933," *Monde*, 19 Aug. 1933.

31. Fanny Jezierska to Tasca, 3 Feb. 1932, insert in Quaderno 22. See also Jezierska to Tasca, 1 Dec. 1931, and Tasca to Jezierska, 21 Oct. 1931, and 7 Jan. 1932, in AT, Corrispondenza, fasc. 1931.

32. For the Paris-Berlin-Moscow idea, see Rossi, "Paris-Berlin-Moscou," *Monde*, 12 Dec. 1931.

33. Rossi, "Vers la troisième Reich," *Monde*, 2 July 1932; also "La poussée di Hindenburg," *Monde*, 19 Mar. 1932; "La contre-révolution en Allemagne," *Monde*, 30 Apr. 1932; "Second ou troisième Reich," *Monde*, 11 June 1932, and "Hitler entre Weimar et Potsdam," *Monde*, 13 Aug. 1932.

34. "Un mort, qui ira bien," *Monde*, 7 Nov. 1931, in which Tasca criticized the Labour party and De Man for lacking an international perspective. See Quaderno 11, p. 147; Rossi, "Perspectives de la résistance ouvrière," *Monde*, 25 Feb. 1933; Georges Monnet, "Paris-Berlin-Moscou," *Monde*, 4 Mar. 1933; Barbusse, "Paris-Berlin-Moscou," *Monde*, 9 Jan. 1932.

35. See "Elections à gauche," *Monde*, 7 May 1932; Rossi, "Vers la nouvelle chambre," *Monde*, 14 May 1932; "La philosophie des élections selon 'Monde.'" *L'Humanité*, 20 May 1932, and Paul Vaillant Couturier, "'Monde? Non. Un nouveau Monde? Oui," *L'Humanité*, 28 June 1932. Jean Freville called Tasca a renegade "chassé de l'Internationale." See "Les Livres: Perspectives révolutionnaires d'Espagne," *L'Humanité*, 9 Feb. 1932.

36. On the background to the Amsterdam-Pleyel meetings, see Herbert R. Lottman, *The Left Bank: Writers, Artists and Politics from the Popular Front to the Cold War* (Boston; Houghton Mifflin, 1982), pp. 50—51.

37. See Lottman, *The Left Bank*, p. 59; Paul Nizan, "Littérature révolutionnaire en France," *Révue des vivants*, September—October 1932, pp. 393—400.

38. "A propos de Congrès de Kharkov: Exposé fait au comité de rédaction de Monde," 5 Nov. 1931, Quaderno 16 (end 1931—January 1932), pp. 77—115, *Annali 1968*, pp. 384—420, citation p. 393; "Du réalisme au socialisme," *Monde*, 2 Apr. 1932.

39. For the manifesto of *Monde*, see "Article proposé par Barbusse et que la rédaction a refusé de publier en le remplaçant par le Manifeste paru le 5 Décembre 1931," AT, Francia, fasc. 254 *Monde*; see "Monde," "L'écrivain et la révolution," *Monde*, 5 Dec. 1931; "Notre débat sur la littérature prolétarienne," *Monde*, 26 Dec. 1931; "Les livres: Le manifeste de l'Association des Ecrivains et Artistes Révolutionnaires," *L'Humanité*, 29 Mar. 1932.

40. "Lettre de Victor Serge, fin janvier 1933," insert between pp. 76—77 in Quaderno 24. On the Victor Serge affair, see Lottman, *The Left Bank*, pp. 92—93.

41. See Rossi to A. Wauters, Directeur du *Peuple*, 20 May 1933, AT, Corrispondenza, fasc. Wauters; "Il faut que les soviets rendent la liberté a Victor Serge," *Le Peuple*, 3 June 1933.

42. Lottman, *The Left Bank*, pp. 92—96.

43. Tasca had been in and out of trouble over his reluctance to tolerate excessive praise of the USSR. He accepted an article by Georges Friedmann on professional education in the USSR but edited out a reference that placed Stalin on the same level as Marx as a theorist. Friedmann protested, and Tasca was forced to apologize; Tasca to Barbusse and Werth, 14 Jan. 1932, Quaderno 16, p. 280 annesso, in *Annali 1968*, pp. 422—23. For Tasca's views on Barbusse, see the notes on *Clarté* and on *Le Feu*, in Quaderno 21, pp. 84, 104—66, and his review of Barbusse's *Zola*, "Du realisme au socialisme," *Monde*, 2 Apr. 1932; Tasca to Barbusse, 6 Mar. 1932, in Quaderno 22, pp. 1—14, *Annali 1968*, pp. 508—12; Barbusse to Rossi, 14 Mar. 1932, Quaderno 32, p. 12.

44. "Prévision budgetaire, janvier à décembre 1932," AT, Francia, fasc. 254, *Monde*. See also "Lettre au Conseil d'administration du journal," 10 Oct. 1933, AT, Corrispondenza, fasc. *Monde*.

45. For the letter announcing the change in policy for salaries, see Barbusse to editors, 21 July 1933, AT, Corrispondenza, fasc. *Monde* and Rossi to Barbusse, 3 Aug. 1933; also Barbusse to Rossi, 12, 22, 26 Feb. and 6 and 19 Mar. 1933, AT, Francia, fasc. 254 *Monde*. The correspondence relating to the dispute between Tasca and *Monde* is contained in AT, Corrispondenza, fasc. *Monde*.

CHAPTER 7

1. Tasca to Blum, 12 May 1932, and Blum to Tasca, 14 May 1932, in Quaderno 22, pp. 132—33 and insert.

2. Tasca to Vandervelde, 20 May 1932, Quaderno 22, pp. 166—67.

3. See Tasca to Vandervelde, 4 Aug. 1933; Tasca to Landsvreegt, 7 Aug. 1933; Tasca to Silone, 30 Aug. 1933; J. Maurin to Tasca, 7 Sept. 1933, AT, Corrispondenza, fasc. "Marxismo 1933." Tasca to De Man, 7 Aug. 1933, and De Man to Tasca, 11 Aug. 1933, in AT, Corrispondenza, fasc. De Man. Tasca to C.-A. Julien, 22 Feb. 1933, Quaderno 24, pp. 18–22.

4. On Paul Desjardins, see *In Memorian Paul Desjardins*, (Paris: Editions de Minuit, 1949), pp. 12–20.

5. Interview with Charles André Julien, 16 Mar. 1981. On Carlo Rosselli and Pontigny, see Franco Venturi, "Carlo Rosselli e la cultura francese," *Giustizia e Libertà nella lotta antifascista* (Florence: La Nuova Italia, 1978), p. 169. See also Desjardins to Tasca, 14 Aug. and 20 Nov. 1933, AT, Corrispondenza, fasc. Desjardins, and the critique of Tasca's presentation at Pontigny, 30 Aug. 1934, in AT, Corrispondenza, fasc. Recensioni varie.

6. On the Concentrazione antifascista, see Santi Fedele, *Storia della Concentrazione antifascista 1927–1934* (Milan: Feltrinelli, 1976), pp. 88–89.

7. See Tasca to Rosselli, 6 Mar. 1931, AT, Corrispondenza, fasc. Carlo Rosselli. See also Tasca to Boatti, 24 July 1931, and Boatti to Tasca, 1 and 25 July 1931, and 10 May 1932 in AT, Corrispondenza, fasc. Boatti. Boatti was working as a day laborer and was experiencing extreme financial difficulties when Tasca tried to help him.

8. See the article by Tasca and the editorial note, Tasca, "Opinioni sulla Germania," *Quaderni di Giustizia e Libertà*, June 1933, pp. 9–14. On Rosselli's views, see Ariane Landuyt, "Rosselli e Modigliani: Due socialismi a confronto," *Giustizia e Libertà nella lotta antifascista*, pp. 104–5. For a general study of Rosselli's life, see Aldo Garosci, *Vita di Carlo Rosselli* (Florence: Vallecchi, 1973).

9. Santi Fedele, *Storia della Concentrazione antifascista*, pp. 98–101.

10. On the *Giornale degli operai*, see Rosselli to Tasca, 9 Jan. 1934, and 26 Mar. 1934, in AT, Corrispondenza, fasc. Carlo Rosselli; Faravelli to Rosselli, 3 Jan. 1934, Archivio di Giustizia e Libertà, Istituto per la Storia della Resistenza, Florence, Fondo Rosselli, sottofasc. 46 Faravelli; Faravelli to Tasca, 26 Feb. and 10 Mar. 1934, AT, busta 7, PSI-PCI 1930–1934, fasc. 1934; the report of 26 Feb. 1934, to the Capo Div. Polizia Politica, and the telegrams from the Italian Embassy in Paris to the Foreign and Interior ministries, 16 Mar. and 10 Aug. 1934, in ACS, CPC, 5040/24848; "Che cosa vogliamo," *Giornale degli operai*, March 1934.

11. Santi Fedele, *Storia della Concentrazione antifascista*, pp. 168–71. See Modigliani to Rosselli, 25 Feb. 1934, and Rosselli to Modigliani, 26 Feb. 1934, Archivio di Giustizia e Libertà, Fondo Rosselli, I 1, sottof, 75 Modigliani.

12. Nenni to Tasca, 14 Apr. 1934, and Tasca to Nenni, 18 Apr. 1934, in AT, Corrispondenza, fasc. Nenni.

13. Nenni to the Direzione of the PSI, 28 Apr. 1934, AT, busta 7, 1930–1934, fasc. 1934.

14. Nenni, "La crisi della Concentrazione antifascista e la riclassificazione dell'emigrazione," *Politica socialista*, August 1934, p. 30.

15. Tasca to Rosselli, 1 May 1934, in Stefano Merli, ed., *Documenti inediti dell'archivio Angelo Tasca: La rinascita del socialismo italiano e la lotta contro il fascismo dal 1934 al 1939* (Milan: Feltrinelli, 1963), pp. 83–84.

16. Rosselli to Tasca, 1 May 1934, in *Documenti inediti*, pp. 85–87.

17. Tasca to Faravelli, 18 May 1924, AT, busta 7 1930–34 PSI-PCI, fasc. 1934; Tasca, "Il problema delle generazioni," *Nuovo Avanti*, 26 May 1934; "La commedia degli equivoci," *Nuovo Avanti*, 23 June 1934.

18. Tasca to Lussu, 2 Aug. 1934, in *Documenti inediti*, pp. 100–1. In the

August issue of *Politica socialista,* Tasca accused Lussu (Tirreno) of trying to form a rival party on Marxist lines and affirmed that the whole venture of GL was illogical: "Le riviste: Giustizia e Libertà," *Politica socialista,* August 1934, pp. 88−93. On the break between Tasca and Rosselli caused by Faravelli's meddling, see Tasca to Rosselli, 23 July 1934, AT, Corrispondenza, fasc. Rosselli. A year later, when Rosselli broke all relations with Faravelli, he continued to blame him for the rupture with Tasca. See Rosselli to Faravelli, 25 Dec. 1935, Archivio di Giustizia e Libertà, Fondo Rosselli, sottofasc. 46 Faravelli.

19. See John T. Marcus, *French Socialism in the Crisis Years, 1933−1936: Fascism and the French Left* (New York: Praeger, 1958), pp. 73−78, for the stipulation of the French Unity of Action pact.

20. On the Communist position, see the meeting of the Ufficio politico of the PCI, 12 and 17 July 1934, APCI, 1934, busta 1194/4, pp. 98−99, 101−2; "Per l'unità d'azione del proletariato," *Lo stato operaio,* July 1934, pp. 489−93. For the reaction of the PSI, see Leonardo Rapone, "L'età dei fronti popolari e la guerra (1934−1943)," in Giovanni Sabatucci, ed., *Storia del socialismo italiano* (Rome: Il Poligono, 1981), vol. 5 *Gli anni del fascismo,* pp. 196−200.

21. Nenni to the Direzione of the PCI, 23 July 1934, and the PCI's response of 24 Aug. 1934, in APCI, 1934, fasc. 1210/1, pp. 1−3. For the citation from Nenni's article, see "Nuova fase e nuovo fronte," *Nuovo Avanti,* 28 July 1934. On the course of the negotiations, see "Punti presentati dalla delegazione comunista alla prima riunione della delegazione dei due partiti," APCI, 1934, fasc. 1210/3, pp. 20−21.

22. For Longo's remarks, see the meeting of the Ufficio Politico of the PCI, 3 Aug. 1934, APCI, 1934, fasc. 1894/4, pp. 110−16.

23. See the draft agreement, dated 6 Aug. 1934, in AT, busta 7 PSI-PCI 1930−1934, fasc. 1934.

24. Tasca to Nenni, 7 Aug. 1934, AT, busta 7, PSI-PCI 1930−1934, fasc. 1934; Faravelli to Tasca, 14 Aug. 1934, ibid.

25. Rugginenti to Tasca, 18 Aug. 1934, and also Nenni to Tasca, undated (August 1934), AT, busta 7, PSI-PCI 1930−1934, fasc. 1934.

26. Delegation of the PCI to the delegation of the PSI, 16 Aug. 1934, APCI, 1934, fasc. 1210/3, p. 32; for the text of the agreements, see Rapone, *Storia del socialismo,* pp. 464−68, and "I limiti dell'accordo," *Nuovo Avanti,* 25 Aug. 1934; for a comparison with the French text, see Marcus, *French Socialism in Crisis,* p. 78.

27. Tasca to Nenni, 19 Aug. 1934, AT, busta 7 PSI-PCI 1930−1934, fasc. 1934.

28. On the relationship between Tasca and Nenni, see Leonardo Rapone, "Il Partito socialista italiano fra Pietro Nenni e Angelo Tasca," *Annali della Fondazione Giangiacomo Feltrinelli 1983/1984* (Milan: Feltrinelli, 1984), pp. 661−710. For Tasca's critique of Nenni's style of leadership, see Tasca to Faravelli, 28 Sept. 1934, in *Documenti inediti,* p. 13; see also the sympathetic portrait of Nenni in Vera Modigliani, *Esilio* (Milan: Garzanti, 1946), p. 152.

29. See Tasca, "Episodio Caldara," *Politica socialista,* August 1934, pp. 37−38; Saragat, "Prospettive," *Problemi della rivoluzione italiana,* September 1934, pp. 3−5.

30. For a discussion of the socialist CSI, see Rapone, *Storia del socialismo,* pp. 180−93; see also Alessio (Luzzatto), "Il fronte unico," and Maro (Luzzatto), "Frammenti e prospettive della vita italiana," *Politica socialista,* December 1934, pp. 113−20.

31. Joseph (Faravelli), "L'azione socialista in Italia," *Politica socialista*, August 1934; Faravelli to Tasca, 26 Aug. 1934, AT, busta 7 PSI-PCI 1930–1934, fasc. 1934.
32. See Tasca to Faravelli, 2 Oct. 1934, and 20 Nov. 1934; undated (December 1934), AT, busta 7 PSI-PCI 1930–1934, fasc. 1934.
33. Tasca to Nenni and Rugginenti, 20 Nov. 1934; Rugginenti to Tasca, 19 Dec. 1934, AT, busta 7 PSI-PCI 1930–1934, fasc. 1934.
34. Tasca, "Serietà proletaria e fiera piccolo borghese," *Nuovo Avanti*, 2 Feb. 1935; E. Lussu, "La situazione italiana e l'antifascismo all'estero," *Giustizia e Libertà*, 1 Mar. 1935. On Lussu's role in trying to reconcile GL to a clear proletarian position, see Lussu to Rosselli, 1 Jan. 1935, and 29 Jan. 1935, in Archivio GL, fondo Rosselli, I, 1, sottofasc. 69. For Rosselli's proposals, see GL to the other antifascist parties, 22 Dec. 1934, APCI, 1934, 1210/2, p. 99; "Classismo e antifascismo," *Giustizia e Libertà*, 25 Jan. 1935.
35. Silone to unknown, 6 August (no year), copy in AT, busta 8 PSI-PCI 1935–1936, fasc. 1935. The letter was clearly written in an earlier period.
36. Blasco (Tresso) to Pasquini (Silone), undated, 1930–1931, AT, busta 8 PSI-PCI 1935–1936, fasc. 1935, sottofasc. Articoli di Feroci.
37. On Ravazzoli, see Santini, "Per l'unità organica," *Nuovo Avanti*, 23 Feb. 1935; "Partito unico-politica nuova," *Politica socialista*, August 1934, pp. 77–80, especially p. 80; Ravazzoli to Tasca, 1 Feb. 1933, AT, Corrispondenza, fasc. Ravazzoli. See also Rapone, *Storia del socialismo*, p. 265. For Tasca's hopes to bring Leonetti and Tresso into the PSI, see Tasca to Joseph (Faravelli), 17 Feb. 1935, busta 8 PSI-PCI 1935–1936, fasc. 1935; Leonetti, "Ritorno al Barnum," *Nuovo Avanti*, 16 Mar. 1935.
38. Tasca to Faravelli, 8 Mar. 1935, in *Documenti inediti*, p. 125. Joseph to Tasca, 11 Mar. 1935, AT, busta 8 PSI-PCI 1935–1936, fasc. 1935.
39. 'Politica socialista' [Tasca], "Il partito in formazione," *Politica socialista*, March 1935, pp. 195–203; for Nenni's views, see "Azione socialista: l'unità d'azione tra socialisti e comunisti," *Politica socialista*, December 1934, pp. 104–12.

CHAPTER 8

1. See Simona Colarizzi, *Classe operaia e ceti medi* (Venice: Marsilio editori, 1976), pp. 22–32; Sternhell, pp. 165–66. For Mosley's position, see Robert Skidelsky, *Politicians and the Slump: The Labour Government of 1929–1931* (London: Macmillan, 1967), pp. 167–89. The most complete biography in English of Henri De Man is Peter Dodge, *The Faith and Works of Hendrik De Man* (The Hague: Martinus Nijhoff, 1966).
2. A. Rossi, "La scission socialiste au congrès de Paris," *Monde*, 22 July 1933; see also "Le problème du pouvoir au congrès socialiste," *Monde*, 29 July 1933. Tasca also warned Paul Marion that, although he was moved by a hatred of dictatorship, his socialism might prove "encore plus vide et plus abruttisant" than the ideas against which he rebelled; see Tasca to Marion, 18 Aug. 1933, Quaderno 24, pp. 144–45. For an interesting analysis of neosocialism, see Sternhell, pp. 168–70. On the Congress of Paris, see Marcus, *French Socialism in the Crisis Years*, pp. 165–66.
3. André Philip, *Henri De Man et la crise doctrinale du socialisme* (Paris: Gambier, 1928), p. 131; see also pp. 20–23, 57, 61; H. De Man, *L'idée socialiste* (Paris: Grasset, 1935), pp. 17–19, 32, 160, and Sternhell, pp. 139–40.
4. H. De Man, *Le socialisme constructif* (Paris: Alcan, 1933), pp. 52–53;

also Philip, *De Man*, pp. 66, 70, 74; H. De Man, "Le nationalisme économique," *Revue de l'Université de Bruxelles*, February—April 1934, pp. 19.

5. De Man, *Réflexions sur l'économie dirigée* (Brussels: L'Eglantine, 1932), pp. 28—32, and *Pour un plan d'action* (Le Mans: Imprimerie ouvrière, 1934), p. 5.

6. De Man, *Pour un plan d'action*, p. 7; for the outline of the plan, p. 29; also Dodge, *Faith and Work of Hendrik De Man*, pp. 129—72, for the history of the Plan.

7. Tasca, Quaderno 25, pp. 118—37; Tasca to Paul Desjardins, 15 Aug. 1934, AT, Corrispondenza, fasc. Desjardins; Sternhell, p. 149.

8. Colarizzi, *Classe operaia*, pp. 37—47.

9. See the letters Joseph (Faravelli) to Tasca, 5 and 8 Apr. 1935, and Tasca to Joseph, 10 Apr. 1935, in AT, busta 8, PSI-PCI 1935—36, fasc. 1935.

10. Joseph to Tasca, 8 Apr. 1935, and Tasca to Joseph, 10 Apr. 1935, AT, busta 8 PSI-PCI 1935—36, fasc. 1935; Joseph to a "corriere per l'Italia," *Documenti inediti*, pp. 130—32.

11. Joseph to Tasca, 25 May 1935, *Documenti inediti*, p. 139; Tasca to Nenni, 31 May 1935, and Nenni to Tasca, 31 May 1935, in AT, Corrispondenza, fasc. Nenni.

12. See the minutes of the Ufficio Politico of 1 and 11 Apr. 1935 in APCI, 1935, 1269/3, pp. 73—74, 78—79; meeting of the Ufficio Politico, 21 and 31 May 1935. in APCI, 1935, 1269/4. pp. 96, 102; see also Tasca to Nenni, 31 May 1935, AT, Corrispondenza, fasc. Nenni.

13. See "Problemi essenziali dell'ora," *Lo Stato operaio*, March 1935, pp. 161—67, for citation, pp. 166—67.

14. "Fronte popolare e lotta contro la guerra," *Lo stato operaio*, June 1935, pp. 333—39, especially pp. 336—37; see also the meeting of the Ufficio Politico, 29 June 1935, APCI, 1935, 1269/5, pp. 120—21.

15. "I lavori del Consiglio generale del Partito," *Nuovo Avanti*, 20 July 1935.

16. See the minutes of the Ufficio Politico, 26 July 1935, APCI, 1935, 1269/6, pp. 128—36.

17. Egidio Gennari, "La via verso il partito unico della classe operaia," *Lo stato operaio*, July 1935, pp. 424—27.

18. Tasca to Joseph, 4 June 1935, *Documenti inediti*, pp. 143—44.

19. Ercoli, "Problemi del fronte unico," *Lo stato operaio*, August 1935, pp. 497—510. On the development of Comintern policy in these years, see E. H. Carr, *Twilight of the Comintern, 1930—1935* (New York: Pantheon Books, 1982), especially pp. 239—55, for Italian developments.

20. Pietro Nenni, "L'unità d'azione," *Politica socialista*, April 1935, pp. 299—305; see also Léon Blum, "La garantie de l'unité d'action," *Le Populaire*, 27 Feb. 1935, and "L'unité d'action et l'unité organique," *"Le Populaire*, 28 February 1935. See also the comments of Colarizzi, *Classe operaia*, p. 65.

21. Rugginenti to Nenni, Modigliani, Tasca, and Saragat, 5 Sept. 1935, AT, busta 8, 1935—36, fasc. 1935.

22. See the minutes of the Ufficio Politico, 8 Aug. 1935, APCI, 1935, 1269/7, pp. 152—53.

23. Minutes of the Ufficio politico, 13 and 27 Sept. 1935, APCI, 1935, 1269/7, pp. 157—61, 166—67. For Nenni's views on the applicability of the Popular Front to Italy, see P. Emiliani (Nenni), "Ritorno all'Aventino," *Nuovo Avanti*, 31 Aug. 1935; "In tema di alleanze," *Nuovo Avanti*, 21 Sept. 1935, and "Il settimo congresso di Mosca rafforza l'unità d'azione," *Nuovo Avanti*, 14 September 1935.

24. Tasca to Nenni, 15 Aug. 1935, in AT, busta 8 PSI-PCI 1935–1936, fasc. 1935; see also "Progetto di risposta alla lettera del 26–VIII–35, AT, busta 8 1935–1936, fasc. 1935.

25. See the minutes of the Comitato Centrale, October 1935, APCI, 1935, 1266/1, p. 19 and 1266/4, pp. 71–73, 132. For a description of the congress of Brussels, see the *Nuovo Avanti*, 14 Oct. 1935.

26. "Nel solco dell'unità d'azione proletaria," *Nuovo Avanti*, 7 Dec. 1935; Gallo to Direzione of PSI, 7 Dec. 1935, and Nenni to the Ufficio Politico of the PCI, 12 Dec. 1935, APCI, 1935, 1286/2, pp. 47, 50–52; Ufficio Politico to Direzione PSI, 28 Dec. 1935, APCI, 1935, 1286/2, pp. 55–59.

27. See Joseph to Tasca, 10 Nov. 1935, AT, busta 8 PSI-PCI 1935–1936, fasc. 1935. See also Tasca to Nenni, 20 Dec. 1935, ibid.

28. Modigliani encouraged Faravelli to use the CSI as a counterweight to the effort to strengthen Unity of Action. See Joseph to Tasca, 21 Oct. 1935, AT, busta 8 PSI-PCI 1935–1936, fasc. 1935. On the position of the CSI, see Il Centro Socialista Interno, "Criteri d'orientamenti dell'azione," December 1935, *Documenti inediti*, pp. 153–55; "Come l'unità d'azione è vista in Italia," *Nuovo Avanti*, 14 Dec. 1935, and "Il centro socialista interno alla direzione del PSI," early January 1936, *Documenti inediti*, pp. 180–81.

29. Nenni to Tasca, 1 Jan. 1936, *Documenti inediti*, p. 158; "Che cosa si deve intendere per minimalismo," *Nuovo Avanti*, 4 Jan. 1936, and "Chi mette in pericolo l'unità d'azione," *Nuovo Avanti*, 11 Jan. 1936; Ercoli to Furini, 1 Jan. 1936, APCI, 1936, 1352, pp. 1–2. On the growth of anticommunism within the PSI, see Rapone, "Il Partito socialista italiano fra Pietro Nenni e Angelo Tasca," pp. 681–94.

30. For Tasca's letter, see Direzione del PSI to Ufficio Politico of the PCI, 14 Jan. 1936, *Documenti inediti*, pp. 159–62; Nenni to Tasca, 10 Jan. 1936, AT, busta 8 PSI-PCI 1935–1936, fasc. 1936.

31. Grieco to the Direzione of the PSI, 4 Feb. 1936, *Documenti inediti*, pp. 163–66. See also "Rapporto Adami [Romano Cocchi] su un sopraluogo a Bruxelles, Anversa e Amsterdam," 18 Jan. 1936, APCI, 1936, 1393/1, in which Adami (Cocchi) noted that Alberto Jacometti and others in Brussels were much more forthcoming on cooperation.

32. Nenni to Tasca, 7 Feb. 1936, AT, busta 8 PSI-PCI 1935–1936, fasc. 1936; see Direzione PSI to Ufficio Politico of the PCI, 12 Feb. 1936, APCI, 1936, 1395/1, pp. 17–18. For the negative reaction of the Socialists, see "La politica socialista delle alleanze e del fronte popolare in Italia," *Nuovo Avanti*, 1 Feb. 1936; Saragat, "Ritorno alla concentrazione?" *Nuovo Avanti*, 15 Feb. 1936; Agostini to the Direzione, February–March 1936, *Documenti inediti*, pp. 188–92.

33. "Il partito, il fronte unico e i problemi organizzativi dell'unità d'azione," *Nuovo Avanti*, 4 Apr. 1936; Alessandro Bocconi, a dissident member of the PSI, threatened to break ranks to serve in an official capacity in the Fronte Unico organization; see the meeting of the PCI representatives to the Unity of Action Committee, 4 Apr. 1936, APCI, 1936, 1394/1, pp. 3–4. The SFIO passed a similar ban against belonging to "united front from below" organizations; see Marcus, *French Socialism in the Crisis Years*, p. 60.

34. See the minutes of the Unity of Action Committee, 10 Apr. 1936, APCI, 1936, 1394/1, p. 5.

35. On the negotiations for the renewal of the Unity of Action pact and its expansion to GL, see "Progetto comunista," AT, busta 8 PSI-PCI 1935–1936, fasc.

1936; Tasca to Nenni, 14 Mar. 1936, AT, busta 8 PSI-PCI 1935−1936, fasc. 1936; Comitato Centrale of GL to the Direzione of PSI, 24 Apr. 1936, AT, busta 8 PSI-PCI 1935−1936, busta 1936; "Per l'unità d'azione," *Giustizia e Libertà*, 1 May 1936; Rosselli to Di Vittorio, 7 May 1936, and Di Vittorio to Rosselli, 8 May 1936, Segreteria PCI to GL, 18 May 1936, APCI, 1936, 1397, pp. 8−9, 11−12.

36. "Le elezioni politiche nel Belgio," *Nuovo Avanti*, 30 May 1936.

CHAPTER 9

1. On Blum's policies, see Michel Bilis, *Socialistes et pacifistes ou l'impossible dilemme des socialistes français* (Paris: Syros, 1979), pp. 37, 49−50. An excellent study of Blum's entire career with special emphasis on the years from 1933 to 1940 is Joel Colton, *Léon Blum: Humanist in Politics* (New York: Alfred A. Knopf, 1966); for Blum's foreign policy views, see pp. 83−85.

2. Bilis, *Socialisties et pacifistes*, pp. 23, 29.

3. Ibid., pp. 82−94; Colton, *Blum*, pp. 81−83.

4. André Leroux (Tasca), "Pilsudski et Hitler," *Le Populaire*, 8 Feb. 1934. On Austria, see A. L., "Le problème autrichien," *Le Populaire*, 10 Feb. 1934; André Leroux, "Les entretiens de Rome," *Le Populaire*, 14 Mar. 1934.

5. A. L., "Nouvelles internationales: Les problèmes du jour," *Le Populaire*, 22 Mar. 1934; "Le bilan d'un régime fort: le fascisme italien," *Le Populaire*, 25 Mar. 1934, and "Nouvelles internationales: Les corporations sont nées en Italie," *Le Populaire*, 12 May 1934.

6. Politica Socialista, "La politica estera dell'Italia," *Politica socialista*, December 1934, p. 102; A. Leroux, "L'accord Laval Mussolini," *Le Populaire*, 9 Jan. 1935; "Les accords franco italiens en Afrique," *Le Populaire*, 12 Jan. 1935; Tasca, "Il patto italo francese," *Nuovo Avanti*, 12 Jan. 1935.

7. See "Mentre a Stresa si fa del realismo," *Nuovo Avanti*, 13 Apr. 1935; "L'Abissinia, problema europea," *Nuovo Avanti*, 27 Apr. 1935; André Leroux, "Les résultats de Stresa," *Le Populaire*, 14 Apr. 1935.

8. André Leroux, "L'accord naval anglo allemand," *Le Populaire*, 19 June 1935; see also the article on the same subject in the *Nuovo Avanti* of 29 June 1935.

9. For the evolution of Tasca's views on the crisis, see "Tappa dell'anti Europa," *Nuovo Avanti*, 5 Oct. 1935; "Sanzioni o compromesso?" *Nuovo Avanti*, 9 Nov. 1935; "Il compromesso Hoare Laval," *Nuovo Avanti*, 14 Dec. 1935; "Il fascismo e la guerra d'Africa," *Almanacco socialista 1936* (Paris: Partito Socialista Italiano, 1936), pp. 16−30.

10. Tasca to J. R. Nitchison, 8 Mar. 1935, AT, busta 8 PSI-PCI 1935−36, fasc. 1935.

11. On the Franco Soviet Pact, see A. L., "Pacte franco soviétique, pacte de la SDN et pacte de l'Est," *Le Populaire*, 4 May 1935; "Conseguenze e sviluppi del patto franco sovietico," and Ennio (Nenni), "L'opinione degli altri," *Nuovo Avanti*, 25 May 1935.

12. *** (Tasca), "Il crepuscolo della Società delle Nazioni si illumina di sinistri bagliori," *Nuovo Avanti* 11 July 1936; "Mussolini e Hitler si associano contro la sicurezza collettiva," *Nuovo Avanti*, 20 July 1936; G. E. Modigliani, "Da Zimmerwald a Zimmerwald," *Nuovo Avanti*, 20 June 1936.

13. [Tasca], "Lo sconcertante processo di Mosca," *Nuovo Avanti*, 24 Aug. 1936.

14. "Le esecuzioni di Mosca," *Nuovo Avanti*, 5 Sept. 1936.

15. On the development of the Spanish Civil War, see Gabriel Jackson, *The Spanish Republic and the Civil War, 1931–1939* (Princeton: Princeton University Press, 1965). For the policy of the Comintern and the Communist parties, see E. H. Carr, *The Comintern and the Spanish Civil War* (New York: Pantheon Books, 1984).

16. Carr, *The Comintern*, p. 5.

17. "Le elezioni francesi e la politica europea," *Nuovo Avanti*, 9 May 1936; "Elezioni politiche e unità socialista in Spagna," *Nuovo Avanti*, 7 Mar. 1936; "Les problèmes du jour," *Le Populaire*, 14 May 1936. On the first reactions to the outbreak of the war, see "L'effort des troupes républicaines se concentre sur Orviédo, sur Saragosse et sur Grenade," *Le Populaire*, 1 Aug. 1936; A. L., "Les événements d'Espagne," *Le Populaire*, 4 Aug. 1936; "Il fronte spagnolo della lotta mondiale contro il fascismo," *Nuovo Avanti*, 8 Aug. 1936.

18. "La Direzione del Partito e gli avvenimenti spagnoli," 15 Aug. 1936; "Loro e noi," *Nuovo Avanti*, 1 Aug. 1936; Nenni, "Ciò che rappresenta il governo Caballero," *Nuovo Avanti*, 12 Sept. 1936. Nenni's exception to the United Front was the anarchist movement, with which he felt that a conflict was inevitable: Nenni to Rugginenti, 13 Aug. 1936, and Nenni to Tasca, 16 Aug. 1936, AT, Corrispondenza, fasc. Nenni. On the exchange between the PSI and PCI, see Grieco to Nenni, 8 Oct. 1936, APCI 1936, 1395/1, p. 52; Ufficio Politico of PCI to Direzione PSI, 9 Oct. 1936, APCI 1936, 1395/2, pp. 54–55; "I problemi dell'unità d'azione," *Nuovo Avanti*, 24 Oct. 1936.

19. Nenni to Tasca, 16 Oct. 1936, AT, busta 8 PSI-PCI 1935–1936, fasc. 1936.

20. The entire correspondence between the parties, including the debate over Modigliani, is reproduced in the *Nuovo Avanti* of 14 Nov. 1936, and in *Grido del popolo* of 7 Nov. 1936.

21. Tasca to Faravelli, 7 Dec. 1936, *Documenti inediti*, p. 211; Vice (Rugginenti), "Sostegno con la corda," *Nuovo Avanti*, 12 Dec. 1936.

22. "Le nouveau gouvernement catalan et les tendances politiques en Espagne," *Le Populaire*, 21 Dec. 1936, and "Il governo della Catalogna e le prospettive sociali della lotta in Spagna," *Nuovo Avanti*, 26 Dec. 1936.

23. Tasca to Nenni, 21 Dec. 1936, AT, Corrispondenza, fasc. Nenni.

CHAPTER 10

1. Interviews with Valeria Tasca, 18 Mar. 1981, and Charles André Julien, 16 Mar. 1981; Fernández, like too many other intellectuals, began on the Left and eventually passed to a collaborationist position during World War II: see Lottman, *The Left Bank*, pp. 104, 145, 199–200.

2. Julien approached Tasca about collaborating on the *Oran Républicain*, C.-A. Julien to Tasca, 31 July 1936, AT, Corrispondenza, fasc. Julien.

3. N. Greene, *Crisis and Decline: The French Socialist Party in the Popular Front Era* (Ithaca: Cornell University Press, 1968), pp. 187–93, 206.

4. For Tasca's continuing interest in Roosevelt's New Deal, see "Il messaggio di Roosevelt," *Nuovo Avanti*, 11 Jan. 1936; "La lumière vient de l'Amérique," *Le Populaire*, 2 Dec. 1936; "Dans un discours retentissant," *Le Populaire*, 6 Oct. 1937.

5. On the Moscow trials, see Paolo Spriano, *Storia del Partito Comunista Italiano*, vol. 3 *I fronti popolari, Stalin, le guerre* (Turin: Einaudi, 1970), p. 163.

6. Alberto Jacometti, "Ritorno dall'Urss," *Nuovo Avanti*, 16 Jan. 1937, and Spertia (Saragat), "Viaggio in Russia," *Nuovo Avanti*, 30 Jan. 1937.

7. "Un altro processo di Mosca," *Nuovo Avanti*, 30 Jan. 1937, and "Aujourd'hui commence a Moscou le deuxième grand procès contre les Trotzkistes," *Le Populaire*, 23 Jan. 1937.

8. G. Lombardi (Faravelli), "Note ai processi di Mosca" and "Avvenimenti spagnoli e processo di Mosca," *Nuovo Avanti*, 13 Feb. 1937.

9. "La lezione di un processo," *Lo stato operaio*, February 1937, pp. 81–89, especially pp. 84, 88–89.

10. F. Furini (Dozza), "Di qui non si passa," *Grido del popolo*, 20 Feb. 1937, and "Applicare il patto," *Grido del popolo*, 7 Mar. 1937. On the rupture with Faravelli, see G. Niccola and F. Furini of the Ufficio Politico to the Direzione of the PSI, 20 Feb. 1937, AT, busta 9 PSI-PCI 1937.

11. Tasca to Nenni, 6 Mar. 1937, AT, busta 9 PSI-PCI 1937.

12. On Faravelli, see Joseph to Tasca, 23 Feb. 1937, and 8 Mar. 1937, AT, busta 9 PSI-PCI 1937. On Morgari, see Morgari to Rugginenti, 3 Feb. 1937, AT, Corrispondenza, fasc. Morgari, and "A proposito dei fucilati di Mosca," *Nuovo Avanti*, 13 Mar. 1937. Morgari's caution had little effect because in the end his visa was not renewed and he was forced to leave Moscow; see O. Morgari, "Perchè fui sfrattato dall'Urss," *Nuovo Avanti*, 24 June 1937.

13. Carlo Roncoli (Montagnana), "Unità d'azione: ma tra antifascisti," *Grido del popolo*, 21 Mar. 1937; for the attack on Tasca, see "Un passo in avanti e due indietro," *Grido del popolo*, 3 Apr. 1937.

14. On Tasca's support for the Popular Front in France and Spain and his justification of Russian arms aid to Spain, see "Prospettive e compiti del 1937" and "Il passo anglo francese e il giuoco di mosca cieca," *Nuovo Avanti*, 2 Jan. 1937; "La battaglia diplomatica sul non intervento," *Nuovo Avanti*, 16 Jan. 1937; "L'initiative britannique pour la non intervention," *Le Populaire*, 11 Jan. 1937; "Non intervento e blocco," *Nuovo Avanti*, 24 Apr. 1937. For Grieco's effort to divide Tasca from the other leaders of the PSI, see "Intervista con il compagno Pietro Nenni," *Grido del popolo*, 9 Jan. 1937, and Grieco, "Non c'è tempo da perdere," *Grido del Popolo*, 16 Jan. 1937. For Tasca's response, see "Polemiche sulla questione del non intervento," *Nuovo Avanti*, 23 Jan. 1937.

15. See the announcement of the congress of the UPI, *Grido del popolo*, 3 and 17 Apr. 1937; also "A proposito di un quotidiano antifascista," *Giustizia e Libertà*, 9 Apr. 1937. On the Bocconi case, see "Ancora sul fronte unico," *Nuovo Avanti*, 23 May 1936.

16. See "Il congresso del Fronte Unico," and Modigliani, "Per i partiti, per il partito," *Nuovo Avanti*, 3 Apr. 1937, and "Alleanze si, ma con le mani libere," *Nuovo Avanti*, 10 Apr. 1937; Joseph to the Direzione of the PSI, 6 Apr. 1937, AT, busta 9 PSI-PCI 1937.

17. On Nenni's proposal, see Pietro Emiliani, "Per una unità d'azione estesa e rafforzata," *Nuovo Avanti*, 10 Apr. 1937. On the reaction to it, see Modigliani, "Bipartitismo contro socialismo," *Nuovo Avanti*, 17 Apr. 1937, and "Fedeltà a noi stessi," *Nuovo Avanti*, 24 Apr. 1937; Saragat, "Convergenze," *Nuovo Avanti*, 17 Apr. 1937. In defense of Nenni, see vice (Rugginenti), "Unità d'azione," 1 May 1937.

18. Tasca, "Una perdita irreparibile," *Nuovo Avanti*, 8 May 1937, and "Ritorno a Gramsci e Gobetti," *Giustizia e Libertà*, 7 May 1937; also "Contro una sfacciata menzogna," *Nuovo Avanti*, 26 June 1937.

19. Berneri had been in contact with Tasca since the early 1930s and had provided him with information about Spain, but the two men were not politically close; see Berneri to Tasca, March 1935, AT, Corrispondenza, fasc. Berneri; also

Berneri to Tasca, undated, written from Barcelona, AT, Corrispondenza, fasc. Berneri; Tasca to Jacometti, 19 May 1937, AT, Corrispondenza 1939; Tasca, "Camillo Berneri," *Nuovo Avanti*, 2 May 1937; N. Chiaromonte to Tasca, undated (early 1937) and 15 June 1937, AT, Corrispondenza, fasc. Chiaromonte.

20. For Nenni's position, see Pietro Emiliani, "Tre punti chiari," *Nuovo Avanti*, 26 June 1937, and "Relazione del compagno Nenni," "Supplemento al *Nuovo Avanti*," 31 July 1937, pp. 6–10. See also Rapone, "Il PSI Tra Nenni e Tasca," pp. 677–79.

21. Tasca, "Problemi di tattica e problemi di principio," *Nuovo Avanti*, 26 June 1937.

22. "Il discorso del compagno Tasca," "Supplemento al *Nuovo Avanti*," 31 July 1937, pp. 10–13; see also Spriano's account of the congress and the differences between Nenni and Tasca, *Storia del PCI*, III, pp. 216–17; Rapone, "Il PSI tra Nenni e Tasca," p. 679.

23. For the debates, see the "Supplemento al *Nuovo Avanti*," pp. 16–20; "La nuova Direzione del Partito," *Nuovo Avanti*, 3 July 1937.

24. On Silone, see Tranquilli to Tasca, 29 July 1937, AT, Corrispondenza, fasc. Tranquilli; also Tasca to Tranquilli, 4 June 1937, and Tranquilli to Tasca, 8 July 1937. On Chiaromonte's efforts to draw Tasca out and Tasca's to draw him in, see Chiaromonte to Tasca, undated (early 1937), 4 June, and 8 July 1937, AT, Corrispondenza, fasc. Chiaromonte.

25. Tasca to Chiaromonte, 21 Aug. 1937, AT, Corrispondenza, fasc. Chiaromonte; Chiaromonte to Tasca, 29 Aug. 1937, ibid.

26. Nenni made it clear that he accepted Communist positions against the anarchists. Nenni, "Situazione attorno alla Spagna," *Voce degli italiani*, 5 Aug. 1937, and "Un anno di guerra e di rivoluzione," *Nuovo Avanti*, 17 July 1937; on the refusal to criticize the USSR while the war in Spain continued, see Italicus (Nenni), "L'unità d'azione e il movimento operaio internazionale," *Nuovo Avanti*, 14 Aug. 1937. Nenni was aware of the problems between the Communists and other political groups in Spain but felt that the Socialists were not sufficiently strong numerically to act without the Communists: See Nenni, "Rapporto del segretario del Partito alla Direzione," AT, busta 9, PSI-PCI 1937.

27. Saragat, "Il nostro dovere," and Spertia, "Critica e realtà," *Nuovo Avanti*, 28 Aug. 1937.

28. Tasca's remarks appear in Quaderno 33, pp. 267–68.

29. "La nuova carta d'unità d'azione fra il nostro partito ed il Partito comunista," and "L'adesione dei socialisti all'Unione Popolare," *Nuovo Avanti*, 31 July 1937; Nenni, "Socialisti e comunisti hanno firmato la nuova carta di unità d'azione," *Voce degli italiani*, 31 July 1937.

30. Tito Mocellin, "Il dovere della disciplina per tutti i compagni," *Nuovo Avanti*, 4 Sept. 1937. The position of the *Nuovo Avanti* was contained in a note of the editor with the article.

31. Rugginenti to Tasca, 20 Aug. 1937, and Tasca to Rugginenti, 21 Aug. 1937, AT, busta 9 PSI-PCI 1937.

32. Tasca to Nenni, 13 Aug. 1937, *Documenti inediti*, p. 252.

33. Saragat to Tasca, 16 Oct. 1937, AT, Corrispondenza, fasc. Saragat.

34. xxx [Tasca], "L'asse di guerra Berlino Roma," *Nuovo Avanti*, 2 Oct. 1937. Also Lynx (Tasca), "Lumières sur le monde," *Lumière*, 13 Aug. 1937; André Leroux, "De la conquête éthiopienne à l'intervention en Espagne," *Le Populaire*, 25 Sept. 1937; "Note per il rapporto Nenni all'IOS, Londres 10–11 mars 1937," Quaderno 30, p. 215. On the coordination of Fascist policy, see Lynx, "Lumières

sur le monde," *Lumière*, 1 Oct. 1937, and Angelo Tasca, "La santa alleanza degli Stati fascisti," *Nuovo Avanti*, 13 Nov. 1937.

35. "La plebiscite soviétique," *Le Populaire*, 13 Dec. 1937, and Lynx, "Lumières sur le monde," *Lumière*, 24 Dec. 1937.

36. Tasca, "Socialismo e dittatura del proletariato," *Problemi della rivoluzione italiana*, December 1937, p. 9, also pp. 5, 10–13.

37. Quaderno 33, p. 291.

CHAPTER 11

1. Tasca, *Nascita e avvento*, pp. 23–24, 93–94. The book was published in 1938 in France as *La naissance du fascisme* and in Italy after the war. All references are to the Italian edition.

2. Ibid., pp. 9, 150.

3. Ibid., pp. 20–22.

4. Ibid., pp. 152–55, 157, 164.

5. Ibid., pp. 192–93.

6. Ibid., pp. 251, 320–21; for the negative role of the IC, see p. 331. See also "Primo epilogo," pp. 540–41.

7. Ibid., p. 559; also pp. 298–99, 554–57.

8. Quaderno 25, p. 89; "Dopo dieci anno," *Nuovo Avanti*, 9 June 1934; *Nascita e avvento*, pp. 548–51, 47.

9. Tasca, "Dodicesimo anno," *Nuovo Avanti*, 27 Oct. 1934.

10. A. Leroux, "Economie de guerre en Italie," *Le Populaire*, 30 Mar. 1936; *Nascita e avvento*, p. 556.

11. Quaderno 8, pp. 62–91.

12. *Nascita e avvento*, p. 563.

13. Quaderno 34, entry for April 1938, pp. 91–92; see also *Nascita e avvento*, p. 571.

14. See Subalpino (Calosso), "Tasca vivo," *Giustizia e libertà*, 4 Nov. 1938; also Tirreno (Lussu), "La Naissance du fascisme," *Giustizia e libertà*, 29 Apr. 1938; Otto Bauer, "Zur Geschichte des Faschismus," *Der Sozialistische Kampf*, 30 July 1938.

15. See Buozzi, "La Naissance du fascisme o il processo al socialismo italiano," *Problemi della Rivoluzione italiana*, September 1938, pp. 3–6; O. Morgari, "Il trionfo del fascismo," ibid., pp. 7–10. See also Pietro Emiliani, "La nascita del fascismo in Italia," *Nuovo Avanti*, 16 Apr. 1938.

16. For the debates on the future of the Popular Front, see G. Di Vittorio, "La forza del Fronte popolare," *La voce degli italiani*, 23 Jan. 1938; Gino Bagni, "I socialisti e l'Unione popolare," *La voce degli italiani*, 6 Jan. 1938; "Il Fronte popolare nel parlamento e nel paese," *Nuovo Avanti*, 29 Jan. 1938; Alberto Jacometti, "Sul Fronte popolare," *Nuovo Avanti*, 22 Jan. 1938; mag. (Aldo Garosci), "Esperienze in clima democratico," *Giustizia e libertà*, 21 Jan. 1938.

17. "Direzione del Partito," *Nuovo Avanti*, 7 Jan. 1938, and "Fronte popolare e l'unità d'azione," *Nuovo Avanti*, 26 Feb. 1938.

18. For Tasca's quote, see André Leroux, "Le nouveau procès de Moscou," *Le Populaire*, 2 Mar. 1938. Tasca continued to write on the subject: "Le procès de Moscou," *Le Populaire*, 3 Mar. 1938; "I processi di Mosca," *Nuovo Avanti*, 5 Mar. 1938; "La politique extérieure: France et Urss," *Le Populaire*, 4 Mar. 1938. For Berti's comment, see "Il Nuovo Avanti alla ricerca delle cause," *Lo stato operaio*, 1 Apr. 1938, pp. 89–92; also "Il processo di Mosca," *Voce degli italiani*, 3 Mar.

1938. For the official position of the PSI, see "Il nostro Partito e la situazione internazionale," *Nuovo Avanti*, 19 Mar. 1938.
   19. Quaderno 34, pp. 19–20.
   20. Quaderno 34, entry for 14 Mar. 1938, p. 23.
   21. Quaderno 34, p. 148. On the fundamental weakness of British policy, see A. Leroux, "Grande Bretagne et Espagne," *Le Populaire*, 23 Mar. 1938; "Grande Bretagne, Italie et Espagne," *Le Populaire*, 24 Mar. 1938; "Les conservateurs anglais finiront-ils pour comprendre?" *Oran Républicain*, 1 Apr. 1938. On the need for firmness with Mussolini, see "Mon programme, c'est le fait," *Lumière*, 13 May 1938; "Mussolini ed Hitler si preparano per una conflagrazione generale," *Nuovo Avanti*, 14 May 1938; "Le programme européen de Mussolini," *Oran Républicain*, 13 July 1938.
   22. See Saragat, "Per la Spagna e per la pace," *Voce degli italiani*, 20 Jan. 1938, and "La condizione essenziale della lotta per la pace e l'unità degli antifascisti," *Voce degli italiani*, 11 Feb. 1938; "Il socialismo, il neoreformismo e la guerra," *Problemi della Rivoluzione italiana*, April 1938; see also O. Morgari, "Il fattore bellico nella lotta dell'antifascismo," *Nuovo Avanti*, 16 Apr. 1938, and "La guerra è sempre reazionaria?" 30 Apr. 1938; "Il nostro partito e la situazione internazionale," 12 Mar. 1938, AT, busta 10 PSI-PCI 1938.
   23. Modigliani, "Contro la guerra e per il partito," *Nuovo Avanti*, 28 May 1938; Santini, "La tesi guerresca di Morgari," *Nuovo Avanti*, 21 May 1938. For Saragat's counterposition, see "La Spagna contro drama dell'Europa e del socialismo," *Nuovo Avanti*, 4 June 1938, and Modigliani, "Risposta a Saragat," *Nuovo Avanti*, 11 June 1938.
   24. See Tasca's preface to Bruno Maffi, *Echi: La politica delle classi medie e di planismo* (Paris: Partito socialista italiano, 1938), p. ix.
   25. Ibid., p. xi–xii.
   26. See Joseph to Tasca, 8 Mar. 1938, AT, busta 10 PSI-PCI 1938. In June Nenni resumed his collaboration. See Joseph to Tasca, 2 June 1938, AT, busta 10 PSI-PCI 1938.
   27. Lino Boscardin to Tasca, 15 Mar. 1938, and the report from Boscardin to the Direzione, 10 Mar. 1938, AT, busta 10 PSI-PCI 1938. Boscardin was a socialist representative to the International Brigades. On Pacciardi, see Charles Delzell, *Mussolini's Enemies* (Princeton: Princeton University Press, 1961), pp. 150–53, 161; G. Di Vittorio, "Dove va il Partito repubblicano," *Voce degli italiani*, 15 June 1938.
   28. On the background to the *Problemi della Rivoluzione italiana*, see Ariane Landuyt, *La Comune di Vienna e l'antifascismo italiano* (Cosenza: Lerici, 1979), pp. 96–103; Volterra, "Fronte popolare italiano," *Giustizia e libertà*, 13 May 1938; Volterra to Tasca, 12 Feb. and 15 Mar. 1938; Tasca to Volterra, 19 Feb. and 8 Apr. 1938, in AT, Corrispondenza, fasc. Volterra-Virgili.
   29. See Tasca, "Per finire," *Nuovo Avanti*, 16 July 1938; see also about GL's offer "Il convegno di GL: La carta ideologica del Movimento," *Giustizia e libertà*, 17 June 1938, and Tasca, "Due convegni, due documenti," *Nuovo Avanti*, 2 July 1938.
   30. Quaderno 34, p. 248, entry for 19 Sept. 1938. On Faure's position, see Paul Faure, "Les heures d'espoir," *Le Populaire*, 30 Sept. 1938.
   31. For the May conversations with Blum, see Quaderno 32, pp. 232–40, in *Annali 1968*, pp. 632–33. The citation is from *Annali 1968*, p. 664. Tasca almost lost his position at *Le Populaire* when he met the opposition of Jean Longuet, who did not think that he wrote a sufficiently forceful column on foreign policy. See

Tasca to Longuet, 23 Mar. 1936, and Longuet to Tasca, 24 Mar. 1936, AT, Corrispondenza, fasc. 1936. On Rosenfeld, see Bilis, *Socialistes et pacifistes*, pp. 72—73. Tasca expressed his growing sense of isolation at *Le Populaire* in Quaderno 34, p. 28, in *Annali 1968*, p. 660.

32. Entry for 7 Aug. 1938, Quaderno 34, pp. 218—20, in *Annali 1968*, pp. 674—75; Tasca to Ascoli, 2 Oct. 1938, and Ascoli to Tasca, 16 Oct. 1938, AT, Corrispondenza, fasc. Ascoli.

33. Rossi to Rosenfeld, 5 Oct. 1938, and Rosenfeld to Rossi, 16 Nov. 1938, AT, Corrispondenza, fasc. 1938; Quaderno 34, entry for 30 Nov. 1938, pp. 305—6.

34. For the evolution of Tasca's views on Czechoslovakia, see the relatively optimistic "La ferme attitude anglo-tchecoslovaque a sauvegardé la paix," *Oran Républicain*, 24 May 1938; "La politica estera del Signor Chamberlain," *Nuovo Avanti*, 4 July 1938; "La missione Runciman in Tchécoslovaquie," *Nuovo Avanti*, 20 July 1938. On the actual crisis, see "Un accord est entrevenu, déclare a minuit M. Daladier," *Oran Républicain*, 19 Sept. 1938; "Verso la catastrofe," *Nuovo Avanti*, 17 Sept. 1938; "Dans quelle mésure Hitler a-t-il cédé," *Oran Républicain*, 1 Oct. 1938, and "L'Europe trouvera-t-elle son nouveau équilibre?" *Oran Républicain*, 2 Oct. 1938.

35. Pietro Emiliani, "Socialismo-Democrazia-URSS," *Nuovo Avanti*, 1 Oct. 1938; also "I processi di Mosca," *Nuovo Avanti*, 10 Sept. 1938, and "Il super-tradito Trotzki ha la parola," *Nuovo Avanti*, 24 Sept. 1938.

36. See Saragat, "I nuovi doveri," *Nuovo Avanti*, 8 Oct. 1938; "La nostra posizione," *Nuovo Avanti*, 1 Oct. 1938, and Direzione del PSI, "Ai lavoratori in patria, in esilio e nell'emigrazione," *Nuovo Avanti*, 8 Oct. 1938.

37. Nenni to Tasca, 12 Oct. 1938, and the draft proposal of Nenni, in AT, busta 10 PSI-PCI 1938.

38. "Prospettive sulla situazione interna ed internazionale," *Nuovo Avanti*, 29 Oct. 1938.

39. "Prospettive sulla situazione interna ed internazionale," *Nuovo Avanti*, 4 Nov. 1938.

40. For the reaction of the Communists, see Roncoli, "Contro gli agenti del disfattismo," *Voce degli Italiani*, 9 Nov. 1938; "Il nemico della classe operaio," *Lo stato operaio*, 15 Nov. 1938, pp. 349—51. For Nenni's reaction, see "Appunti a degli appunti," and "I problemi tattici e la politica unitaria del Partito," *Nuovo Avanti*, 12 Nov. 1939.

41. C. Valai to Faravelli, 14 Nov. 1938, AT, busta 10 PSI-PCI 1938; also Volterra to Tasca, 13 Nov. 1938, AT, busta 10 PSI-PCI 1938; Jacometti to Faravelli[?], 16 Nov. 1938, and 'Prode' (Orlandini) to Faravelli, 14 Nov. 1938, AT, busta 10, PSI-PCI 1938.

42. "Prima e dopo Monaco," *Nuovo Avanti*, 19 Nov. 1938.

43. Tasca, "La posizione del nostro partito," *Nuovo Avanti*, 26 Nov. 1938.

44. Saragat to Tasca, 19 Nov. 1938, AT busta 10 PSI-PCI 1938; Saragat, "Il socialismo al bivio," *Nuovo Avanti*, 19 Nov. 1938, and "La nostra posizione," *Nuovo Avanti*, 3 Dec. 1938.

45. "Mozione di Nenni al Consiglio Nazionale," AT, busta 10, PSI-PCI 1938; for Tasca's speech, see Quaderno 37, pp. 14—33, and "La politica internazionale e il problema russo," *Nuovo Avanti*, 3 Dec. 1938; the results of the meeting of the Consiglio Nazionale are in "Dichiarazione politica votata dal Consiglio Nazionale del Partito," *Nuovo Avanti*, 10 Dec. 1938.

46. A. G., "Il Consiglio Nazionale del PSI," *Lo stato operaio*, 15 Dec. 1938, pp. 385—86 and "Una vittoria dei fautori dell'Unità d'azione al Consiglio Nazionale,"

Voce degli italiani, 6 Dec. 1938; also "Fine d'anno 1938," Quaderno 34, pp. 323–24, in *Annali 1968,* p. 683.

CHAPTER 12

1. Blum, "Devant l'Axe," *Le Populaire,* 4 Jan. 1939, and "La motion de Montrouge," *Le Populaire,* 8 Jan. 1939; also "Le Conseil National du Parti socialiste," *Le Populaire,* 6 Mar. 1939, and Mag. (Garosci), "Note sul congresso nazionale del Partito SFIO," *Giustizia e Libertà,* 6 Jan. 1939. See also, Greene, *Crisis and Decline,* pp. 240–51; Georges Lefranc, *Le mouvement socialiste sous la Troisième République* (Paris: Payot, 1963), pp. 368–74.

2. Monnet, "Plus de concessions au fascisme," *Agir,* 15 Mar. 1939; Pierre Viénot, "La France peut-elle être sauvée par Londres?" and Pierre Brossolette, "Un bloc des nations pacifiques," *Agir,* 1 Apr. 1939.

3. On Tasca's views on the United States, see Lynx, "Lumières sur le monde," *Lumières,* 13 Jan. 1939; A. Leroux, "Le discours historique du Président Roosevelt," *Oran Républicain,* 6 Jan. 1939; on the need to bring England and the USSR closer, "Lumières sur le monde," *Lumière,* 7 Apr., 19 May, and 23 June 1939. Brossolette expressed similar views in "Pour la réalisation du bloc des états pacifiques," *Le Populaire,* 12 Apr. 1939, and "Après le message de M. Roosevelt," *Le Populaire,* 17 Apr. 1939.

4. See "Le départ de M. Litvinov a fait sensation en Europe," *Oran Républicain,* 5 May 1939, and "Il caso Litvinoff e la politica dell'Urss," *Nuovo Avanti,* 13 May 1939; "Necessità di concludere fra Londra e Mosca," *Nuovo Avanti,* 8 July 1939; A. Rossi, *Deux ans d'alliance germano-soviétique* (Paris: Fayard, 1949), p. 197.

5. A. Leroux, "Socialisme et communisme," *Agir,* 15 May 1939.

6. A. Leroux, "Assez de verbalisme et de course aux mandats," and G. Monnet, "Le socialisme est un combat," *Agir,* 1 May 1939.

7. "Estratto d'una lettera diretta a un compagno che mi aveva chiesto appunti," copies to Joseph and Modigliani, undated (early 1939), AT, busta 12 PSI-PCI, pt. 2.

8. Joseph to Menè (Modigliani), Tasca, Buozzi and Santini, 6 Jan. 1939; also Joseph to unknown, 29 Jan. 1939; Joseph to Tasca, 15, 23, and 25 Feb. 1939, all in AT, busta 13 PSI-PCI 1939.

9. Comitato sezionale di Marsiglia to Direzione PSI, 6 Feb. 1939, Federazione del Sud-est e Centro Francia, 6 Feb. 1939, and Sezione di Marsiglia to Direzione PSI, 18 Feb. 1939; and the report of Masetti, the fiduciario per la Spagna of the PSI to the Direzione, AT, busta 13 PSI-PCI 1939.

10. Nenni to Tasca, 17 Jan. 1939, and Tasca to Nenni, 19 Jan. 1939, AT, busta 13 PSI-PCI 1939.

11. Nenni to Tasca, 7 Mar. 1939, AT, busta 13 PSI-PCI 1939.

12. Joseph to Tasca, 25 Feb. 1939, AT, busta 13, PSI-PCI 1939.

13. "Appunti di Modigliani," March 1939, AT, busta 13 PSI-PCI 1939; Modigliani, "Un punto di storia da ritenere," *Nuovo Avanti,* 11 Mar. 1939.

14. See "o.d.g. [ordine del giorno ("motion")] Tasca respinto con 317 mandati contro 69," March 1939; "Mozione della Federazione della Senna," 12 Mar. 1939; Joseph to Tasca, undated (March 1939), AT, busta 13 PSI-PCI 1939.

15. On GL's proposal, see "Decidere e subito," *Giustizia e Libertà,* 3 Mar. 1939, and "L'unità dell'antifascismo è una necessità immediata," *Giustizia e Libertà,* 7 Apr. 1939. For the Communist position, see C. Roncoli, "L'unità d'azione,"

Lo stato operaio, supplement to n. 5, 15 Mar. 1939, and "L'unità d'azione di fronte ai problemi attuali dell'antifascismo," *Voce degli italiani*, 29 Apr. 1939. On the recruitment of Italians for a volunteer corps that the Communists and the UPI officially supported, see "La direttiva dell'UPI a proposito del decreto sul reclutamento degli immigranti per il caso di guerra," *Voce degli italiani*, 31 Mar. 1939, and "Pro memoriam," AT, busta 12, pt. 2 PSI-PCI 1939.

16. "Problemi e discussioni: Pregiudiziale repubblicana," *Lo stato operaio*, 30 Mar. 1939, pp. 141–42.

17. Nenni to Tasca, 24 Mar. 1939, AT, busta 13 PSI-PCI 1939.

18. "La reazione in Europa contro il colpo di forza di Hitler," *Nuovo Avanti*, 25 Mar. 1939, and "Panorama dei problemi italo-europei," *Nuovo Avanti*, 5 Apr. 1939.

19. Pietro Emiliani, "Ultimi giorni della Spagna repubblicana," *Nuovo Avanti*, 22 Apr. 1939.

20. See on Modigliani's resignation, Nenni, "Quo vadis Internazionale?" *Nuovo Avanti*, 20 May 1939; Modigliani, "Grido d'allarme," and Nenni, "Il bolscevismo col cotello fra i denti," *Nuovo Avanti*, 27 May 1939; "La crisi dell'Internazionale socialista," *Giustizia e Libertà*, 26 May 1939; "Direzione del Partito," *Nuovo Avanti*, 3 June 1939; Modigliani, "Quo vadis Partito Socialista italiano?" and Nenni, "Per una internazionale combattiva," *Nuovo Avanti*, 16 June 1939.

21. "Direzione del Partito," *Nuovo Avanti*, 3 June 1939. On Faravelli's efforts to organize the anti-Nenni forces, see the letters from Gorni to Faravelli, 20 and 29 June; 10 July 1939; Joseph to Tasca, 21 June 1939; Gorni to Joseph and Modigliani, 12 June 1939; Costa to Joseph, 1 Aug. 1939; Elvio Coccia to Joseph, 4 Aug. 1939, AT, busta 12 pt. 2 PSI-PCI 1939.

22. See "Sull'unità d'azione," *Giustizia e Libertà*, 23 June 1939; "Sull'alleanza antifascista," ibid., 7 July 1939; Luigi Gallo, "L'alleanza antifascista dev'essere conclusa," *Voce degli italiani*, 29 June 1939; "Alleanza antifascista," *Nuovo Avanti*, 7 July 1939.

23. The purpose behind the conference was to create conditions for party unity. See Pierre Viénot to Charles Spinasse, 4 Aug. 1939, and Tasca to Spinasse, 4 Aug. 1939, AT, busta 11 PSI-PCI 1939, pt. 1. Also Quaderno 35, entry for 19–20 Aug. 1939, p. 238. Georges Lefranc in his study of the SFIO characterizes Tasca as the major force behind the conference: See Lefranc, *Le mouvement socialiste sous la Troisième République*, p. 374. The list of participants and other organizational details are also included in AT, busta 11, PSI-PCI 1939, pt. 1.

24. For the citation, see "Progetto di manifesto in data 24 o 25 agosto," see also "Pro memoria per i membri del Consiglio Generale del Partito, 31 agosto 1939," AT, busta 11 PSI-PCI 1939, pt. 1.

25. For the Communist protest against the Socialist actions, see Ufficio Estero del CC del PCI to Direzione PSI, 29 Aug. 1939, AT, busta 11 PSI-PCI 1939, pt. 1; see also Mario Montagnana, "Fatti acquisti," *La voce degli italiani*, 24 Aug. 1939, and "Per il disfatto del fascismo," *La voce degli italiani*, 25 Aug. 1939. Both of these articles seemed almost apologetic about the pact.

26. For Nenni's general position, see "Il voltafaccia della politica sovietica," *Nuovo Avanti*, 31 Aug. 1939; for the debate within the PSI, see "Pro memoria per i membri del Consiglio Generale," AT, busta 11 PSI-PCI 1939, pt. 1.

27. Faraboldi to Tasca, 29 Aug. 1939, and "Il comitato direttivo della Sezione socialista italiana di Parigi," AT, busta 11 PSI-PCI 1939, pt. 1.

28. E. Lussu to Tasca, 26 Aug. 1939, AT, Corrispondenza, fasc. Lussu; for a

dissenting view, see Silvio Trentin, "Riesame dell'antifascismo sul piano unitario," *Giustizia e libertà*, 1 Sept. 1939.

29. See Tasca's notes for the Consiglio Generale, 1 Sept. 1939, and Morgari to Tasca, undated (early September 1939), in AT, busta 11, PSI-PCI 1939, pt. 1; "Il Comitato nazionale," *Giustizia e libertà*, 8 Sept. 1939; Pietro Nenni, "Congedo," and "Unione Popolare Italiano," *Nuovo Avanti*, 7 Sept. 1939.

30. "Pour le congrès national du parti," *Le Populaire*, 5 May 1939.

31. See Blum, "Silence acablant," *Le Populaire*, 19 Sept. 1939; "Le gouvernement dissout le Parti communiste," *Le Populaire*, 27 Sept. 1939; A. Rossi, *Les communistes français pendant la Drôle de Guerre* (Paris: Les Îles d'Or, 1951), pp. 26–27, 35, 123.

32. See O. Rosenfeld to Rossi, 31 Aug. 1939, AT, Corrispondenza, fasc. 1939; Quaderno 37, entry for 4 Nov. 1939, pp. 83–84, cited in Berti, *Annali 1968*, p. 721. Blum often used Tasca's articles as the basis for his commentary, thus increasing their importance. See "La Situation," *Le Populaire*, 16 Sept. 1939, which was cited by Blum on the following day in "Le mystère stalinien."

33. See "Les armées russes et allemandes ont pris contact à Brest Litovsk," *Le Populaire*, 20 Sept. 1939. For the parallel views of Tasca and Blum on Baltic policy, see XX, "La Situation," *Le Populaire*, 27, 28, and 29 Sept. 1939, and Blum, "La paix de Hitler et de Staline," *Le Populaire*, 29 Sept. 1939.

34. See entry in Quaderno 37, p. 35; also "La Situation," *Le Populaire*, 1 Nov. 1939, and Quaderno 37, pp. 166–92, also pp. 146–47, 153–54.

35. See "La Situation," *Le Populaire*, 1 May 1940. Blum made an open appeal to Mussolini in a series of editorials in *Le Populaire* on 27, 28, 29, and 30 Apr. and 5 May 1940, but by early May little optimism remained: See Blum, "Mussolini et l'Italie," *Le Populaire*, 5 May 1940, and Tasca's articles, 'La Situation," *Le Populaire*, 15, 17, 25, 27, 30, and 31 May and 4 and 5 June 1940.

36. On Tasca's efforts to influence Blum, see Quaderno 37, entry for 29 Sept. 1939, p. 73, which related his report to Blum on foreign policy. For the views of Tasca and Blum on Finland, see XX, "La Russie a ouvert les hostilités contre la Finlande," *Le Populaire*, 1 Dec. 1939, and "La Situation," *Le Populaire*, 3 Dec. 1939; Blum, "La crise," *Le Populaire*, 5 Dec. 1939.

37. XX, "La Situation," *Le Populaire*, 21 Jan. 1940.

38. In a letter to Carlo Rosselli, written in 1933 or 1934, Tasca stated his position clearly: "Il socialismo è il problema della nostra generazione. Il socialismo è più una necessitá che un'aspirazione. La coincidenza degli interessi generali delle classi lavoratrici con quelli di tutta l'umanità non la si deve scovare nel sottosuolo della storia; esso si esprime ogni giorno da tutti i problemi della società contemporanea." See Berti, *Annali 1968*, pp. 564–65.

39. See Quaderno 35, pp. 309–24, in Berti, *Annali 1968*, p. 708.

40. Quaderno 29 (1934), pp. 261–342, in Berti, *Annali 1968*, especially p. 544.

41. Quaderno 35, entry for 2 Mar. 1939, pp. 220–21; on the affinities and defects of both Marxism and liberalism, see Quaderno 35, pp. 93–95.

42. Quaderno 34, entry for December 1938, p. 307.

43. Quaderno 35, pp. 77–78, in Berti, *Annali 1968*, p. 685. Berti omitted the last sentence of the entry that was published in the *Annali*.

44. Direzione del PSI, "Progetto di documento politico, risale agli inizii d'ottobre 1939," Quaderno 35, pp. 257–61.

45. Modigliani to Tasca, 2 Nov. 1939, AT, busta 11, PSI-PCI 1939, pt. 1.

46. Pietro Nenni, "Il Partito socialista italiano nella guerra," 15 Dec. 1939, in Merli, *Documenti inediti*, pp. 302–10.

47. Tasca, "La situazione internazionale," 15 Dec. 1939, presented 17 Dec. 1939, AT busta 12, PSI-PCI 1939, pt. 2, especially pp. 6–8; "Il Partito socialista italiana e la situazione internazionale," "Atti della Direzione," and Comitato esecutivo, "Socialisti e comunisti," *Nuovo Avanti*, 23 Dec. 1939.

48. Tasca(?) to Compagni dell'Esecutivo, 23 Dec. 1939, AT, busta 11, PSI-PCI 1939, pt. 1.

49. Tasca to Ernest Labrousse, 2 May 1940, Quaderno 38, pp. 140–41. Planning for the postwar period was to be one of the main tasks of the new review.

50. Nenni to Adler, 2 Jan. 1940, AT, busta 13 PSI-PCI 1940.

51. Tasca, "Contro certi sofismi," *Nuovo Avanti*, 20 Jan. 1940, and "Il partito e la guerra," *Nuovo Avanti*, 3 Feb. 1940.

52. Tasca to the Direzione of the PSI, 29 Feb. 1940, AT, busta 13 PSI-PCI 1940. For the meeting of 2 Feb. 1940, see the report, dated 14 Mar. 1940, to the Ministero dell'Interno, ACS, CPC, 5040, fasc. 24848.

53. Joseph to Tasca, 14 and 23 Mar. 1940, AT, busta 13 PSI-PCI 1940.

54. G. Lombardi [Faravelli], to the Federations and Sections, 1 Apr. 1940, announcing the meeting, AT, busta 13 PSI-PCI 1940; "A bandiera spiegata," *Nuovo Avanti*, 11 May 1940; Vera Modigliani, *Esilio* (Milan: Garzanti, 1946), p. 306.

CHAPTER 13

1. Tasca, "Da Parigi a Vichy," *Il mondo*, 5 July 1952; on the withdrawal of the Ministry of Information personnel, see Philippe Amaury, *Les deux premières expériences d'un 'ministère de l'information' en France* (Paris: Librairie générale de droit et de jurisprudence R. Pichon et R. Durand-Auzias, 1969), p. 30. On the collapse of France, see Marc Bloch, *Strange Defeat* (New York: Norton, 1968).

2. Tasca, "Da Parigi a Vichy," *Il mondo*, 5 July 1952; see also Marc Sadoun, *Les Socialistes sous l'Occupation* (Paris: Presses de la Fondation Nationale des Sciences Politiques, 1982), pp. 35, 40–41, 47, 50–51, 56–57, about Paul Faure. The best general history of Vichy in English is Robert Paxton, *Vichy France: Old Guard and New Order, 1940–1944* (New York: Norton, 1972).

3. Interviews with Charles-André Julien, 16 Mar. 1981, and with Valeria Tasca, 18 Mar. 1981. Apparently Chaumette would not follow him to Vichy, and he could not return to Nazi-controlled Paris.

4. See the autobiographical manuscript of September–October 1940 in AT, Corrispondenza, Processo contro A. Tasca, p. 11; also "Da Parigi a Vichy ," *Il Mondo*, 5 July 1952.

5. Autobiographical manuscript of September–October 1940, AT, Corrispondenza "Processo contro A. Tasca," pp. 18–19.

6. Ibid., p. 19; for a later effort to explain himself, see "Note sur l'activité résistante et militante de J. A. Tasca (Rossi)," AT, Corrispondenza "Processo contro A. Tasca," p. 2; "J'ai espéré pendant quelques semaines qu'une collaboration put s'opérer autour de Pétain."

7. "Au sujet de mon attitude en été 1940," Quaderno 40 (1945), pp. 59–67.

8. "Appunti per la Divisione AAGGeRR," prepared by the Divisione Polizia Politica, 28 Nov. 1940, ACS, CPC 5040, fasc. 24848.

9. Moysset actively intervened with the Vichy authorities, using Tasca's services to Vichy as justification for giving him better treatment. On Moysset, see Maurice Martin du Gard, *Chronique de Vichy, 1940–1944* (Paris: Flammarion,

1948), pp. 97, 233; Amaury, *Les deux premières expériences*, pp. 171–74; Henri Du Moulin de Labarthète, *Les temps des illusions* (Brussels-Paris, La Diffusion du Livre, 1946), p. 143.

10. See the analysis from September 1940, inserted into Quaderno B: France Juillet–Novembre 1940, p. 9; also p. 13, note 1.

11. Ibid., p. 14.

12. Ibid., pp. 16–17.

13. Tasca, "L'avventura di Darlan," *Il mondo*, 9 Aug. 1952, and "Comunisti e maquis," *Il mondo*, 2 Aug. 1952.

14. On the organization of the Ministry of the Interior under the Third Republic and Vichy, see Amaury, *Les deux premières expériences*, pp. 27–37, 52, 56, 59–66, 78–85, and the organizational chart on pp. 220–21. For Paul Marion, see pp. 162–63, 229–37.

15. On the Service du Propagande Anticommuniste, see ibid., p. 335; for the central organization of propaganda, see pp. 332–51; for the Bureau d'Etudes, pp. 330, 333–34. For Tasca's own description of his work, see AT, fasc. Situazione francese: Periodo di Vichy, pp. 1–10.

16. Alfonso Leonetti mentioned Tasca's work with the Minister of Labor Belin and on the Vichy Charter of Labor. Interview of 27 Jan. 1981. On Moysset's involvement in the Charter, see Maurice Martin du Gard, *Chronique de Vichy*, pp. 232–33; on the drafting of the Labor Charter, see Fondation Nationale des Sciences Politiques, *Le gouvernement de Vichy, 1940–1942: Institutions et Politiques* (Paris: Armand Colin, 1972), pp. 157–94. The French socialist Gilles Martinet, who had married the daughter of Bruno Buozzi, contacted Tasca at Vichy on behalf of Modigliani in late 1941 or early 1942 to determine whether the old socialist leader was in danger of arrest. Martinet recalled that he visited Tasca at an office in the Ministry of the Interior, where he seemed to be gathering material about the French Communist party. Tasca was able to tell him that Modigliani was indeed in danger and urged him to leave France (interview with Gilles Martinet, 16 Mar. 1981). Tasca wrote that he tried to contact Modigliani during the war to explain his true role but that they were unable to meet. See "Comunisti e maquis," *Il mondo*, 2 Aug. 1952.

17. On the school at Mayet de Montagne, see Amaury, *Les deux premières expériences*, pp. 222–23, 347–48; M. Martin du Gard, *Chronique de Vichy*, pp. 288–89.

18. "La doctrine marxiste," lecture to the fifth syndical session, June–July 1942, AT, Varie, Conferenze sul marxismo, p. 14.

19. "Révolution nationale et révolution économique," lecture to the Cadres de Jeunesse, 17–27 Aug. 1942, pp. 12, 28–29, AT, Varie, Conferenze varie.

20. "Le role de l'état," lecture of 19–29 Apr. 1943, p. 9, AT, Varie, Conferenze varie; see also "Le role de l'état," lectures of 5–9 Apr. 1943, pp. 1–13. Tasca also was concerned that parliamentary democracy could not deal with bureaucratic, military, and economic power and was incapable of formulating true policy for the state. See Quaderno AC (1940–41), p. 145.

21. "Le role de l'état," lecture of 5–9 Apr. 1943, p. 21, AT, Varie, Conferenze varie.

22. "De notre observateur: Les minorités aux Indes: Où il s'agit aussi du marxisme," *Effort*, 24 Apr. 1942.

23. "Le marxisme et les classes moyennes," Conference of 28–31 Mar. 1943, p. 13, AT, Varie, Conferenze sul marxismo, in which Tasca also expressed a favorable judgment on De Man, pp. 7–8.

24. See "Le communisme," Conference prononcée à l'École des Cadres civiques du Mayet de Montagne, 22–27 May 1944, p. 20 (first citation), p. 4 (second citation), AT, Varie, Conferenze sul Comunismo.

25. "Les doctrines extraverses," Quaderno A-C 1941–42, pp. 111–23, especially pp. 115 and 117 for citations.

26. See the lecture of 7–14 Mar. 1943, "Aux cadres ouvriers," p. 11, AT, Varie, Conferenze sul marxismo.

27. "Philosophie marxiste de l'homme," Conference aux Instituteurs, 18–19 Apr. 1943, p. 11, AT, Varie, Conferenze sul marxismo; also Quaderno AF, pp. 62–63, 66–67.

28. Tasca, In Francia nella bufera (Modena: Ugo Guanda, 1953), p. 73, also p. 97; also Sadoun, Les Socialistes sous l'Occupation, pp. 78–79.

29. The fact that a prominent socialist lent his name to Effort gave much satisfaction to the Italian Fascist government; see the report from the Prefect of Cuneo to the Ministry of the Interior, 31 Jan. 1941, ACS, CPC 5040, fasc. 24848.

30. Paul Rives, "De l'ordre du travail," Effort, 4 Aug. 1940; Spinasse, "Notre ambition," Effort, 6 Aug. 1940; Sadoun, Les Socialistes sous l'Occupation, pp. 78, 85–88.

31. Rives, "Explication d'un vote," Effort, 7 Aug. 1940; "Bilan d'une expérience," Effort, 12 Aug. 1940; "Les institutions et les hommes," Effort, 19 Aug. 1940; Spinasse, "Ce que nous sommes," Effort, 8 Aug. 1940; "Les fins sociales de l'économie nouvelle," Effort, 25 Aug. 1940.

32. J. Arnol, "Regards sur le passé," Effort, 9 Sept. 1940; Victor Marguerite, "Deux routes? Non, un seul," Effort, 27 Aug. 1940; Marcel Déat, "Evolution du socialisme," Effort, 25 Sept. 1940; Spinasse, "Il n'y a pas de collaboration sans espoir," Effort, 10 Oct. 1940; Rives, "Droit avant nous," Effort, 3 Nov. 1940; Julien Peschadour, "A propos de collaboration," Effort, 14 Mar. 1941; Rives, "Propos sur le méthode," Effort, 19 Feb. 1941.

33. "Vues sur le monde: "L'évolution soviétique," Effort, 25 Aug. 1940; see also "Vues sur le monde," Effort, 10, 16, and 20 Aug. and 27 Sept. 1940. On Soviet foreign policy in general, see "Vues sur le monde," Effort, 19, 20, 21, 24, 25, and 26 May 1941; on the Soviet state, see the articles for 30 and 31 May and 1, 2, 7, 8, 10, 13, 15, 16, 20, and 21 June 1941.

34. See the articles signed "R," "La guerre à l'Est," Effort, 24, 25, and 26 June and 3 July 1941. Tasca wrote the lead editorial "La campagne de Russie," Effort, 7 Aug. 1941.

35. "La surprise dans le Pacifique," Effort, 26 Dec. 1941; also "De la guerre éclair à la guerre d'usure," Effort, 24 Dec. 1941. On the evolution of United States policy and the reaction of the USSR, see "Fin de la neutralité américaine," Effort, 12 Nov. 1941, and subsequent articles of 15, 16, and 20 Nov. 1941.

36. See "L'économie allemande," Effort, 20 and 30 May 1942; "Afrique et Méditerranée," Effort, 19 June 1942; "De notre observatoire," Effort, 31 July 1942, minimizing the British victory at El Alamein; "Tournant décisif à l'Est," Effort, 6 Aug. 1942, and "De notre observatoire," Effort, 12 Aug. 1942, on the failure of the Soviet army.

37. See Quaderno XX (1942), p. 53; E. Gaillard to Rossi, 3 Sept. 1942, and Spinasse to Rossi, 12 Sept. 1942, AT, Corrispondenza, fasc. Charles Spinasse. For the circumstances that led to Tasca's break, see Quaderno AC (Spoglio della Stampa 1941–42), pp. 91–92; and Quaderno AB, entry for 19 Jan. 1943; Sadoun, Les socialistes sous l'occupation, pp. 85–88; Bertram Gordon, Collabora-

tionism in France during the Second World War (Ithaca: Cornell University Press, 1980), p. 55.

38. See Quaderno F (Crise de décembre 1940), pp. 123–33; Quaderno AC (1941–42), pp. 158–75, for Tasca's continued sympathy for Pétain.

39. See the insert, dated 19 May 1941 in Quaderno AA (France 7 mai–5 juin 1941) and Quaderno XX (1942), pp. 25–32, 34–37, for conversations with Marion.

40. Quaderno AB (1942), p. 132. See also the conversations with Marion, Quaderno AB, pp. 101–2, 104, and with Frossard, p. 144; on the Soviet army, see pp. 160–66.

41. Quaderno AB, conversation with Brice P., 15 Mar. 1943, pp. 176–77, 187.

42. "Tactique de la Troisième Force," beginning of April 1943, a conversation with A. P., Quaderno AB, pp. 192–98.

43. Quaderno AE (September–October 1943), p. 81, and Quaderno AF (February–March 1944), pp. 76–77.

44. Tasca, "Il programma di Pétain," *Il mondo*, 19 July 1952, and "Comunisti e maquis," *Il mondo*, 2 Aug. 1952; see P. Cavyn to P. H. Spaak, 31 Oct. 1944, explaining the circumstances of Tasca's service to the Belgian Resistance, and Cavyn to Tasca, 24 Oct. 1944. On Tasca's efforts to help Faravelli and the others, see the telegrams from Modigliani to Tasca of 23, 24, and 25 March, informing Tasca that Faravelli, Levi, and Faraboldi had been arrested and were in the Vernet camp. Tasca recalled the events in a later letter to Faravelli, 16 Jan. 1947, AT, Corrispondenza, fasc. Faravelli. Nenni was informed of Tasca's intervention in favor of the Italian Socialists by Saragat, who learned from Modigliani, but Saragat rejected any real role by Tasca. See Pietro Nenni, *Venti anni di fascismo* (Milan: Edizioni dell'Avanti, 1964), entry for 11 Apr. 1942, p. 327. For Tasca's efforts to help Nenni, see *In Francia nella bufera*, pp. 134–35. For Tasca's vague connection with 'Libérer et Fédérer," see "Nasce la resistenza," *Il mondo*, 12 July 1952, and "Note sur l'activité résistante et militante de J.-A. Tasca," AT, Corrispondenza, Processo contro A. Tasca.

45. Bruno Trentin to Salvemini, 14 Oct. 1952, AT, Corrispondenza, 1952.

CHAPTER 14

1. Quaderno AG (August 1944), p. 73.

2. Interview with Elena Dogliani, 9 Mar. 1981. Tasca's daughter Catherine was born in February 1941; see the reference to her in Quaderno AE, p. 10 and the letter from Tasca to Mme. Chaumette, 13 Mar. 1944, and the letter from Tasca to an unnamed correspondent, 1 Dec. 1943, also in Quaderno AE, pp. 46–47, 124–25.

3. For Tasca's hopes in the Viénots, see Andrée Viénot to Tasca, Quaderno 40 (1944), pp. 14–17, and Quaderno AG (June 1944), pp. 17, 34–35, 61–63. On the death of Brossolette and Martorelli, see Quaderno AI (November 1945), p. 71, and Quaderno AK, entry for 31 July 1945, p. 126.

4. On his arrest and interrogation, see Quaderno AG, pp. 96, 140–49. Copies of the letters sent to members of the government at the time of his arrest are in Quaderno AG, pp. 113–17, 121–23, and 130–32 and in AT, "Processo contro A. Tasca." On Tasca's efforts to win recognition from the Belgian government for his services, see Tasca to Jef Rens, 3 Nov. 1944, AT, Corrispondenza, fasc. Cavyn; Tasca to Cavyn, 17 Oct. 1944, Quaderno AG, pp. 138–39. For Tasca's conviction that the Liberation regime was fundamentally unjust, see Quaderno AI, pp. 5–11.

5. Entry for August 1944 and 3 Sept. 1944, Quaderno AG, pp. 84, 102–11, and entry for November 1946, Quaderno AN, pp. 44–45, on the Marxist view of the state.

6. Quaderno AI, pp. 39 for citation; also pp. 34–37.

7. Quaderno AI, p. 40.

8. Quaderno AI, pp. 43–44.

9. Quaderno AI, pp. 45–46.

10. Quaderno AI, p. 49.

11. Quaderno AI, pp. 62–63. On the need to create a new form of democracy, Quaderno AG (June 1944), p. 13, and Tasca to Carlo Tasca, 26 Feb. 1948, Quaderno AN, pp. 194–96.

12. Quaderno AL, entry for 24 Nov. 1945, pp. 129–30. On Tasca's socialism, see Quaderno AK (1945), p. 138, and the long analysis in Quaderno B (1949–51), pp. 106–25.

13. Tasca to C. Vallon, 24 Mar. 1945, Quaderno AK, pp. 46–47, and p. 126.

14. On the Catholic Church, see Quaderno AK (1945), p. 17, and the letter to Carlo, 25 Jan. 1948, Quaderno 40 (1948), p. 376; also see Quaderno AL, p. 1 and pp. 114–15 for a statement of Tasca's vision of Christianity.

15. Quaderno AL (November–December 1945), pp. 144–52; on Tasca's relations with the survivors of Vichy, see Marion to Tasca, 17 Dec. 1948, and Tasca to Marion, 3 Jan. 1949, AT, corrispondenza, fasc. Marion; Quaderno AM, pp. 248–49, entry for 18 Jan. 1949.

16. Quaderno AK (1945), p. 82.

17. See Quaderno AQ, p. 8; on Blum, see entry for 3 July 1946, Quaderno AN, p. 55; Quaderno AO, pp. 82–88, and Quaderno 40, entry for 17 Jan. 1948, pp. 369–71.

18. "Où va la France," Mouvement National Révolutionnaire, 30 Sept. 1944, and "Pour une République moderne," Mouvement Nationale Révolutionnaire, 5 Dec. 1944; see also Jean Servant, "Le programme du CNR est-il un programme de gouvernement?" and "Nous voulons une République moderne," La République Moderne, 15 Nov. 1945; see also Quaderno AK, p. 1, and Quaderno AL, pp. 193–97, for further elaboration of Tasca's political position while he wrote for La République Moderne. In 1947 Robert Aron and Alexandre Marc began to write for the review, which assumed the subtitle "Cahiers du socialisme et du syndicalisme fédéralistes."

19. Entry for 20 Nov. 1947, on Tasca's meeting with Gaullist leaders, Quaderno 40, pp. 315–22, citation from p. 321. See also Tasca to Lucien Laurat, 6 Nov. 1948, and Tasca to Vallon, 3 Dec. 1948, AT, corrispondenza, fasc. 1948, refusing to adhere to the Gaullist movement.

20. Tasca to Charles Vallon, 3 Dec. 1948, AT, corrispondenza, fasc. 1948.

21. A. Rossi, Physiologie du Parti Communiste Français (Paris: Editions Self, 1948), p. 346.

22. Roger Maria, "Un triste personnage de l'antisoviétisme," La France Nouvelle, 7 May 1949.

23. Maria was condemned on 19 Jan. 1951, to pay 35,000 francs. The penalty was reduced on appeal in 1952. Also see the interview with Gilles Martinet, 16 Mar. 1981.

24. Faravelli to Ornella Buozzi, 16 Sept. 1946, copy in Quaderno AN, p. 28; for the reconciliation between Tasca and Faravelli, see Tasca to Faravelli, 13 Nov. 1946, Quaderno AN, p. 30.

25. See Quaderno XLV, entry for 25 Sept. 1949, pp. 151–53; on Tasca's col-

laboration with *Il mondo*, see Aldo Garosci to Tasca, 21 Feb. 1950, and Tasca to Garosci, 24 Feb. 1950, AT, corrispondenza, fasc. Garosci; Mario Pannunzio to Tasca, 25 Mar. 1950, AT, fasc. Polemica Silone-Togliatti.

26. On the debate in *Il mondo*, see "Lettere scarlatte," 24 May 1952; Salvemini to *Il mondo*, 28 June 1952; Alberto Jacometti to *Il mondo* and Salvemini's reply, 16 Aug. 1952; Fausto Nitti to *Il mondo*, 25 July 1952. Tasca's recollections of his life in France during the war appeared in *Il mondo* in July and August 1952 and was published as *In Francia nella bufera* (Moderna: Ugo Guanda, 1953). On Tasca's relations with Salvemini, see Tasca to Salvemini, 15 Mar. and 21 Apr. 1952, and Salvemini to Bruno, Franca and Giorgio Trentin, 16 Sept. 1952, AT corrispondenza, fasc. 1952.

27. See Faravelli to Montana, 18 Mar. 1948, and Tasca to Montana, 24 Oct. 1948, AT, corrispondenza, fasc. Montana; also Tasca to Edward Page, American Embassy Rome, in AT, Corrispondenza, fasc. 1949.

28. Vanni B. Montana, *Amarostico* (Livorno: U. Bastogi Editore, 1975), pp. 166—67. Tasca's correspondence with Montana contained references to "pezzi grossi" in the American diplomatic service. In April 1946 Montana told Tasca that he met with "l'amico," later identified as "Chip" (Bohlen?). Other references were to "Ray" (possibly Raymond Murphy of the State Department) and to "Hay." See Montana to Tasca, 20 April and 7 June 1949.

29. Tasca to Montana, 27 Sept. 1950, and Montana to Tasca, 23 Oct. and 20 Dec. 1950, AT, corrispondenza, fasc. Montana.

30. On Tasca's unsuccessful efforts to obtain a fellowship in America, see Tasca to Ruth Fischer, 14 Oct. and 11 Nov. 1948; Ruth Fischer to Tasca, 2 Nov. 1948 and 18 Jan. 1949, AT, corrispondenza, fasc. Ruth Fischer. See also Tasca to Montana, 22 July 1953, AT, corrispondenza, fasc. Viaggio in America.

31. Tasca to Francis B. Stavers, Office of Eastern European Affairs, Department of State, 25 Sept. 1953, AT, corrispondenza, fasc. 1953. A Freedom of Information Act request has been made to the Central Intelligence Agency; unfortunately, the document relating to Tasca cannot be released for security reasons.

32. On Tasca's possible collaboration with the review *Problems of Communism*, see Bernard E. Brown to Tasca, 12 Nov. 1953, and "Operations memorandum to USIS from USIA: IPS, Washington, 23 Oct. 1953, in AT, corrispondenza, fasc. Problems of Communism. Tasca's activities on behalf of the Congress for Cultural Freedom were contained in AT, fasc. Amis de la Liberté.

33. Quaderno B (1950), entry for 15 June 1940 [1950], p. 61.

34. Tasca to Tristano Codignola, 9 Apr. 1957, AT, corrispondenza, fasc. Codignola; Tasca to Mario Bergamo, 21 June 1958, Fondazione Feltrinelli, Carte Leonetti, fasc. Tasca; on Tasca's work conditions in his last years, interview with Valeria Tasca, 18 Mar. 1981; on Tasca's illness, see Mme. Liliane Tasca to unknown, 7 Apr. 1959, Carte Leonetti, fasc. Tasca.

Bibliographical Essay

Any research on Angelo Tasca or on Italian socialism and communism during the interwar period must start with the Tasca Archive at the Fondazione Giangiacomo Feltrinelli in Milan. The archive contains four main collections: newspaper clippings, including the material on the French Communist party during World War II; a large library of books and newspapers that has been integrated into the regular collection of the foundation; a vast collection of documents relating to the Socialist and Communist movements in the 1920s and 1930s; and the diaries that Tasca kept in several series from 1927 to the mid-1950s. Part of this documentary material on the history of the PCI has been published by Palmiro Togliatti, *La formazione del gruppo dirigente del Partito comunista italiano nel 1923–1924* (Rome: Riuniti, 1962) and by Giuseppe Berti, *I primi dieci anni di vita del Partito comunista italiano: Annali della Fondazione Feltrinelli, 1966* (Milan: Feltrinelli, 1966). Some of the material on the 1930s, including excerpts from the diaries, has been published by Giuseppe Berti, *Problemi del movimento operaio: Scritti critici e storici inediti di Angelo Tasca: Annali della Fondazione Feltrinelli 1968* (Milan: Feltrinelli, 1969) and by Stefano Merli, *Documenti inediti dell'Archivio Angelo Tasca: La rinascista del socialismo italiano e la lotta contro il fascismo dal 1934 al 1939* (Milan: Feltrinelli, 1963). Berti's introductions to both volumes are invaluable for their insights and are useful to reevaluating Tasca from the Communist side. Other useful archival material can be found in the Archivio Centrale della Stato (Rome), in the Archives of the Italian Communist Party at the Gramsci Institute of Rome, and in the archives of Giustizia e Libertà at the Instituto per la Storia della Resistenza in Toscana in Florence.

Turning to the secondary literature, the following works proved useful in the preparation of this study. For more detailed references and for newspapers, however, the chapter notes should be consulted. There are no complete biographies of Tasca. The best work on the early years is Alceo Riosa, *Angelo Tasca socialista* (Venice: Marsilio, 1979). The articles that Tasca wrote for *Il Mondo* on his role in the early history of the PCI have been published as *I primi dieci anni del PCI* (Bari: Laterza, 1971). On the other major protagonists there is a growing body of literature. For Bordiga, see Andreina De Clementi, *Amadeo Bordiga* (Turin: Einaudi, 1971) and Franco Livorsi, *Amadeo Bordiga: Il pensiero e l'azione politica* (Rome: Riuniti, 1976); on Togliatti, see Giorgio Bocca, *Palmiro Togliatti* (Bari: Laterza, 1973). From the point of view of the historian, the best works on Gramsci are Giuseppe Fiori, *Vita di Antonio Gramsci* (Bari: Laterza, 1966); Leonardo Paggi, *Antonio Gramsci e il moderno principe* (Rome: Riuniti, 1970); and John Cammett's fine standard, *Antonio Gramsci and the Origins of Italian Communism* (Stanford: Stanford University Press, 1967). Umberto Terracini has left an interesting account of his views and memories in *Intervista sul comunismo difficile* (Bari: Laterza, 1978).

By far the best history of the Italian Communist party is the multivolume work by Paolo Spriano, *Storia del Partito comunista italiano*, volume 1, *Da Bordiga a Gramsci* (Turin: Einaudi, 1967); volume 2, *Gli anni della clandestinità* (Turin: Einaudi, 1969); volume 3, *I fronti popolari, Stalin, la guerra* (Turin: Einaudi, 1970). On the early years, with strong emphasis on the organization of the party, see Renzo Martinelli, *Il Partito comunista d'Italia, 1921–1926* (Rome: Riuniti, 1977). The best general history of the Italian Socialist party is the recent collective work, edited by Giovanni Sabatucci, *Storia del socialismo italiano* (Rome: Il Poligono, 1981). Volume 4 by Bruno Tobia and Leonardo Rapone covers the period from 1926 to 1943. A useful documentary history of the PSI is by Gastone Manacorda, *Il socialismo nella storia d'Italia: Storia documentaria dal Risorgimento alla Repubblica* (Bari: Laterza, 1970). Also useful is Luigi Cortesi, *Il socialismo italiano tra riforme e rivoluzione* (Bari: Laterza, 1969).

The Turinese working-class society that produced Tasca is described in Stefano Musso, *Gli operai a Torino, 1900–1920* (Milan: Feltrinelli, 1980); student socialist politics are well covered by Renzo Martinelli, "Gramsci e il *Corriere universitario* di Torino," *Studi storici*, XVI (1973), pages 906–916, and by Giovanni Gozzini, *Alle origini del comunismo italiano: Storia della Federazione giovanile socialista* (Bari: Dedalo, 1979). The late Alfonso Leonetti, who knew both Gramsci and Tasca, has given us a wonderful memoir of his early years, *Da Andria contadina a Torino operaia* (Urbino: Argalia Editore, 1974).

On the postwar crisis in Italy, Giuseppe Maione's *Il biennio rosso: Autonomia e spontaneità operaia nel 1919–1920* (Bologna: Il Mulino, 1975) was especially useful, as was Tasca's masterful *La nascita e l'avvento del fascismo* (Bari: Laterza, 1965). The crisis that led to the formation of the PCI is described in T. Detti, *Serrati e la formazione del Partito comunista italiano* (Rome: Riuniti, 1972). Much information on the relationship between the PCI and the Communist International (IC) is contained in the memoir of the IC representative in Italy, Jules Humbert Droz, *De Lénine à Staline: Dix ans au service de l'Internationale communiste* (Neuchatel: A la Bacannière, 1971) and in his *Il contrasto tra l'Internazionale e il PCI, 1922–1928* (Milan: Feltrinelli, 1969). Aldo Agosti's *La Terza internazionale: Storia documentaria*, in three volumes (Rome; Riuniti, 1976) provides analysis and documentary material on the Third International. Useful, although hostile to Tasca, is Camilla Ravera, *Diario di trent'anni* (Rome: Riuniti, 1973).

Ariane Landuyt has traced the politics of the Left from the elections of 1924 through the murder of Matteotti and the consolidation of the dictatorship in her *Le sinistre e l'Aventino* (Milan: Franco Angeli, 1973). Pietro Secchia, one of the hard-liners in the late 1920s, has edited a volume of documentary material on the PCI's actions against the Fascist regime, *L'azione svolta dal Partito comunista in Italia durante il fascismo, 1926–1932: Annali della Fondazione Feltrinelli 1969* (Milan: Feltrinelli, 1970). By far the best work on Bukharin is Stephen Cohen's *Bukharin and the Bolshevik Revolution* (New York: Vintage Books, 1975). The debates within the Italian party over the nature of fascism during the late 1920s have been studied by Giulio Sapelli, *L'analisi economica ei comunisti italiani durante il fascismo* (Milan: Feltrinelli, 1978), who has underlined the importance of Tasca's contributions.

Ferdinando Ormea covers the years of the *svolta*, or purge, of the PCI with a good deal of sympathy for Tasca and the others in *Le origini dello stalinismo nel PCI* (Milan: Feltrinelli, 1978). Silone has given his account of the purge in *Uscita di sicurezza* (Florence: Vallecchi, 1965), as has Umberto Terracini in *Sulla svolta: Carteggio Clandestino dal carcere, 1930–1932* (Milan: La Pietra, 1975). Tasca recounted some of the conditions surrounding his own break with the PCI in "Per una storia politica del fuoruscitismo," *Itinerari*, October 1954. For the politics of the exiled parties up to 1934, consult Santi Fedele's *Storia della Concentrazione antifascista, 1927–1934* (Milan: Feltrinelli, 1976). Giustizia e Libertà (GL) and Carlo Rosselli have been studied in the collective work *Giustizia e Libertà nella lotta antifascista* (Florence: La Nuova Italia, 1978) and in Aldo Garosci, *Vita di Carlo Rosselli* (Florence: Vallecchi, 1973). The best general history of the Italian exiles remains that by Charles Delzell, *Mussolini's*

Enemies (Princeton: Princeton University Press, 1961). For the antifacist press, see Frank Rosengarten, *The Italian Antifacist Press, 1919–1945* (Cleveland: Case Western Reserve Press, 1968).

A controversial analysis of the connection between neoreformism and the rise of fascism in France is offered by Zeev Sternhell in *Ni droite, ni gauche: L'idéologie fasciste en France* (Paris: Editions du Seuil, 1983). The literary and political background is given in Herbert R. Lottman, *The Left Bank: Writers, Artists and Politics from the Popular Front to the Cold War* (Boston: Houghton Mifflin, 1982). On De Man, the standard biography is Peter Dodge, *Beyond Marxism: The Faith and Works of Hendrik De Man* (The Hague: Martinus Nijhoff, 1966). The parallel debates over neoreformism that occurred within the Italian party are covered by Simona Colarizzi, *Classe operaia e ceti medi* (Venice: Marsilio Editore, 1976) and by Leonardo Rapone, "Il Partito socialista italiano fra Pietro Nenni e Angelo Tasca," *Annali della Fondazione Giangiacomo Feltrinelli 1983–1984* (Milan: Feltrinelli, 1984). French socialism during the interwar years has received far more coverage than its Italian counterpart. On the role of foreign and domestic policy in splitting and paralyzing the party, see John T. Marcus, *French Socialism in the Crisis Years, 1933– 1936: Fascism and the French Left* (New York: Praeger, 1958); Michel Bilis, *Socialistes et pacifistes ou l'impossible dilemme des socialistes français* (Paris: Syros, 1979); N. Greene, *Crisis and Decline: The French Socialist Party in the Popular Front Era* (Ithaca: Cornell University Press, 1968). Although the most recent biography of Léon Blum by Jean Lacouture, *Léon Blum* (Paris: Seuil, 1977) contains some useful personal information, the best study for the purposes of this book remains Joel Colton's *Léon Blum: Humanist in Politics* (New York: Alfred Knopf, 1966). Robert Paxton's *Vichy France: Old Guard and New Order, 1940–1944* (New York: Norton, 1975) and Bertram Gordon's *Collaborationism in France during the Second World War* (Ithaca: Cornell University Press, 1980) provide a good view of the various currents within Vichy and in Paris during the war. Tasca's own works, *Les communistes français pendant la Drôle de Guerre* (Paris: Les Îles d'Or, 1951) is also useful, as is his *In Francia nella bufera* (Moderna: Ugo Guanda, 1953). An extremely good study of the organization of propaganda in France is Philippe Amaury's *Les deux premières expériences d'un 'ministère de l'information' en France* (Paris: Librairie générale de droit et de jurisprudence R. Pichon et R. Durand-Auzias, 1969). On the French Socialists who collaborated during the war, see Marc Sadoun, *Les Socialistes sous l'occupation: Résistance et collaboration* (Paris: Presse de la Fondation Nationale des Sciences Politiques, 1982).

Index